UN

Fighti

UNBROKEN
Fighting To The Bitter End

Emily Reilly

2016

Copyright

First Printing: 2016

ISBN 978-1-326-70115-4

Emily Reilly
Brisbane, Queensland 4000

www.facebook.com/officiallyunbroken

Ordering Information:
Special discounts are available on quantity purchases by corporations, associations, educators, and others. For details, contact the publisher at the above listed address.

U.S. trade bookstores and wholesalers: Please contact Emily Reilly

Email : emilyunbroken@gmail.com

Dedication

For those that are yet to be Unbroken and for those who feel they are stuck in a situation that they cannot get out of.

Always remember that you can be UNBROKEN

Contents

Acknowledgements

My Dearest Pa, thank you for always being there when I needed you and for being my hero. I would never have known what a man should have been if you didn't set the benchmark.

Mum, I can never put into words what you have done for me or what you mean to me. Thank you for all the sacrifices you made for Barry and I. You are the most selfless human I have ever met. Thank you for being our Mum and Dad. As I always tell you "If I had to pick a Mum when I was born it would have been you"

Barry, thank you for always being there for me, standing up for me and just for being you. I know the words "I Love You" don't leave your mouth often but I feel it when I am with you. I love you mate.

Ava, what can I say? I have done the best I can to give you all I could. I truly am grateful that you have grown to be the person you are, you are someone who loves with all her heart, strives to do her best at everything and would give her last dollar to help a friend or family member. You were my little rock for such a long time when it was just you and me. I wish for you to always be happy. Thank you for making me tell my story. I love you xx Mum xx

There are two other very special people in my life that I will introduce to everyone later. You both know who you are.

The first is the one I gave my heart and soul to years ago and will be forever grateful for your love and support. We have had ups and downs but we still stand strong. I love you xx

The second was a blessing, such a beautiful human being. I am so proud of you and love you very much xx

Lastly I would like to thank all those people on my Facebook page who have supported me over the last few years while I have been writing my story. You were there from day one when I click post. You will never know how much it has meant to me having you there along the way. Don't forget what I said at the start of my journey "as you can tell my story is far from over, you will all form a part of my last few chapters".

Take Care and Stay Unbroken xx Emily xx

Foreword

Be prepared to witness the most incredible, inspirational, strongest and loving girl/woman you would ever have the pleasure to get to know by reading her life story.

By reading this you will smile, you will laugh but also you will find it breaking your heart for her tears well up in your eyes feeling her pain wanting to help her, knowing you can't as it is all in the past.

Be prepared for a journey of love, heartbreak and happiness. Stay UNBROKEN. This is Emily's life story, she is incredible someone to look up to and inspire to be.

That's what I tell my friends and family ~ Nadine Seagar

Chapter 1: We're Just Playing

Well here it goes...

My name is Emily and this is my story. I am telling my story for the first time ever in detail and this just happens to be to people I don't know (you). I know a lot of people will not believe this story but I can guarantee you this did happen and it happened to me.

All names have been changed in order to protect those I love and care for.

I was born in Auburn (Sydney Australia) to a beautiful lady and a not so perfect Father. We lived in a two story brick town house. When you enter the door to our home you look directly into a small lounge room that held a two seater lounge, directly in front of that was a small coffee table that held a television. When you are in the lounge room, you turn to the right and there you see a staircase that ascended to the upper level. The stairs were covered in a fluffy cream coloured carpet, when you reach the top of the stairs if you turn to the right you look directly at the door that led to my Mother and Father's room and to the left led you to Barry's and my room, the bathroom and toilet.

My Mum came from a large family with eight brother's and sister's. They lived on the North Shore of Sydney. When she was younger she danced the part of the Swan in Swan Lake (ballet), she danced professionally. Living on the North Shore gave the family a stigma of being well off, life was not easy for them as my Grandfather would work his fingers to the bone to support their large family but they never went without, he made sure of that.

My Father was also from a large family of nine children, him being the eldest child. His eldest sister whom I am named after died at a young age. The family lived in a small house and didn't have a

UNBROKEN

lot. They lived in the Western Suburbs so in the eyes of those from the North Shore he was a bad boy.

The song Uptown Girl by Billy Joel always reminds me of my Mother and Father. Maybe Mum was trying to rebel by falling for someone on the wrong side of the tracks, well she succeeded and they married and had me and eighteen months later Barry arrived. Mum stayed at home to look after myself and my baby brother (Barry) whilst my biological father went to work all day then the pub until late every day.

•

My earliest memory is from when I was about two years old. People say that you cannot remember back that far, I guess that is true when you have a normal life but when you have witness something that rocks your world you will remember, believe me.

My Daddy (as I called him back then) had come home and was drunk as usual and none too happy. He was ranting and raving and then took my Mum up to their room at the top of the stairs. I heard a noise and decided to go investigate I worked my way up the staircase. I was partly crawling as the stairs were pretty difficult for a two-year-old to navigate. When I got to the top of the stairs I remember feeling the long soft carpet under my feet. I turned to the right and headed towards the noises. I got to my Mum and Dad's bedroom, the door was ajar so I pushed it open further, what I saw before me has never left my mind, scaring me for life. My Mum was laying on the bed with my Dad kneeling on her arms whilst sitting on her chest pinning her to the bed. Mum's face was covered in blood and I witnessed him punch her in the face for what had to have been the hundredth time just as I walked in the door. He stopped turned in my direction and glared at me, his eyes were vacant, almost black. My Mum looked over at me and said obviously in pain managed to say "Mummy is OK Emily! I will be down in a minute and we can play a game" she paused then added

"Daddy and Mummy are just playing" I turned around following my Mum's instructions, went down stairs, sat on the lounge and cuddled my little brother as he was crying. I tried to soothe him but the muffled, pained sounds Mum was making scared him and I couldn't calm him down. Isn't it funny how noises can affect us, even without seeing what they are, even as children you know when something is not right. It was a while before Mum came down stairs as she had to wait for my Father to stop hitting her and for him to pass out from his drunken fury.

I remember her face to this day. She had wiped away the blood the best she could from her face but the split lip, cheeks, eyebrow and black eyes forming could not be hidden. She looked ashamed but not scared. I can't remember any more of this night but I know it was terrifying and scarred my soul forever.

The next morning my Father had to go to work and as usual my Mum made his lunch and got us all breakfast. I remember when he walked out the door he turned and looked my brother and I and said harshly "Don't let that fucking kitten out the door!" whilst pointing down at a black and grey kitten.

Later that day I got a little chair and opened the front door, I'm not sure why I did this but as I did the kitten got out. My Father's words rang through my mind like an echo. I followed it with my little brother but it seemed the more we followed that little kitten the further it went. We arrived at another town house in our complex as we were about to grab the kitten a man came out and looked down at us both. He was smiling and had huge big work boots on. I remember looking at him and thinking how huge he was. He looked me directly in the eyes and raised his boot up high then slammed it down. He squashed our kitten! right in front of

UNBROKEN

Barry and me. I was screaming and crying. Mum was hanging clothes on the line when she heard the screams it was at this time she must have realised we were outside. She came running down towards the screams and saw what had happened, she was so bruised from the beating she had taken the night before, she picked us both up and took us inside not saying a word to the big man. Not long after Mum had taken us inside the man dumped the kitten at our front door. When my Father arrived home he was furious as we had disobeyed him. I remember Dad getting a garbage bag from under the kitchen sink, walking out the front and putting our kitten inside it. Dad walked around the back of the complex and disappeared but not for long. When he came back inside he started yelling at us and my Mum said she had let it out accidentally when she went to hang the clothes on the line. Mum always protected us no matter the consequences and never put herself first. Dad grabbed her arm pulling at her roughly as they went back upstairs and started playing games again. The sound of him abusing my Mum will never leave me. I cannot really remember what else happened the last time my Dad took my Mum upstairs to "play".

•

My Mother is such a wonderful lady. She NEVER said bad things about my Dad to either Barry or myself as we grew up even though she could have been justified in doing so. She wanted us to see our Father as she felt all children needed a Dad.

My mother is the strongest person I know. When I was little I used to look up at her with her beautiful blonde hair, dark skin and size eight body and think '*I want to be just like my Mummy, she is so beautiful*'. She always put us and still puts us first after all these years.

She went through these beatings for years and would have still gone through them if my Father did not try and start on my brother and me. The day he hit us was the day Mum moved us to the Mid North Coast of NSW where my Pa, Nan and other family lived (so much more on my Pa to come) to protect us. I asked her when I was old enough about my Father's Father (my Paternal Grandfather) and she told me a story that is chilling.

My Grandfather (Dad's Father) use to beat my Grandmother and the nine children daily. He too worked all day then drank every afternoon. He would come home and would wipe his fingers over the bench tops and if there was one speck of dust he would beat my Nan till she could not move and if the kids tried to stop him he would beat them also.

When my Father took my Mother (aged seventeen) to tell his Dad that she was pregnant with me my Grandfather punched her in the stomach and hit my Father too. He had hit her so hard that Mum started to bleed. When my Nan heard and saw what had happened she took my Mum to the hospital. Luckily for me she did not lose me then and there as he had hit her so hard that she should have lost me. His temper was triggered by the smallest things and he wasn't the kind of man to speak calmly and discussions were few and far between.

A few months after this beating the police turned up to my Father's family home. My Father, Mother, his siblings and his Mother where all there at the time. The police knocked at the door and told my Nan that my Grandfather died, he had driven off the Granville bridge. Nan was devastated, even after all he had done she still loved him. They then stated that he had left a suicide letter blaming her and the children for his death and that she was not to get any insurance money. What? This man was pure evil yet my Father still to this day idolises him. Years later when Father tried to speak about him to me in a positive light I would change the subject. I guess even if he was bad Dad subconsciously wanted him to be good and had probably blocked out the evil deeds this man had done.

My Nan had to raise all eight children on her own with very little money and no work skills as she was never allowed to leave the house whilst my Grandfather was alive. Nan eventually got a job then she very quickly had to get more work to cover the costs of raising her children alone. Nan worked three jobs working long hours and did whatever she had too to get by. This meant the children were looked after by the older children whilst she was away. One of my Aunt's was sent to a girl's home for a year or two, whilst there she was abused (she was the youngest girl and a bit if a rebel). Maybe this is why my father was the way he was but I do not believe you have to follow in anyone's footsteps, you can break the pattern.

When we moved to the Mid North Coast we lived in a beachside town in a flat. I remember my Mother constantly checking the doors and windows were locked. There was always a feeling of fear in this little flat as my Mother had not told my Father where we were at this stage. I suppose she wanted some peace, even just for a little while. She would call him weekly and let him speak to us, on a lot of occasions she didn't let him talk to us at all, I didn't know at the time why but Mum told me not so long ago it was because he was drunk and threatening. Mum didn't want us to speak to him like that as he had a tendency to cry and get us upset, leaving Mum to calm us and make us feel better.

As my Nan and Pa lived not far from us we would go and visit them daily, a little routine in a hugely difficult time for both Mum and us. We did have peace for a few months.

Months later Mum decided it was time to let our Father see us again and provided him with our address, our peace was soon shattered. One night when I was taken to bed just as I started to

Emily Reilly
drift off to sleep I heard the sound of smashing glass. My Mum
came into our room to check on us then she told us "Close the door
and do not come out no matter what. Do not come out!" Mum
kissed our foreheads then turned and shut the door. I could hear her
running around as she did routinely making sure the windows and
doors were locked, but this time it was different, she was frantic.
What I heard that night will never be forgotten. I heard drunken
ranting and more glass smashing then I heard Mum scream

"NO!" then I heard loud thuds coming from down the hallway.
My Mum and Dad were playing games again only this time I knew
it wasn't a game and this time I was petrified, frozen in my bed.
Barry was holding me around the waist so tight shaking just as
much as me.

"Sissy is Mummy OK?" he said almost stuttering due to his
shaking. This beating was vicious and seemed to go forever, we
could do nothing but sit and wait as Mum had said. I heard the
sound of sirens as our front door slammed closed, he had left.
When the sirens stopped a few seconds later there was rapid loud
banging on the front door, both Barry and I jumped and thought it
was going to start again. I held him tighter and whispered

"It's OK, everything is going to be OK" Mum somehow made
her way to the door. When she opened the door there stood two
Police Officers. One sat with Mum and the other went searching for
our Father. They had no luck finding him that night. Mum
remembered we were in our room and asked the second Police
Officer to check on us after he had arrived back from his search. I
don't remember much of him only the feeling that we were now
safe. I do remember him picking up Barry and telling him the bad
man has gone now. Due to the state of my Mother the Police called
an Ambulance to check her over. They were there talking to my
Mum for a very long time and the Ambulance Officers tended to
her wounds the best they could. They wanted to take Mum to the

UNBROKEN

hospital but she would not go. She did not want to leave us after this night and there was no way she was dropping us off to our Nan and Pa's for them to see her like this.

The Police and Ambulance finally left and we went out to Mum. We all got in to Mum's bed and she sang us a song to try and make us feel safe. I remember not feeling safe at all that night, my little mind was running on over drive, every little sound outside would make me jump and move just a little closer to my Mum and Barry. I did not sleep a wink that night and I am sure Mum did not close her eyes either. So much for trying to do the right thing and let our Father see us! I know now that she got a restraining order but back then I didn't as I couldn't have known what that was.

The violence that occurred that night was so traumatising for myself and my little brother. I have spoken to him about things now that we are grown but he doesn't remember much of it.

Back then I thought Dad was great when this was not happening, whenever I was with him alone he would spoil me but add alcohol and you saw a whole other side and it was evil just like I could imagine his Father was.

Mum always told people when they saw her that her bruises and cuts were from running in to a door, falling over or some other lame excuse. I remember thinking to myself *that is not true, why don't you tell someone the truth*' I did not know at the time but I was to find out later in my young life that it is not that easy to speak up. I instinctively knew at the time not to say anything to anyone and to be honest this last time I did not witness what happened at the time it happened but I heard everything, just one look of Mum told the story.

Emily Reilly

I wish I could say this was the last time this happened but it was far from over. I was still so young. What would follow and the life I was about to lead scares me even now

Chapter 2: Pa My Hero

During my childhood I had one very strong and consistent influence in my life and he will be the positive in my story as I go through my childhood.

This was my Pa.

Pa was always so good to us, like Mum when we were with him he always made us feel special. He made me feel like I was the most important person in the room even if the room was full of all our family. It wasn't an effort for him to do this as it came naturally to him. His family was his life and he made each and every one of us know this without words. Everyone that connected with my Pa loved him. Pa was quiet around strangers at first, never rude he was just taking it all in and trying to understand the person in front of him.

Imagine a man that had dark skin and his body was always toned, he had hair that encircled his head that was always cut short, atop of his head was bare apart from a few strands hairs that were always combed to the side (a bit like curly from the three stooges, which just happened to be his favourite TV show outside of the Road Runner cartoon). He used to go to the hairdressers and say to the lady

"Short back and side, take care with the hair on top its precious" when he told me this I always laughed as he had maybe four hairs if he was lucky on top. He had piercing blue/grey eyes like the clear sky in summer. If you looked closely enough into his eyes you could almost see his soul, it was pure and loving. His eyes always told a story, his emotions were always clear if you looked into them. When he smiled his eyes smiled first with tiny creases to each side. Pa didn't have to speak words for you to know what he was thinking or about to say these eyes, they said it all.

My bond with this great man was something that I wish everyone in the world could have with at least one person. Our bond always made me feel safe and loved not matter what could have been going on in the background.

He was in WW2 as a soldier. He use to have scars on the bottom of his legs. I would as a young child ask him about them and he only ever said "I got them helping a friend" we were always told that he enrolled in the Army as a general soldier and got his trade as a Mechanic. I later found out that he didn't become a Mechanic until after he got out of the Army. Those scars (in official records held in Canberra) were from him jumping out of a plane. His mate jumped first and landed on a mine and the shrapnel torn my Pa's legs to pieces. He was in the Special Forces or something like that. Pa tried to save his mate but it was too late for him. He was not afraid to tell the story he just didn't, like so many other brave men that had served their country and saw and did things that no person should have too. He would never have wanted to be painted as a hero he was just a man doing a job. But you will see he was my hero.

When my Mum ever went to Sydney to see other family members we would be allowed to stay with my Nan and Pa. She would always leave groceries and money in case we wanted to go to the pool. Mum would never leave us without knowing that she had provided for us and that Nan and Pa were not out of pocket. This was not expected by her parents but Mum just did it. She took her responsibilities seriously and we were her responsibility.

Pa use to always joke with my little brother and I. Every morning he would sit at the kitchen table and have a cup of tea whilst we had breakfast. He used to say "Do you want to see a spoon burn?" of course we would say

"Yes! Please Pa" manners were enforced by my Mother so we were always polite but it didn't matter with Pa as I never wanted to disappoint him. He stirred his cup of tea then shook off the excess tea, blew on the spoon and touched my hand with it, it didn't burn as he had cooled it, it was just warm I would instinctively pull my hand away then go in to a fit of giggles. Funny, this is such a small thing but it stays with me to this day. He would take his false teeth out and sit them beside my dinner place. This creeped me out the first few times but in the end I always ended up rolling around laughing. He was just a fun loving person.

One day I asked if I could go to the pool as I had planned to meet my Aunt in-law (we'll call her Kylie) and her baby for a swim. Pa said "Here is five dollars, you can pay to get in, this will be fifty cents, get a packet of chips another fifty cents and a drink another fifty cents. Bring home the change, do not pay for Kylie!" he said in a way that you knew you should not disobey him, his eyes slimmed to a couple of slits. I agreed and set off to the pool.

The pool was about one kilometre away from my Nan and Pa's house, you could see it from their home, you had to trek through a huge flat paddock to get there. The paddock was full of long grass and in bare feet you would find all the tiny rocks and sticks along the way. I got to the pool and Aunt Kylie and my Cousin were waiting. She asked if I could pay her in and as I was only young I didn't know how to say no to my family, so I went against my Pa's wishes and paid her in. When we got in to the pool area I went over to the little shed that was a canteen and brought her a packet of chips and we shared my drink. My cousin was only a baby so I didn't have to pay for her and she couldn't eat chips or have soft drink. I loved going to the pool not only for the swim but for the chips and drinks as we never had these things at home. We always had home cooked meals and the closest we got to soft drink was cordial. I had a great time splashing around in the pool whilst Aunty Kylie watched on, every now and then she would bring our baby cousin in for a splash but mostly she just sat on her towel sunbathing. I always had to be home before dark so a few hours later when the sun was going down and the pool was about to shut we packed up and head home me with my two dollars fifty change in hand ready to give it to my Pa. As soon as I walked in I gave the change to Pa "Where is the other dollar?" he asked ever so calmly as he was always calm. I told him what I had done and not amused or impressed he said

"That is stealing, Emily" this was the first and very last time I saw my Pa disappointed in me. He didn't have to say anything more I took myself off upstairs to my room and stayed there and cried until a little while later he came in to talk to me and explain why he was disappointed. I was not crying because Pa did anything wrong but for the fact that I had disappointed him. Not long after he came in to the room, held me and explained why he was disappointed. I apologised hugged him tight and kissed his check, I then took myself off to the bathroom to wash my face and clean myself up, after this Pa led me downstairs to have dinner. All was forgiven but he was still disappointed with Kylie.

The next morning early my Uncle and Aunty Kylie came over. Pa was none too happy with Kylie. I am not sure why but you could always tell that he had little time for her. He was unusually quiet this morning and very cold towards Kylie, Nan held most of the conversation. I don't know if Kylie could read my Pa but I could and I never wanted to see those eyes looking at me that way ever. I didn't hang around too long as I had organised with one of my other cousins to go to splash rock for the day. I asked Pa if I could go and see my cousin and he said "Go on have fun but be home before dark"

UNBROKEN

When I arrived at my cousins house we didn't stay long. I had enough time to knock on her door and call out "Hello" to my Aunt. We made our way up to the golf course. The golf course crested two hills, when you look over the edge of these hills where they joined you saw a small secluded beach. The drop was huge for such small children and the non-existent path down to the beach was perilous, the rocks below your feet would slip from under you, you really had to watch where you placed your feet and make sure that it was going to hold your body weight. When you reached the bottom and landed on the sand it was like another world. The feeling of freedom that you had was amazing, no adults, no one but you and the fun ahead. As soon as you get down the first thing you want to do is go into the caves that are only visible when it is low tide, when high tide hits the water level is above the caves so you have a limited window of time to go in. I always thought that I would find treasure in those caves, I guess I did they are the memories that I have of these times. After messing around in the caves we decided to take the big step of swimming out to splash rock. Splash rock was the largest rock in a group of rocks that jutted up out of the water. We would leap into the oncoming waves, only to be washed around the rock, which we would then climb back up and jump off again. Sometimes we would try and hold on and let the wave go over our heads but this was no easy task and almost always we would end up in the water hoping not to get caught in the regular rip that would send you out in to the ocean to be swallowed up whole. As children we did not think of the consequences that may occur from doing this all we thought about was the fun and the freedom we felt. If our families knew we did this, we would have been in so much trouble but this day we were not spotted and that suited us just fine. When we had finished up and before the sun had started to go down we made the trip back up the hill making sure to peek over the top ensuring that there was no one on the golf course that could see us. The only problem we ever had in this town was that everyone knew our family, if anyone had spotted us we knew that this would get back to Pa something we didn't want to happen. This day we were lucky.

Pa smoked DR Pat tobacco in a pipe, every now and then when he had just about run out he would ask me to go the shop and get his DR Pat. The people at the shop had no problem giving this to us as they knew this was at Pas request, however I am sure that a few of my old cousins used this to get themselves some tobacco whilst under age. I always loved doing this for Pa as he would always give me a dollar and I would buy myself a pizza pie, the best pies ever! This was a meat pie base with bacon and a whole egg placed on top with a little cheese, yum.... To this day these little trips for DR Pat make me smile. Not so long ago I was at an antique store and saw a DR Pat tin, I brought this as a memento.

•

When I was about five my Father came to visits us. I was so excited as he always brought me the best present. Isn't it funny how as children you tend to forget the bad things that you have seen people do when you are spoilt by that very person. My little Brother was never spoilt like me as Dad always said to my Mum that Barry wasn't his, I'm telling you all now that he looks exactly like my Father only with darker skin and lighter hair. Barry has a temper to match but he also has a filter and knows the difference between anger and evil, something our Father did not understand.

I remember being in a little back yard playing around in the soft green grass making clover necklaces when a bee stung me on the leg. I didn't know at the time what had happened just that it was extremely painful. I screamed and my Father came running over, he tried to calm me down but I would not stop jumping up and down long enough for him to look and see what had actually happened. All I kept saying between screams and tears was "I want my Pa" so my Father picked me up and carried me down the street to a garage

UNBROKEN

where my Pa worked as I continued to cried and scream all the way. For him it must have been so frustrating but in this case he didn't get angry maybe because he was sober. He put me down when we got there and as soon as I was on my feet I started crying saying

"I want my Pa; I want my Pa" the whole time sobbing until a man ran in who knew us to get him. They must have thought I had broken my leg the way I was carrying on. My Pa came running out and picked me up all I could manage through my tears were the words

"It bit me" Pa smiled at me whilst he led me inside the workshop, went to his huge tool box and got a pair of pliers. He pretended to remove the bee sting. What I didn't know at the time was that my Father had already removed it. Something Pa told me later in my life. He then got the brown stuff (Betadine) put it on the sting then lifted my shirt to draw a smiley face on my belly with it.

"All gone now Emily, Pa fixed it" he kissed my little leg and in my mind I was immediately fixed, he had kissed it better. The brown stuff always fixed me and I use it to this day.

"Pa has to go back to work now but I will come over after work and make sure you are OK" he said then he looked up at my Father and nodded his head once whilst waving goodbye to me.

My Father carried me back on his shoulders as I had no shoes on. After a little while I had forgotten about that bite and went back outside to play again. This time a green frog jumped on my leg, I got a shock and thought it was a bee again so off we went and the whole process started again. My Pa always seemed to fix me. Just being in his presence made me feel safe.

There are so many little things that you will hear throughout my story about this wonderful man and how he saved my tiny soul and showed me that there are good men out there. I was going to find out they are few and far between...

Chapter 3: Staying with Nan

We moved house again so that my Father couldn't find us but Mum did the right thing again and allowed my Nan (my Father's Mother) to know our phone number so we could communicate with our Father and his family. Mum truly did not want us to miss out on having a Father, it was important to her that we were happy no matter what the consequence may have been to her.

After the last attack made by my Father he ran all the way back to Sydney to his Mother's house. This was normal behaviour for him, a simple habit he could not break. He called us regularly, even though most of the time he was drunk so we didn't get to talk to him. Mum got to the point when he called she wouldn't say his name so we didn't get upset because we could speak with our Dad. He also wrote letters to my Mum and us but we never saw them till my little brother found them in Mum's cupboard when we were older. We read these letters and got really upset as our Father was wanting her to allow us to go to him. He would rave about missing Mum and us. In some spots we could see tear stains that he had obviously spilt whilst writing these letters. He always apologised for the way he had treated Mum and professed his undying love over and over again. Looking back on these letters as a grown adult myself, I see that he was trying to play mind games, making Mum feel sorry for him, hence allowing him back in to her/our life to do the same thing over again.

My Mum worked really long hours from memory as we spent a lot of time with my Pa and Nan until Mum got home. It was always just after dark when she would arrive and Pa would always have us bathed and feed.

Months had pasted since the attack and Mum started to allow us to go Sydney to see our Father at Christmas Holidays. We always stayed at his Mother's house (I will call her Nanny M). Nanny M always had a bottle of TAB cola in her fridge (funny I remember that little detail). My Dad would work during the day at the factory, so Nanny M would watch us. I tried to help her clean the house once and once only... She got really angry and said "No one is allowed to help clean the house, I have to do it just right" This obviously was ingrained in her because of my Grandfather (her husband). Nanny realised how she had spoken to me.

"Run along Emily and play with your brother, I'll finish up here" she said a smile crept over her face. I don't ever remember doing much when we visited.

•

Our Father took us to Underwater World and I remember seeing large sharks whilst being pulled around under a large aquarium on a flat escalator weaving in and out of tunnels. He brought me a big fluffy grey Elephant with pink inside its ears, it was almost as big as I was back then. I still have it to this day sitting up in my cupboard and when I look at it I remember the person he was at the very moment he gave it to me. I don't think my brother got much on that day.

Our Father was so bad to Barry when I look back on these times we spent with him. An example of this was the time my Father brought me a bag of sweets and didn't buy any for my brother. I couldn't understand this at the time but I would always save them and share them out when we got back to Nanny M's house. I always tried to protect my little brother making sure where possible his feelings didn't get hurt, but I was only young and this I could not do. I can only imagine how he felt as this was his Father and Barry was not looked upon as his child even though our Father never said this out loud around us his actions spoke far louder than

UNBROKEN

his words. I remember thinking this was mean at the time but I also remember our Father had a temper and to save us both I never said anything that could enrage him.

Another day during our trip our Father went to work, we had the best day ever as my favourite Uncle was there he was about 16 at the time, we will call him Timmy. Timmy had a Mechano set and would sit and help us built stuff. I remember looking up at him and thinking he was so big, I idolised this man. This day my Uncle said "Emily! Do you want to see a magic trick?"

"Yes please Uncle Timmy" was my response.

"Well go outside and Uncle Timmy is going to disappear, when you come back in you need to look at the picture on the wall and I will be in it" I did what I was told and when he called me back in he was gone! Wow! Magic! He started talking to me and telling me he was in the picture. I looked up and there was his face. Wow I was amazed. After a while of chatting to me he said

"Emily, go outside and I will come back" so I did what I was told and when I went back into his room he was there sitting on his bed. It wasn't till I was about eighteen I found out that he was in the cupboard next to the picture, he had stuck a small photo of himself onto the large picture on the wall. This was one of the best memories I have of being there. Uncle Timmy always took time with us, he was patient and very attentive. We loved him with all our hearts.

That night Nanny M ran me a bath. When I got into the bath I noticed on the side of the bath was a rubbery thing so I put soap on it and started to wash myself thinking it was some special sponge for bathing. A little later my Nanny came in and said the weirdest thing to me "Emily! have you seen Nannies booby?" I immediately pointed to where her boobs were (her chest)

"There silly" she looked down at me and that rubbery sponge I was using. Well let's just say it was not a sponge at all. She took it from me and wiped it off then proceeded to put it back in her bra. I didn't know what breast cancer was at the time or that people had fake boobs

"Eww" I said squinting my face in horror. Nanny M had breast cancer, she had to have a double mastectomy and these were her artificial boobs. I think back now and laugh at how naive I was but a kid is a kid.

Later that night just as we were going to bed I heard someone banging at the door. Nanny M checked and it was my Father. I use to like to sleep next to him on a mattress when we stayed but this night I felt that terror come back and sleeping next to my Father was not an option. Nanny M opened the door with the latch still on and she told him to go away and sober up before he could see us. Let's just say he had no intention of waiting. He kicked the door in and pushed past Nanny, she obviously knew what was to come so she said to us as calmly as possible "Go and pop into Nannies bed, I'll be in shortly" All I could hear was screaming, Nan was screaming at my Father to leave and he was screaming back at her. I remember thinking that the evil was back. I wanted to run out of the room and tell Nanny to run and hide! but I was frozen still on Nannies bed with the covers pulled up over our heads. Isn't it funny how you think that a sheet over your head and you not being able to see can protect you from anything when you are young? Barry was so terrified that he involuntarily wet his pants, all I could do was tell him

"Everything will be OK, he will leave soon Barry I promise nothing will happen to you" my Nanny was a hard lady and she was also very loud so her screams must have been heard by the entire apartment complex. She was trying to get him to leave. I could hear banging and smashing of glass, it sounded like a bull in a china shop but there was no way those covers where coming off my head. I was muttering to myself

"I wish Uncle Timmy was here, he would help. He wouldn't let anything happen to us or our Nanny" Uncle Timmy had gone out that night so he wasn't there to protect us. I heard more screaming this time it was my Nanny and she was obviously in pain. I knew that sound by now as we had heard it many time before but with Mum. Our Father was beating his own Mother, the woman who gave birth to him, the one that raised him on her own with no outside help. Was there nothing that this man would not do? The screaming seemed to get further away until we could hardly hear it. It was at this time that I got the courage up to get out of the bed and open the door just a little. When I spied out the door I could no longer see them. The lounge room was a mess from all of the broken furnishings and glass scattered everywhere. The front door was wide open and as I snuck out of the room and got closer to the door I could hear my Nannies screams getting louder so I turned and ran back to the room, slammed the door, jumped on the bed and furiously tugged the covers back over Barry and my head. Our Father had dragged her out to the front lawn of the apartment complex and continued to beat her. By this stage I am sure that the entire street could not only hear what was going on but also see it. His beating of his own Mother was relentless, she tried to fight back but he was so much larger than her so her fighting back was to no avail.

We even as young children knew that if he was like this it was best to just not say anything that would provoke the evil. His Mother was obviously not aware of this, though to be honest I now know she was, but maybe she was thinking she of all people could talk some sense in to him. One of the neighbours must have called the police and when they finally arrived he was thrown in the back of the police van and locked up. The officers brought our Nan back inside. We could hear them speaking to her "I think you need an ambulance" one officer stated.

"No, no ambulance, I have his two children in the room. They must be terrified" Nan replied. The door to the bedroom opened but we were not moving from the safety of the covers. I heard a few footsteps then the covers were pulled back slowly.

"Are you OK?" said a tall dark haired officer.

"Yesss" I stuttered.

"Nanny, where's our Nanny?" Barry spat out through his tears. The officer could see that the ordeal had really shaken us up. He must have noticed the puddle of Barry's urine that we were sitting in.

"Your Nanny is fine now, we are here to help" he continued speaking with us until we were comfortable enough to come out of the room. He obviously wanted to question us about what we may have seen or heard but he knew too well he could not do that without my Nannies permission. The officer picked Barry up in his urine soaked pants and to his credit he did not react at all to it. Barry held him so tightly around his neck that the poor officer almost could not breathe. When we arrived in to the lounge room I ran up to Nan but Barry would not leave the comfort and protection of the officer. Barry turned his head away from Nan and when she stood to grab him from the officer Barry tightened his grip. I would say that the mess that our Father had made of Nan's face frightened Barry enough to not want to go to her. She really should have gone to the hospital but she refused. We were questioned by the police but we were too afraid to speak out for fear that our Father would find out and this could happen. I eventually coaxed Barry to let go of the officer so they could return to their job of saving others. The officers took our Father away again this night and that was that. After Nan had changed her bed linen and dried the urine from her mattress she popped us in to her bed. I did not sleep at all that night.

The following morning Nanny was obviously sore as she was walking hunched over. She made us breakfast and then she called our Mum. Nan told her what had happened and I could hear the voice on the other end of the phone "Are you OK?"

"Are my children OK?" the voice said frantically.

"The children are fine love, I am fine." Nanny proceeded to tell our Mum that she was sending us back the next day. Nanny warned Mum to stay away from him that he was crazy. This I think my Mum already knew. Nanny took us to the airport the next day, we kissed her goodbye. I remember my Nanny saying to me just before we got on the plane

"We love you Emily, you know that don't you?"

"Yes Nanny, I know" was my reply. These words may have been my Nannies farewell to me. Maybe she thought that this was the last time she would ever see us. I got the feeling also that this was the last time so as we heading down the passageway to board the plane I turned and ran back to my Nanny. I grabbed her around the legs and cried my little eyes out. The last call was made and my Nanny signalled to the air hostess to come and get me. The hostess pried me off my Nanny and picked both Barry and I up and took us to the plane. I remember seeing my Nanny very blurry through my tear stained eyes. She was covering her face and wiping her tears in turn. Once onboard the hostess fastened our seat belts, gave us colouring books and biscuits. She comforted us until we finished crying then she went about her job of getting others seated and ready to take off. We had to sit with the hostesses as we were minors but this didn't worry us as they were always great with us.

Mum offered for us to go back to Sydney to see our family after this but when she stopped paying for the full flights there and back and asked that my Father pay half, well we stopped going. He did come to see us though. But the last time I remember being with my Father we didn't go home to Mum for a while. Let's just say Mum's heart was almost completely broken by then..

Chapter 4: Kidnapped

We moved again to a neighbouring town, about fifteen minutes away from Pa and Nan. The new house was in the housing commission area. It was a three-bedroom brick home and it was brand new. Mum hand made all the curtains for this nice little house that we would call home. We had a huge back yard with a clothes line that we would hold on to and swing around (Hills Hoist) most Aussie kids did it and not many parents were happy about it.

We had been there a while when Mum's new boyfriend moved in. If Mum yelled at us he would always say "It's alright love!" we thought, he was ok but he wasn't our Daddy.

The school holidays were coming up and my Father called Mum to ask if we could go to Queensland and stay with him at his cousins house our Aunty Gail. Mum agreed as she wanted us to see our Dad and she always hoped he would change for the better. Mum also knew Aunty Gail from when she was with my Father so it was final we were going to see our Father again.

Mum told us the plans that had been made and we were so excited! We were to be picked up by Aunty Gail's husband Paul in a HUGE semi-trailer truck and go with him over night to Queensland where we would meet our Father.

The weekend after our Father called we were picked up by Paul. Paul was very tall and lean with shoulder length black curly hair. The whole trip was a blur apart from us being able to pull the cord for the horn to blast which was just to the right of where Paul sat. We also got to sleep in the cabin. Being young it fit us both in with two little curtains that could be pulled together to keep the lights from oncoming traffic away from our eyes, enabling us to fall fast asleep. We must have slept for a while as when we woke he said "Won't be long now kids and you'll be seeing your Daddy" wow were we excited a truck ride and we got to see our Dad!

We stayed at Mt Tamborine which is located in the Gold Coast Hinterland. I didn't know where we were then but I do now. I don't remember seeing much of our Father whilst we were there but I do remember what happened to my poor Mother. One-night Aunty Gail got a call from our Father. He told her he had been arrested for drunk driving and assaulting police officers. The story that is to follow was told to me by my biological Father a few years later.

•

He had been driving drunk and as the police were trying to pull him over he started to drive down the main road (a one-way street) in Surfers Paradise the wrong way. A high speed chase occurred instigated by my drunken Father. A police car finally pulled him over when it was safe and away from others. One Police Officer ran to the driver side window which was where my father was and the other Officer was on the passenger side of the car. The officers tapped on the windows on either side of the car and demanded that the windows be wound down. Paul was in the passenger side. Dad wound down the window and so did Paul. The officer with Paul asked his name and Paul proceeded to tell him his real name, whilst the other officer asked the same question of my Father who proceeded to say his name was Paul, he was not going to give his real name as he had warrants out for his arrest. The officer asked my Father "Didn't you see the arrows?" the arrows signalled that this was a one-way street and my Father ever the smart arse said

"Nope Officer, and to tell you the truth I didn't see no Indians either" The officer frustrated by this time asked my Father to step out of the car so my Father wound up the window. The police officer then smashed the window on my Father's side and as you all know by now he is aggressive when drunk, so he jumped out of the car and started beating this poor guy really badly. The other officer raced around to help his partner and he coped it too for his efforts. In the end they managed to arrest him. He spent twelve months in Boggo Road Jail for all his outstanding warrants plus what he had done that night.

The night this occurred I only heard one side of the call from my Father but I remember clearly that my Aunty when finished on the call with my Father got straight on the phone and called my Mum. I heard my Aunty Gail say "You have to sell all your stuff to get him out or you will never see your kids again" I started to get scared as I wanted to see my Mummy. These calls continued for about six weeks back and forward. Mum had called the police but she didn't know where we were. We got to speak to her sometimes and she would say

"Where did you go today? What does it look like there etc.?" she didn't want to show us she was scared or make Gail suspicious so they were pretty simply questions that would sound like a normal conversation between children and their mother. I told mum

"We went to a dam where there was a tunnel and the water went over us, I got a leech on my leg whilst we were there. We also went to Magic Mountain and Aunty Gail brought me a toy horse" like most little girls I had a fascination with horses.

After about three of these calls I think the police had an idea of where we were and they contact Queensland Police who found the semi-trailer we had gone to Queensland in and the address we were staying at. This was the end of our kidnap situation. We didn't feel kidnapped though which I guess is a good thing. We got to go for a ride in a police car and they even let us put the sirens on wow we loved this ride. The police took us to the airport from there we flew to a town close to home and Mum was there to meet us. I couldn't understand why she was crying so much but now that I know what happened I can totally understand.

My Father was released from prison and we were never to go away with him again, not on our own. If my Aunty brought him to visit it was ok but all visits were to be supervised. Mum explained at the time that the court man said "He can come but he has to bring our Aunty Tessa" Each holiday after that my Aunty Tessa would bring him up to visit us. We would be allowed to go fishing, to the beach or park but not much further than that. I remember one-time Dad saying

"Let's go away together again"

"No Daddy the court man said no and Mummy will cry" I responded so he took us home. I was really upset every time he left as I truly missed my Daddy and knew that I would not see him again for ages, I was a Daddy's girl. Before I went inside this last time Aunty Tessa seeing that I was distraught said

"Emily! This is my diary you can have it. That way you always have us with you and if you ever miss us write down what you feel and when we come back you can read it to us" I still have that little yellow diary with gold leaf on the edge of the pages and a padlock to this day. My brother was the opposite he always misbehaved for Mum but it was because he didn't want to go with our Father ever.

Chapter 5: The Stepfather

My Mum married her boyfriend Arthur, I was the flower girl and Barry was the page boy at their wedding. It was a beautiful ceremony, I remember my Pa giving my Mother away and he looked awesome as usual, he was so very proud. Mum wore a lilac wedding dress as she had been married before and she couldn't wear white as tradition states. We were having so much fun at the wedding in one day I had gained a Step Brother and a Step Sister both of whom where older than Barry and I, we loved them. They didn't live with us they both lived with their Mother but we saw them every day. That night my new step father got so drunk and I saw something in his eyes I didn't like. I couldn't put my finger on it at that time. Later that night my Mum and my new Step Father went on their honey moon. They went for a week to Sydney whilst we got to stay with Pa and Nan.

You have probably noticed I don't speak much about my Nan. I did love her and as a child you tend to want to love your relatives but my Nan was a funny lady, she had her favourites and my Brother and I weren't one of them. We had 36 cousins on this side of the family and I suppose Nan didn't really have room for us in her favourites list. This was obvious when there were others were around. She wasn't nasty to us she just didn't show us she loved us. I don't ever remember her giving me a hug and if I went to hug her she didn't really give me a hug back.

All this being said we did sometimes misbehave for her. One day one of my cousins came over and we decided it would be a great idea to see what fly spray and a match does. Let's just say after she demonstrated what would happen she handed me the can so I could have a go. I lit the match, pressed the spray and as you all know a huge flame came out. Unlucky for me at this very minute Nan came out the back door and here I was with a can of fly spray alight. She started yelling at us and saying "You wait till your Pa gets home" well we never moved so quickly. We were smart though we started helping Nan clean the house from top to bottom in hopes that she would not tell Pa. When Pa got home not a word was mentioned to him plus my Nan had had a few glasses of beer by then.

When Mum's honeymoon had finished she and Arthur came to pick us up, we went back to our little house. We got home just after dark, Arthur unlocked the door and went inside he noticed that there was mess everywhere, someone had taken our television and smashed all our plates and left half eaten biscuits everywhere. Our house had been broken in to. Arthur told us to stay outside while he checked the house. Once he had checked everywhere and was sure that the perpetrator was no longer there he called us in. Mum took my little brother to his bed, she had carried him from the car as he had fallen asleep on the trip home. I followed close behind my Mum holding on to her dress. Mum then took me to my room, I was frightened, I thought that it was my Father coming to hurt my Mum again. I made Mum check everywhere. When mum checked under my bed she saw a window screen. The person had gotten in to our house through my bedroom window! They used the tap that was below my window to climb up, pulled the screen off and open my glass window then once inside they put the screen under my bed. There was no way I was sleeping in my room that night, I couldn't stop shaking. Imagine being a little child and knowing that the boogeyman came through your window. This is exactly how it felt.

The police were called, when they arrived they checked everything even taking fingerprints samples. I felt safer as one of the officers told me "It's ok now. We will catch the bad guy" Mum laid with me till I fell asleep. Let me tell you it would have been really early in the morning before I actually fell asleep. I love my Mum.

Over the coming weeks we found out the it was a local Aboriginal man well known to the police. That very same night he had broken in to several homes and beating the women inside the houses. He knew where the women lived alone with small children in most cases. Just lucky that Arthur was there also as I can only image what would have happened had we in fact been in that house when he was on his rampage. We also found out that he had beaten his mother almost to death and raped her.

Life seemed settled for a few months and we got a puppy oh how I loved this dog. The puppy followed me everywhere, I taught him tricks, how to sit and also how to howl when I said his name. Mum and Arthur got the dog so that we could have a little more protection and with the hope that this dog would alert us to possible trouble.

My brother and I got bikes for Xmas and Arthur taught us how to ride them in our back yard. Arthur had a greenhouse around the side of our house that we were never allowed to go in as he had "Mexican Tomato Plants" in there that only flower once a year, this is what he told Mum and us kids but it was a marijuana plant.

One day when we were riding our bikes my brother accidentally rode into the greenhouse and crush one of these plants. We didn't say anything as we were so scared of what would happen to us. When he got home from work he went in to his green house to water his beloved plants and saw the mangled plant. He was furious he started yelling "You fucking kids get out here now". We knew what he had found but we went out as we were told. Mum had gone to a neighbours house for a cup of tea as you could leave your kids at home in those days to play in your back yard. After he had stopped ranting and swearing he asked

Emily Reilly

"Who did this?" neither of us said who it was but when he grabbed my arm my little brother stepped forward

"It was me" Arthur grabbed him by the arm and started smacking him so hard whilst swearing at him. The smacking was that hard it was lifting Barry off the ground, Arthur then dragged Barry to a chain that was on the clothes line that had been used for the dog when it misbehaved and chained him to it. I tried to stop him but he just back handed me so hard I fell backwards. I was crying and I am sure the neighbours could hear us but didn't come out.

"You want to act like an animal you will be treated like one" Arthur said this made no sense at all as I look back on it but to him at that time it did. This was a little child that was learning to ride his bike and accidentally ran over his precious plant.

Mum got home about two hours later and I was in my room still crying and my brother was still chained to the clothes line in the blistering heat not making a sound. Arthur explained what had happened, (his version of the truth) he said we were being assholes and my brother started acting like and animal so he chained him up, almost everything that came out of his mouth was a lie. Mum yelled at him and ran out the back to my brother and unchained him. I came out when Mum brought him inside and he hadn't even cried. My brother never really showed much fear. Barry was so red as it was a Saturday and Arthur only worked till lunch time so he had been out there in the heat with no water or shade for hours and was sunburnt.

When Mum finally got Barry inside Arthur was nowhere to be seen and all I could think was *I want my Daddy*, weird I know but that is what went through my mind. I remember a lot of yelling later that night between Arthur and my Mum and a door slam but I

UNBROKEN

don't remember anything else only that when we got up the next morning Mum had breakfast on the table as she always did and Arthur was not there Mum had kicked him out. We were so happy. We had months without Arthur living with us, Barry and I were so happy but Mum was miserable. Arthur used to come around and see Mum and beg to be taken back. Mum finally agreed and he moved back in.

Arthur went down to the pub almost every night after work and played in the local darts competition. Mum hated drinking as you can imagine with what had happened to her. At about 7:30 at night Mum had a call and we were packed in the car to go and pick up Arthur from the pub. He had won the darts comp. When we arrived we all waiting in the car out the front for what felt like forever and Mum was not happy as she had to go in several times to call him out. When Mum went in the last time Barry decided to sit on the car window sill and pretend he was in Dukes of Hazard (this was one of our favourite shows) his legs where inside the car but his body was out and he was holding the top of the window sill. Upon Mum returning to the car with Arthur she yelled at Barry and told him "Get in to the car" Arthur was intoxicated beyond belief. They started arguing all the way home and Mum was furious.

We came to the corner of our street and turned left, we were only doing about 20km an hour as Mum never sped and this corner had a lot of loose gravel. We drove for about 30 meters and our driveway was about another 10 meters up the road on the right when I looked over and my little brother wasn't there. I interrupted Mum and Arthur's argument "Mum ! Barry is not here anymore" Mum was so angry she told him to get back up on the seat and stop messing around. Then Arthur in his intoxicated state looked over his shoulder to where my brother should have been sitting behind Mum, I have never seen or heard someone sober up so quickly he turned to Mum

Emily Reilly

"He is not there!" Mum pulled into our driveway and looked down the road she was in such a panic as what we saw was so frightening. Barry was laying on the road face first as Mum and Arthur ran towards him he got up not a tear to be seen or a cry to be heard and started walking up the road. He had fallen out the car window when we went around the corner. Arthur reached him first and the whole left side if Barry's face was full of gravel and there was so much blood. Mum thought he had lost his eye and started looking for it, she was not thinking straight. Arthur put Barry in the back of the car and he got in the driver's side, Mum got in the back with Barry whilst I sat up in the front of the car. We had a V8 and I had never been in a car doing that speed. The hospital was about 15 kilometers away and we got there in record time. Arthur carried Barry in with blood going everywhere and Mum followed closely behind. I got out of the car and ran to keep up with Mum. When we got inside the Emergency Department they took Barry and Mum into a room straight away. All I could hear was Mum crying and then I heard someone say

"Help her" Mum had passed out just as they had started cleaning Barry ready to stitch the area above his eye. I heard Barry scream and I have to tell you, all I wanted to do was go and hit the doctor and make him stop hurting my little Brother. I have never since that night heard Barry scream. We stayed there all night in that dull hospital waiting room. When Barry came out he had bandages all over his tiny head. Mum was beside herself. We got home, Mum took Barry to bed and to be honest I don't remember much more of that situation. I do know that my Brother had a terrible habit of hurting himself. He used to fall upstairs not down them lol.

I was always protecting Barry we use to catch a bus home from school. Barry was always back chatting bigger kids on the bus and they used to threaten to bash him. Because of what we had been

UNBROKEN

through I used to say "Don't hit him I will tell Mum when we get home and she will smack him" for some reason they believed me. All the way home I would chastise him. Barry and I used to pull a small branch off one of the trees on the way home. We would peel off the outer layer and it left a white stick that was like a whip. We always had magpies swooping down on us so we used the sticks to deter them from attacking us by waving them above our head.

One day after the usual walk home we went inside to find Arthur sitting inside on the lounge. For some reason he was home early and had already had a few drinks. We said hello to Arthur as we went to walk pass and put our bags in our room. I don't remember why but he grabbed the stick I was holding and started whipping me with it, I suppose I must have done something wrong but I really can't remember what, each time he swung the stick it sounded like a whip cutting the air before I felt the burning. I can't remember how many times he hit me with it but Barry got the stick off him and broke it in too little pieces. I ran to my room and closed my door too scared to come out and I could not stop the crying when I heard him get something from the kitchen. He then went in to Barry's room and all I could hear was a muffled sound and every now and then I heard Barry whence. No crying or screaming, I snuck out the front door and went to our neighbours house I was so scared and all I wanted was for them to go next door and help Barry. Our neighbour had Mum's number and she called her. Mum worked just up the road at the Nursing Home so she was home in about five minutes. I saw her pull in to the driveway and then I heard screaming and something being thrown. I then saw Arthur get in to his car and take off.

My neighbour took me home to see my Mum and to check that everything was ok. I don't blame our neighbour for not going over she had two little kids and one of which had a whole in her heart so she really couldn't. Mum was holding Barry and still he would not cry. His eyes were bloodshot and I knew he wanted to cry but he would not give anyone the satisfaction of seeing him cry.

Mum had kicked Arthur out again...

The next day when we went to school Barry had to wear the school uniform but long pants and I had to wear my winter tights and a jumper over my dress. The welts on our legs and arms were terrible. Barry told Mum that Arthur hit him with a wooden spoon and when that broke he used the jug cord on him. I loved my little brother so very much but what could I do to protect him from that? I guess I could have stood in front of him and taken the beating instead of running next door. God knows he would have done it for me. I often think about this and what he has done for me over the years. He was a very brave little boy and he never showed fear, he was like a bouncing clown the type you knock down and they bounce back up. Oh how I loved him..

Chapter 6: It's My Party

My Mum threw a party every year for our birthdays. On my 10th birthday my Mum had a really good friend come over (Julie) I had grown up with her daughter (Shel). I had all my friends there a couple I had known since moving up from Sydney. I will name one in particular as he will become a big part of my story as we go along his name was Nigel, I haven't changed his name as it is too important to keep it the same, I cannot make a name up for him. This is the one and only time this will happen during my story but you will see why later on.

Mum was inside with Julie, our neighbour and all of us kids were out the back playing in our clown water sprinkler. When the water was on the hat went up and when you ran through it the hat dropped, the game was to run through and not get hit by the hat. We were all having such a great time. Mum had set a table up on the back veranda with party food. After a while of playing in the water Mum called us all so I could cut the cake. When I got to the veranda the best cake was sitting on the table, Mum had made me a Barbie doll cake. All the candles were lit and just as I went to blow out the candle there was a huge bang inside the house. Mum ran in to see what it was and it was Arthur he had banged the door open. He started yelling at Mum and ranting saying he wanted her back etc. Julie came running out the back and took all of us out the side gate and around the corner to her house. I was so scared and all the other kids had no idea what was happening. Julie called all the parents and asked them to pick their children up from her house. All I could do was cry, Barry was trying to make sure I was ok. Julie came and sat with me and said "Everything will be ok Emily. You can't cry on your birthday" I was so worried about my Mum. All the kids got picked up pretty quickly but Nigel and Shel were with me still. Shel asked me to go outside and play on her trampoline. When we got there we jumped up so we could see my house as this is what Shel used to do all the time. She would jump up and call out to me. I couldn't see anything. A few hours had passed and the phone rang. Julie said

"Barry, Emily your Mum called and she wants you to come home everything is ok" Julie packed us in her car and drove us there. When we got there Arthur was inside sitting on the lounge. I couldn't even look at him as he had ruined my birthday and I really didn't like him. Arthur moved back in that day, I am not sure why but I think Mum always tried to see the best in people and gave them a second and third chance. Everything seemed to go well for a few months and Mum and Arthur brought a house together on the other side of town just near the river. It was a very nice area.

Before leaving our house to go to the new house I went up to the shop with a friend of mine (Carole). We were always trying to be older than we were. Mum used to sometimes send Barry and I up to the shop to get milk or cigarettes for her and she would always give us a little extra to get some lollies.

This time Carole and I were going to buy cigarettes but not for my Mum. We got to the shop with Carole's money and brought the cigarettes. The guys at the shop never questioned me as I usually got them for my Mum. When we started walking back I said to Carole "If my Mum comes I am going to throw these in the bush and jump in after them" Carole agreed and not one minute later Mum's car came up over the hill. Well I can tell you I threw the bag so far into the bush but I did not get in on time. The car screeched to a stop and Mum came running over.

"What are you two doing up here?" I tried to lie but like Mum always told me I couldn't lie straight in bed. She then asked what I had thrown into the bush.

UNBROKEN

"Nothing" Mum walked over the area I had thrown the bag and found it. Well let's just say I was in trouble BIG time. Mum put us both in the car and she didn't say a word. All the way to Carole's house I tried to say we had brought them for someone else. Mum was not buying this, Carole got out of the car and Mum took me home. She made me smoke the whole packet and I was so sick. I must admit this is something I probably would have done to try and deter my child also. It worked though I didn't smoke again...... until High School lol.

We moved to our new house and it was fantastic. So big with a huge back yard. It was a bit of a walk from our Primary School but we didn't have to catch a bus anymore and it wasn't long before I started High School which was just around the corner. The only problem with our new house was that Arthur's Mother and his brother lived six houses down and his brother was also an alcoholic. Every afternoon Arthur's brother would be at our house and he would get rolling drunk...

We had a house warming party at our house and so many of Arthur's friends were there. Mum didn't have any of her friends over as Arthur didn't like Mum's friends, he didn't like that they supported her and told her she could do so much better than him. This night all the adults were out on our back veranda playing cards and having a few drinks. One of Arthur's friends who was introduced to me said to call him uncle Pat. He seemed really nice he would tickle me and make me laugh. Mum put the TV on in the lounge room for Barry and I so we didn't have to be around the adults. She got us a plate of chips and drink so we could have our own little party. I got bored a few hours later and went back out. Mum went back inside for a minute and everyone was busy chatting when Uncle Pat said "Emily come and sit on my lap" I did what I was told.

Emily Reilly

"Give uncle Pat a kiss" so I went to kiss him on the cheek and this sick man kissed me on the lips and put his tongue down my throat. He held my head so tightly I could pull away. No one saw this as they were all drunk and busy chatting. He must have heard my Mum coming as he stopped and pushed me off his lap. I just stood there not able to comprehend what had happened to me. I was only about eleven at this stage. I was frozen with fear. Mum back came out and told me to go inside and that she would tuck me in to bed. I turned and walked inside. Mum followed me. I kept looking behind me to make sure that Uncle Pat was not there. We went to the lounge room and got Barry. Mum told me to go to my room but I would not leave her side. I don't know why but I felt like it was my fault that this had happened and I didn't want to tell Mum as I didn't want to get in trouble, crazy though as my Mum probably would have tried to kill him if she knew.

After tucking in Barry Mum took me to my room. I got in to my bed (I had a double bed) and Mum tucked me in. After she left I got out of my bed and went straight in to Barry's room. I didn't tell him what happened but I told him I was scared and asked if I could sleep in his room, he tried to calm me and find out what had happened but I wouldn't say and he didn't push me. I got in to the top bunk and felt so much safer. Not long after getting in to bed I heard someone go to my room. I can't say who it was as I was in the top bunk in Barry's room but it wasn't my Mum as she would have come in to see where I was.

I am so glad I went to Barry's room that night....

Chapter 7: Time to Protect Myself

Not long after this I asked if I could join Karate. Our Shihan was an old family friend who had known my Mum's family since she was a teenager when our family holidayed up here (we will call him Matt). Mum told me later in life that when my Father lived in our town every time Matt found out or suspected Dad of hitting my Mum he would beat him up. It wasn't hard to know when this happened as she was so bruised.

Matt took me under his wing. He was extremely hard on me. He loved us like his own kids. I did martial arts for a very long and quickly climbed the ranks within our Dojo. The Dojo was an old tin shed when I went there with blue carpet on the floor. It smelt like sweat as when we were there we worked hard. Everyone was so nice and they became like my second family and I always felt safe with my gee on and my second family around.

On one of the last grading's we went to a seaside down (this was a few years later at this stage I was about fourteen (turning twenty), it was a three-day grading. We were woken every morning at about 3am before the sun came up and our day didn't finish till at least 6pm.

This particular grading, we all had to do 3568 power techniques into a bag within an hour. This number came from one of our masters who had broken this many ice blocks in that time. Most of the girls used their palms but not me I used my fists. At the end of this my cipher knuckles were raw and bleeding. I did not want to stop I was so focused, martial arts became my life and settled me down a bit. We then had to fight 52 rounds of 2 minute fights with black belts. This was full contact. We had pads on our shins and forearms. I was defending during my first round and Matt

Emily Reilly
stopped the fight. He came over to me and said "This video is going to Sydney so you can be graded, you need to fight" I was a bit of a smart arse, not too much as I had to much respect for Matt so I responded

"I am fighting" I was not happy that I was told what to do.

"Emily, if you don't fight you will not be graded" so I entered the ring and was furious. The guy I was fighting had no idea what was coming. He stepped in to throw a punch at me and as he did I punched him in the nose. Blood went everywhere. He covered his face instinctively. I ran in to make sure he was ok when Matt yelled out

"Emily! Get to your corner and kneel down" I turned around and went to my corner. You had to face away from your opponent and kneel down as a sign of respect when they were injured. He was taken away from my ring and another person was brought in to replace him. Again I was just defending and again Matt told me the same thing. I don't know why I got angry at this again or didn't learn from the last time but I'm sure Matt knew exactly what he was doing and it was getting me to win. This time the guy that was in the ring came at me and I did a roundhouse kick that hit him on the hip area. He dropped to the ground, I went in to check on him as all I heard was a crack. Matt yelled again sternly

"Emily! Corner" so I again turned around and went to my corner. He was taken to the hospital as I had dislocated his hip. The rest of the fights I attacked and defected and they went past pretty quickly with minimal injuries.

The next day we got up, went down to the beach and had to stand in the waist high water do punching techniques and our carters in the water for about two hours. It was freezing, as soon as we got out we had to go for a 15 km run to a massive hill called heart break. One of my best friends (we will call her Kylie) was

UNBROKEN

with me and a girl I used to call Sis as everyone thought we were twins. We got on so well (we will call her Melissa). We all ran to the top of this enormous hill. When we got there Matt yelled to us "Back down when you get to the top" so Kylie and I decided to run as fast as we could to the bottom without falling over. Just to put it in to perspective a lot of cars couldn't make it up this hill as it was so steep hence the name "heartbreak". When we got to the bottom we were out of breath. Matt yelled again

"Back up" well let's just say we didn't run that fast down the hill again because everyone else was only halfway down that bloody hill and turned around to go back up and we had to go ALL the way back. This happened another three times but we had smartened up and took our time going down. When we finished this we had to run all the way back to camp. Wow that was a big day and by the end of it we were exhausted.

That night I learned about boys. I had a crush on one of the black belts and he kissed me. We kissed all night (no Matt did not know as it was in our tent) Kylie liked another guy but he got with Melissa. This camp was amazing, we ate good food and laughed a lot but boy did we work out.

Weeks later our grading results came in and I had skipped one full belt. This happened twice to me during grading's I was so very proud. The grading was videoed by Matt and my Mum still has this video to this day it is a VHS tape. I was pretty sporty when I was younger, Barry didn't really like sport all that much he would rather be out playing war games with his mates.

My Mum's family where hockey players. Two of them where representatives. I used to play hockey every weekend. My Pa was a hockey nut. He would always be there when we played. Games started at 9am and we were there all day. Before we played Pa would make sure we warmed up and stretched, he would watch every game and during breaks he would make sure that we had oranges and didn't drink too much water. He would run through the game and what we did wrong and what we did right, he never criticised us he just pointed out the obvious. When the game finished he would lay a towel down on the ground and rub our legs down again. When I was thirteen I was playing in the under fifteen A grade side. My Pa was approached by one of the coaches and asked if I could fill in for the A grade women's team. Pa knew I could so it but he asked if I wanted too. I said ok and from that day on I played in the A Grade women's team as you couldn't really play for more than one team for a whole season. Karate was my first love but Hockey was in my blood or so I was told.

One freezing cold wet day I went out to play a game with a team I had been warned about. They were really aggressive unfortunately for one of the ladies she hit me one to many time with her stick. This particular lady was tripping me over all game and when we came back on she tried it again, however this time I swung my stick and hit her across the face (not nice but I was so young, stupid and a tad angry at her) it knocked her mouth guard out and one of her teeth, I was sent off. Pa was not happy with me at all "Emily! No matter what happens out there you make sure you keep your cool, you are better than that. Go and apologise NOW!" It was killing me to apologise to this woman but I did as I was told. I did feel sorry for what I had done afterwards though as Pa's words sank in.

Between Karate and Hockey, I was pretty busy but I always had time for my friends. We had a tight knit groups which consisted of ten kids. Some lived in town and others lived out of town but we always managed to stay at each other's house. My friends loved my Mum but not my Step Father and not because I said anything but because when they were there when he was drunk and he tried to be cool.

UNBROKEN

Nigel lived in town and we always spent time together. He was from a broken home also. We used to go down town or ride our bikes. Mum brought me a horse something I had always wanted and I used to ride my bike down to the paddock one handle bar had a bucket of water and the other a bucket of chaff. Nigel would meet me there and we would talk for hours. He was one of my best mates. I told him everything and he told me everything. His Mum was really nice but always chose the wrong guys. One of her boyfriends used to beat him really badly all the time. Nigel would escape and come to see me so we could chat. He was the only one who knew about that night I had to sleep in Barry's bunk bed.

Kylie was also always there from me. I used to love going to her house as she lived on property and had horses and motorbikes. She was the one who taught me how to ride a motor bike. It didn't turn out well when I first rode the bike as she told me not to get to top gear but I went all the way to the top of a hill and turned around to come back and I forgot what was the brake and what was the clutch and ran straight in to a gate and crushed my fingers. We were not game to tell her Dad as he was an ex-military man and was very firm. This man was so wise though he once told us (they were dropping me home one night after karate)

"You will only ever make one true friend in your life so cherish them when you do" I will never forget these words and he was so right.

Getting ready to start High School this is when my life was to change   again...

Chapter 8: Year 6 Graduation

It was the day before my year 6 farewell and we were all so excited about going to High School the following year. Mum had made my skirt and top for the big night, I was a bit of a tom boy and really didn't like dresses at this stage. It was the eighties and I had a Fluor pink puff skirt and nice top. Pa had built us a billy cart using a mowers wheels, wooden planks for the seat and rope for a steering wheel. Barry decided we should take it out and have a go on it. We went to a hill down the road and it was a VERY steep hill. I demanded of Barry "You have to keep your feet down all the way to the bottom" I was concerned about falling off and hurting myself and I knew that Barry was a bit of a rough nut. He agreed and I got on the back of the billy cart. He was so cheeky he did what he said he would until we were about a meter from the bottom, then he giggled, picked his feet up and started pulling on either side of the rope making the billy cart go from side to side. As I had feared I came off and slid down the hill on my left leg sideways. I started to cry and yell at him. He ran over to make sure I was ok but I had a lot of skin missing off my thigh. It was like a burn but with gravel in it. If you have ever had this happen, you will realise how much it hurts. I hobbled back up the hill and cried all the way home while Barry dragged the billy cart. All the way home he begged me

"Don't tell Mum what I did" he didn't want to get in trouble.

When I got home Mum came running out to see why I was crying and give me a hug. I just said I came off and slid down the hill no more than that so Barry didn't get in to trouble for being stupid. Mum helped me up the back stairs and walked me to the bathroom where she ran the bath and put in some peroxide, I knew this was going to hurt. I got in the bath and started screaming as it hurt so badly, it was like someone had poured acid on my leg. Mum

UNBROKEN

tried to calm me but all I could say is "Shit that hurts" just was the words left my mouth Mum slapped me on my arm

"Emily! I don't care how much it hurts you DO NOT SWEAR" I knew I shouldn't have done it as Mum was pretty strict about this sort of thing but it was a reaction and I didn't think before it came out due to the pain. Even as an adult I wouldn't swear in front of her out of respect. The next night was my year 6 farewell and all I was worried about was the gravel rash and burn on my leg showing when I had a beautiful skirt to wear. I was so upset.

The big night had arrived and I look beautiful or so Mum said. I was pretty popular at school so no one said anything about my leg the only people who did were Kylie and Nigel and it was just to find out what happened and make sure I was ok. Nigel asked because he was worried it was Arthur. That night we danced the night away and laughed so much. Nigel and I had a dance together which was pretty great because he was one of my best friends ever. I had a lot of friends but a few really good ones. When the night finished none of us cried we all were just too excited as it was the Christmas Holidays and the next year we were all to start High School together.

During the holidays we got to go and stay with Pa for a bit and then we would go camping with Arthur, his family and some of his friends and yes Uncle Pat was there. We stayed in a tent with all the other kids. During the time we were there we would go fishing during the day. One day we found a seahorse skeleton that had washed up on the shore it still had some scales which I thought was weird (Mum kept this for years). We use to go hunting for pippy's so Mum could make rissoles. Pippy's are a shell fish you only ate the tongue similar to a muscle only smaller. We would twist our feet from side to side in the wet sand until we felt a shell then you would dig down until you found it and pick it out to put in your bucket. I did this one time and the pippy was open and clammed

Emily Reilly

down on the side of my finger so hard it couldn't just be pulled off, believe me I tried. Mum took me back to the camping area and she used a can opener to get it off. Yes, I cried and yes it hurt lol.

On the first night we had a camp fire going and we got to roast marshmallows over the fire (yum). The adults were all drinking and someone was playing a guitar. We got told to get to bed as we had to be up early to go for a swim/surf. We all went to the tent. Uncle Pat said he had to go to the toilet and followed closely behind me. He leaned down with terrible beer breathe and said "Give Uncle Pat a kiss good night" I grabbed hold of one of the other kids

"RUN!" I yelled, Mum looked around to see why I had yelled, she got up and followed us to the tent. By the time she got there we were all inside and Uncle Pat had gone back to the camp fire.

"Are you all alright?" Mum asked concerned, we said yes but she knew different I think as she saw my face, I was terrified a look she had seen many times before. I made my way the furthest inside the tent right next to Barry and behind the others.

We got up the next morning at sunrise and went down to the beach. One of Arthur's brothers (Uncle Tim) dove in but he didn't come up quickly. When we saw him he was floating and being pushed around in the waves. We yelled out to Mum and she came running over she yelled out to Arthur "Arthur Tim's hurt, come quickly!" When he arrived we realised that this was not a joke. Tim was face down, by the time Arthur got into the water his other brothers were there and got Tim out of the water. Tim was not awake or able to move on his own. They carried Tim to the camp got the car and drove the 45 minutes to get to the hospital. Mum and some of the other ladies stayed with us kids. They didn't get back till late but Tim was not with them. They thought Tim had broken his neck. After ex rays they found it was not broken but he had dislocated something, when he dove in he hit the bottom. The next morning, we all packed up and went home.

During these holidays Mum was rushed to hospital.....

Chapter 9: Mum's Not Well

Being the school holidays as usually Barry and I were up early ready to spend our day outside in the sunshine. Mum was always up early. I never remember her sleeping in much. The times she did try to sleep in we woke her up, she was not too happy with us for waking her either.

One morning Barry and I were wondering around when we heard crying. This wasn't crying for sadness it was a painful cry. We looked out the back and Arthur's car was not there (we were checking he wasn't in the room). We went in to Mums room and she was curled up in to a little ball on her bed. I asked if she was ok and the reply was "Emily! Please call Arthur" then she continued to cry. I called Arthur and told him something was wrong with Mum (when he was sober he was ok). Not long after he arrived home. Barry and I had waited with Mum but there was nothing we could do to ease her pain. Arthur told us to go and open the door on the car. We waited outside for a minute or so and out came Arthur carrying my mum in his arms, he put her gently on the seat and ran to the driver's side and as he got in he told us to stay home and he would come back and tell us what was going on.

Mum had been to the hospital before with similar pain but we had not ever seen her leave it was pretty devastating seeing your Mum being taken away and you couldn't go with her to know she was ok or what was going on. Barry and I didn't leave the house that day as we were waiting for the phone to ring with any news on our Mum. We decided to clean the house for Mum so when she got home she didn't have to worry about anything as we were sure that she would be back a little later on.

UNBROKEN

Arthur arrived back late that afternoon only to get clothes for Mum and leave again. We asked what was wrong and he just said " Mum is in hospital and she is staying for a few days". I was full of questions but he wouldn't answer them he just went about what he was doing and left the house. I look back now and think maybe he was just really concerned about her and was so focused on Mum that he didn't think to stop and tell her children she was ok. I took a lesson away from this that no matter what I would take the time to explain things to my children as I never wanted them to worry like this about anyone. It's best to try and explain than the say nothing. Young minds always dream up so much.

Arthur arrived back after dinner time so we had made ourselves spaghetti on toast. When he arrived I again ran out to see what was happening with Mum and what was wrong. Arthur went straight to the back fridge and got himself a beer "Your Mother is in hospital; they don't know what is wrong with her now piss off" Devastated!

That night when I went to bed I closed my eyes and prayed for everyone as I always did. I asked God to make sure my Mum was ok and that she would be home soon. I then said the lords pray. I learnt the lords pray from my Mum. Mum gave me a little gold cross on a necklace and in the middle of the cross was a tiny crystal it had the lords pray etched in it. I used to put it to my eye and looking through it, you could make out most of the words. I closed my eyes and went to sleep. The next morning Barry and I got up and ran out to see if Mum was back. There was no sign of her or Arthur. Arthur had gone to work and Mum was still in the hospital. We spent most of our day hanging around the house. Barry decided in the afternoon to go and spend time with his friends. I just called mine on the phone and talked for ages, Mum and Arthur would be none too happy when they got the bill.

Emily Reilly

Later that day when Arthur arrived home (he had been to the hospital first) he got out of his car and went straight to the beer fridge. Barry wasn't home and it was after dark. I was a bit worried. Arthur started yelling and screaming "Where the Fuck is that little prick!" Arthur stopped hitting me when I got my purple belt in karate but he hadn't stopped hitting Barry.

"He should be back soon" as soon as those words left my mouth Barry walked in the back door and Arthur grabbed him by the arm and started kicking him on the backside all the time screaming at him what a useless piece of shit he was and every other swear word you could think of. This did not stop till he threw him in his room and slammed the door. Arthur only needed a beer to do this to us but he was worried since I got my purple belt that I would kick his arse if he did it to me. Arthur disappeared out the back and I ran in to see Barry, had I stepped in Arthur would have gotten so angry and done more damage to Barry, plus I was still a kid even though I thought I was older than I was. He had tears in his eyes and his back, legs and arse were so red. He had been kicked really hard. I sat with Barry all night and said to him

"I will never let him hit you again no matter what" we both cried wanting our Mum but she still wasn't home and we had no idea when she would be or even if she was coming back. That weekend Arthur took us to see Mum, she was so pale. I didn't ask her what was happening, she just said they would fix her and she would be home soon. It was so sad seeing my little Mum in a hospital bed and not coming home with us. She kissed us good bye after a while and Arthur took us home. When we got home he immediately went to the beer fridge and we went to the lounge room to watch a bit of television. Just before our bed time were heard Arthur call us to Mum's room. We both walked towards the bedroom door (this memory only came back to me a lot later in my life, I didn't have any recollection of this for a very long time, it took a shock for this to come back).

Arthur was standing in his doorway with no shirt on his arms where straight up and his hands were holding the top of the door frame. He started talking about sex! (Yes to two children). He was swinging back and forwards on the door frame trying to be cool and was talking about sex in a disgusting way. It made my skin crawl when I remembered this as it was not ok and I knew it. It was sleazy.... I don't know how the conversation ended or why it even started but I know I did not feel comfortable and even worse Mum wasn't home. I know I spent the night with Barry in his room and luckily enough nothing else happened that night.

The next afternoon when we walked in the house after being out all day we noticed that Arthur's car was there. Not thinking much more we walked inside. Arthur spoke really nicely to us which was strange as this wasn't him and how he had been with us especially when no one was around. He said "Where have you both been" Barry expecting a bashing anyway said in his bravest voice

"You're not our Dad! We've been out!" next thing we hear Mum yell out to us

"You two get in here now!" she was not happy. From the way she spoke we knew Arthur had said we had been shits of kids whilst she was in hospital. I will tell you now that this was far from the truth he was a drunk and a coward who beat kids and spoke to them inappropriately. If I was a shit he would have known about it and to be honest I wish I had of stepped in when he beat Barry and knocked Arthur out! Mum told us that we should never speak to Arthur that way and that we needed to respect adults (Mum was a stickler for manners).

Emily Reilly

Later that night Mum explained that she had been bleeding internally and that is why she was away so long but she was getting better. I never did tell Mum about the sex talk or the way he beat Barry. Maybe I should have...

Chapter 10: High School

Up early for my first day of High School. I had my knee length navy blue skirt and white shirt neatly pressed by Mum. Like any thirteen-year-old I was nervous about starting a new school and being the youngest as we had just come from primary school where we were the oldest. The positive was that we had all spoken either on the phone or in person the day before to organise a place to meet.

I arrived at the school and remember thinking to myself this place is huge. The nerves really started to kick in. I met all my friends out the front and we walked in together in one big group supporting each other and trying not to act nervous.

When the bell rang we went to roll call and we were told our grade classes and luckily we were all mostly in the same class (win). We organised a place to meet before we all went to our first class. This was beside A Block and this is where we stayed the entire time I was at school. A teacher asked us if we had any brothers or sisters that went to the school and I said yes a Step Brother and Step Sister. He asked who and I said my Step Brothers name. Big mistake! As much as I loved him I didn't realise he was really bad at school and my year adviser tarred me with the same brush from that moment on. Had I thought about it I should have said my Step Sister as she was loved by all. She was so beautiful on the outside and in.

During my first year not much happened but the second year I ran into a guy in year 11 (we will call him Dan). Dan was about 6-foot-tall dark haired and lean and he smelled amazing (he wore Drakar I found out later). Every time I walked past him he would smile at me and as I was always with my friends they used to say "He so likes you" I used to smell his cologne wherever I went.

Emily Reilly

After about three months I found a letter in my bag from Dan. It was an introduction to him and he said that he liked me and wanted to chat during lunch. I was so excited but had really bad butterfly's so I made Kylie, Nigel and Trish come with me. Not actually with me but stand around and watch for support from a distance.

I started to date Dan. It was so exciting. One day he asked if I would like to go to the movies with him and his friends. I didn't think Mum would let me but I was surprised as she allowed me to go as long as I was home before 10:30pm.

Before I go on I have to give you a bit more information on me at this age. I felt ten-foot-tall and bullet proof and as I did karate Mum knew I could look after myself. I was a typical popular girl (not stuck up just popular). I looked at the world and took it on like a bull at a gate. I was in the school softball team, played hockey and did my karate so I was very fit and my body was perfect (though at that age you don't think so) my skirts got shorter as did all my friends and we walked very confidently around the school. I was also a bitch to people and because of what I had gone through as a kid and what sometimes happened at home I was a hard person. No one ever messed with me at school. I will give a couple of examples of my personality at school.

One day a friend of mine (we will call her Lilly) came to school really upset. I sat with her and found out that her Father was sexually abusing her and bashing her. I took her to the office and asked to speak to the school counselor. When we went to go in the counselor asked me to stay outside. Lilly protested and said she wouldn't go in if I wasn't there. We went in and Lilly told her everything. The counselor advised that she had to speak with our Year Advisor (we will call him Mr. B). After Lilly had pulled herself together we went out and sat with our friends as it was a break. After the break we went to the art block and when we walked past the teachers' lounge we heard them all discussing Lilly and what had happened to her out loud with the door open. Lilly was distraught and I was furious (I was a protector of my family and friends). I told Lilly to go to class and I would sort it out. I walked in and asked them how they found out. One teacher told me it was Mr. B and to go back to class. Well I was having none of that I wanted to punish him for breaking confidence. I stomped off down to the science block where I knew he would be. I didn't realise it at the time but Lilly, Kylie, Trish, Nigel and a few other friends were following me.

When I arrived at the science block I went straight to the teachers' lounge barged in and said "Where is Mr. B?" as you can imagine it was not said nicely. The teacher was shocked and just looked around in the direction of Mr. B. I don't remember moving but I must have as I punched him in the face and next thing I know I am in the Principals Office. The Principal said "For what you have done Emily we are going to call your Mother as this is assault and you will be expelled" I retaliated with a quick tongue

"Well he has breached confidentially by telling everyone about Lilly and I know my rights you have to suspend me before you expel me" needless to say I was sent back to class, my Mum was never called and I didn't get expelled or suspended. Lilly went home that day and never returned to our school I still to this day wonder what happened to her.

I was sitting in the science block and a new girl, who had only been at our school for about three months decided for some strange reason to call my Mum a "SLUT". When she said this I asked what she had said and she repeated it. In my calmest voice I said to her

"It may not be today darling and it may it be tomorrow but I would watch your back" at that age I couldn't really let things go and I had an overwhelming need to defend my family and my friends. After school I walked out the front and Kylie followed me as she knew I was going to get myself in trouble. When I walked out I spotted the new girl, she was mucking around on someone's crutches. I asked her again what she had said and she swung one of the crutches at me. I don't really remember what else happened I must have blacked out as the last thing I remember is her sitting on her backside crying and covering her face. I know from what was told to me what had happened, I had beaten her up. Kylie walked over after and kicked her also.

I walked home as we only lived a block away and Mum was home sitting on the lounge. When I walked in and I said "I might me on assault charges tomorrow Mum" she jumped up and asked me why. When I told her all she could say is

"Sticks and stones, Emily"

A few days later the new girl's Mother called and asked me to leave her daughter alone I was still angry at her "If she comes back I will do the same" I wouldn't have but I really didn't like her, she moved schools. Now I am older I have found out she has changed her religion and is doing ok but back then she was always trying to be popular and not in the right way, by making people feel bad or insulting them and their families. She just did it to the wrong person.

I was walking to the tuck shop to get a can of coke and a pie when this Aboriginal girl came up and went to punch me. I blocked the punch and punched her in the face and I did a round house kick to her hip. I was confused as to why this had happened as I really did get along with all the people at school. This girl was only new and I had never spoken to her. I found out after when I heard the laughter that she was acting tough and talking about how good she was etc. and one of the aboriginals dared her to hit me, they knew I did karate. Poor girl really but I am glad it was me and not one of my friends.

This same year Barry started high school. One day I was walking to the toilets to have a cigarette when I saw him running out of A Block and he had blood coming from his left ear. I ran over and asked what had happened and all he could manage was "She did it and I didn't even do it" I calmed him down and asked again.

"I was flicking my ruler on the desk and the Teacher told me to stop so I did then my friend flicked his ruler, when she turned around she came over and grabbed my ear and pulled it" the pull was that bad that it tore behind Barry's ear hence the blood. Well my blood boiled and I went straight up the stairs with Barry in toe. I stomped in to the class and the Teacher said

"Get out of my class" I ignored her and faced everyone in the classroom

"Who flicked the ruler on the desk the last time" I think they were more scared of me than the teacher. Barry's friend put his hand up and as this happen I walked over to the teacher and punched her in the nose, just as I did this the Head of Geography walked passed and grabbed me by the arms and dragged me down stairs to the Principals Office. He didn't yell or say I was expelled he simply asked what had happened. I explained that she assaulted my brother and I lost it. I stated that no one should very do that to a person and that she was supposed to teach not attack children. I was sent away and that teacher lost her job.

I was a tough nut on the outside but broken on the inside. I do not condone what I did and I would never allow my children to do this. I honestly can say it was a protection mode that I went in to. If

Emily Reilly

I knew then what I know now I would have handled these situations better but I guess we can all say this.

Chapter 11: Chinese

Before I go in to my first date I want to take you back a little. We were in Year 8. We all decided that we would go out and have a party there were about 15 people that I was close too. It was all planned for a Friday night. We all told our respective parents that we were going to have a farewell dinner at a Chinese restaurant down town for a friend. I had a friend stay at my house because she lived out of town and she wouldn't have been able to make it if she didn't stay over. My friends loved my Mum but not Arthur even though he tried to act cool around them. Looking back now he probably looked like a dirty old man. He always tried to joke with my mates.

My house was the place to be, we wagged school all the time. We would go to school then decide we would go back to my house because we couldn't be bothered being at school. Sitting around my house smoking cigarettes and talking was so much better. At lunch times everyone would be at my house and a couple of us (usually Trish and I) would call a cab and go get Chinese for lunch and bring it back. This wasn't easy as we would have to duck down when we went past my Mums work and then again before we went past Arthur's work. We would have to do the same on the way home.

Everyday Arthur would come home at lunch and ask the same question "What are you all doing here" we would lie and say they are watching a movie at school or we had a free period. He believed us if he didn't he never said anything. It was on one of these days our final "party" plans were hatched.

I worked for my Mother on the weekends and most days after school to get some pocket money. One day my friend who was going to stay over (we will call her Pam) came to work with me.

Emily Reilly

She had her school bag which was not unusual. Mum managed a grocery come liquor store. Mum went out the back and we went to work. We rushed over and grab like 5 bottles of alcohol (enough for everyone) we put them in Pam's bag and she left the store to take them to my house (not that far away) and put them under my bed. We were set!

The next day none of us could be bother going to school so it was off to my house again. We were so excited. Everyone left just before the school bell was to ring and caught the bus to their homes. The party was to start at 7:30pm. Pam and I got dressed up and I wore my Mum's skirt. We did our makeup and we got in the car as Mum was dropping us off. On the way down Mum said "Don't burn my skirt Emily!" she knew I smoked, she didn't condone it but she thought she could control it (she would never buy me cigarettes either). Back then smoking wasn't splattered all over the papers and TV as a killer.

We arrived at the Chinese restaurant and as Mum pulled up she bunny hopped the car out the front, she wanted to embarrass me and it worked. We planned this party down to the last minute detail. The girl who was supposed to be leaving walked out of the Chinese restaurant like she had been inside. Our parents had brought it we had them hook line and sinker. After we all arrived we crossed over the road and went down to the river to drink the alcohol that Pam and I had stolen. I drank so much ... We were only there an hour when we decided we would all go and sit in the mall outside a nightclub where my Shihan (Matty) worked.

I was so drunk. I had never had alcohol before so drinking almost a bottle in an hour made a mess out of me. I sat in the gutter outside the night club and all I could say was "Please don't tell Matty" I knew if he found out I would be in so much trouble.

UNBROKEN

Karate was still first in my life at this stage. The only other thing I said was

"Don't burn Mum's skirt" I started to feel really sick and I asked Pam to go upstairs and get Lex, she was an older girl I knew who was a bartender at the club. Matty was the head bouncer.

"Pam, don't tell Matty why just say you need Lex" Pam and my friends were really worried about me they had drunk too just not as much as me. Pam did what I asked and Lex came downstairs only to run back up and get her car keys to take me home.

Lex had a really old valiant. It was red but faded and rusty. She got me in the back and put Pam in the front. She was racing me home when I said "I'm going to be sick" she pulled the car over got me out and I was violently ill. The trip home took us 45 minutes I was told the next day; it should have only taken 5 minutes that is how often I was sick. Lex pulled up one house away from mine and helped me out. Pam grabbed my arm and we walked around the side of my house to go through the back door. Pam whispered to me loudly (yes a loud whisper)

"Emily! Come here and I will hose you down" I remember looking at her and thinking how is hosing me going to help. I turned and started to make my way up the back stairs holding on to both the rails so I didn't trip and I walked really slowly, Pam in toe. I walked in to our laundry past out kitchen left in the dining room then followed the hallway till I go to my room. I didn't stop to look in to the lounge room, I flopped on my bed then I heard Mum say to Pam

"What are you doing home so early? You have been gone under two hours" Pam responded

"I think Emily has food poisoning" Well after hearing that I was set to play the role of my life, or so I thought. Mum rushed into my room. She stood over the bed I had flopped on and all I said was

"Mum the food was terrible" she knew exactly what was wrong and dragged me out to the toilet. When I kept lying to her she got really angry, she hated alcohol. She slapped me across the face and said

"You're just like your Father!" after I had been sick again those words hit me hard. She got me in the car and off the hospital. I had to drink charcoal to pump my stomach. I had alcohol poisoning. I promised myself after this I would never drink again. I had never had a drink before this so needless to say I had never had a hangover. Well that changed the next morning Mum woke me early and made me go to work. I had a terrible head ache and all Mum could say was that is your own fault. Mum asked where I got the alcohol from and I had to tell her the truth. She didn't say anything (it's always scary when Mum says nothing or is calm).

About an hour later the local Police Sargent came in to the shop. He took me out the back and had "the chat with me and told me I could be charged with stealing, underage drinking, public intoxication etc., I was petrified. Mum had called the police on me, luckily I wasn't charged. This was the way Mum dealt with things and I would do the same to my children. What I did was illegal and this taught me never to steal and at the time not to drink again but I also think the hangover taught me that. I was barred for a very long time after this and it meant not leaving the house except for school and no phone calls or friends over. Mum didn't stop karate or hockey though. She knew that karate would sort me out and Pa would also even without words.

I thought all the trouble was over until I had to go to Karate later that day. Mum had spoken to Matty. I didn't know this before

UNBROKEN

I left the house that day. I got to the Dojo and bowed to enter as you always did.

As soon as I stepped foot inside that Dojo Matty called me to the Alter and told me to kneel down. He told me he knew all about the drinking as he had seen me on the cameras out the front of the club. He spoke very calmly to me and asked if I knew all the things I had done wrong. I went through the list and he agreed. He then proceeded to tell me that he could strip me of my belt (degrade me). I started to cry. I had worked so hard for my belts all the way through and this had ruined it for me. I felt stupid and embarrassed but this, this one thing made me realise how stupid I was. Not the police, not Mum but losing something I had worked so hard for and was so proud of.

We spoke for a while and I thought it was over. He then said

"This is your warning Emily! Never ever get in this sort of trouble again or it is your belt!" I agreed and the tears stopped running. He scared the crap out of me..

Chapter 12: Strange Feeling

I know I keep putting off my first date but going through this process gets me remembering all the things that have happened during my life. I promise to get to my first date soon but I have to tell this part of my life as it is important.

After the party incident Mum was really hard on me, I understand now why but back then it was hard for me to comprehend.

One night I went to have a bath after Home and Away (An Australian Soap Opera). I told my family were I was going as usual. I don't know why I did this all the time but I would always say "Going to have a bath" or "Going to the toilet" weird but that's what I still do to this day.

When you walk in to our bathroom which was between Barry's room and mine. To the left you had the shower you walk to the edge of the shower and in front was our bath, straight ahead was the bathroom sink. We had a window above the bath that had misted glass and slid up and down with a latch on top. The bottom left corner of the top panel of glass had about an inch chip in it.

I ran the bath and got in and was washing myself. I had the strange feeling someone was watching me. I looked at the window and I could see an eye peeping through the small chip. I didn't scream I just froze. I was petrified. I yelled out to Mum once I got the nerve. She didn't hear me over the TV. The eye disappeared and I heard the footsteps going across our back veranda. They didn't disappear down the stairs from what I could hear so they must have gone inside. I jumped up and threw my towel over me. I got through the bathroom door then the dining room door and then I saw who it was. It was Arthur. He looked at me and didn't say a word. I think he knew I wouldn't say anything to Mum and I didn't again. I hated Arthur and I was always fighting with him, I missed my Dad. Even though he did what he did I missed him. I guess I was just a kid in a separated family.

I had been allowed to go and visit a friend that lived two doors down. We hatched a plan to run away. We decided we would run away to Sydney to see my Dad. The plan was to go to the bus stop down town near our library that picked people up to go to Sydney (at that stage it was a good 8-hour trip). So at 12pm we put the pillows in our bed and made it look like we were still in them, she at her house and me at mine we left a note for our respective Mum's, got our bags we had had packed for days from the hiding spot under our beds. We walked downtown and waited at the bus stop... I turned to her when we arrived and said "Do you have any money?"

"No" so we turned around and went home. When I walked up the back stairs of my house my Mum was sitting there waiting, she was so upset. She had heard me leave and read my note but didn't follow me as she knew I had no money and would come back as soon as I figured out there was no hope of getting on a bus. She told me to go to bed and we would speak in the morning. The next morning being a weekend I sat with Mum at the table and told her I hated it here and that I wanted to live with Dad.

"If you want to live with your Father I will call him and ask but Emily you will learn the hard way that it won't be as easy as you have it here. It is your decision though"

Mum called my Dad and he agreed I could live with him. I was leaving the next weekend. I was so excited but my Mum was breaking to pieces as at this stage I only thought of my Dad as awesome even after everything he had done but Mum knew him and the real him with alcohol and she must have been scared for me. She never said anything more.

I went to school the next week and said my sad goodbyes to everyone. The day had come and Barry said "You can't leave if you do I will take your room" he was being tough but inside I think it hurt him. We packed my things in the car and Mum, Barry and I went all the way to the Entrance.

The Entrance is a beachside town and as soon as we got there I feel in love with it. I think it was because of my Pa living in a beach side town. We got to the address my Mum had been given and pulled in to the driveway. On the right of the driveway was a lovely house on the left a caravan. Mum got out of the car and as I went to get out the caravan door opened. A tall blond headed lady stepped out. She was pretty but not as pretty as my Mum. After she got close to the car a young girl followed her. The ladies name was Lexi and the child that followed was Corrina (her daughter) she introduced herself to Mum and said she was Dad's girlfriend and that he had to work late and then had AA but he would be home straight after. Mum was nice to her but I could tell she was also being a bit cold. I think more out of worry than anything else.

Mum helped me get my stuff and we took it in to the Caravan (yes that is where they lived). As you walk in the door straight ahead is a table with two seats either side that fit 2 people either side. Directly to your left is a sliding door and a double bed, we turned to the right and walked past the tiny kitchen on the right on the left the toilet into a room at the end that had two bunk beds either side. I was a bit put off as I had my own room at home and here I had to share with this eight-year-old girl that I didn't even know. Once I had everything unpacked it was about 6pm. Mum had by that stage had a coffee and Barry had nothing. Mum turned to me and said "Emily it is getting late and I have a long trip I have to leave now" I ran over to her and hugged her so tight and told her I

UNBROKEN

loved her. You could tell her heart was breaking, Barry gave me a hug when we got to the car. I walked around with Mum and she hugged me again and whispered in my ear

"If you need anything, if anything happens call me I will come straight away, I love you!" I said I would be fine and she got in the car and drove away. Barry just looked out the window staring blankly. I was going to miss him and he didn't even get to see Dad.

It got to about 8pm and Dad still wasn't home. Lexi went in to the house and a guy came out (Paul). She introduced him to me and said "You and Corrina go with Paul down to KFC and get some dinner by the time you get back your Dad should be here" So off we walked. We ordered our food and returned home. It was nearly 9pm when we got back. Lexi said we couldn't eat till Dad got home. I found this strange but who was I to argue. About half hour later the caravan door opened and Dad came in. He came running over and hugged me so tight he told me he missed me etc. etc., he was so drunk he was slurring his words and couldn't stand up straight. Finally, we sat down to dinner to have our KFC. Corrina and I said on one side, Corrina and Lexi were closets to the window Dad and I sat on the outside. We started chatting and all of a sudden mid-sentence he jumped up and started yelling at Corrina for eating the chicken with her fingers

"Corrina how many fucking times do I have to tell you not to eat with your fucking hands" Lexi tried to calm him down by this strange he was standing right next to me and Lexi was stand near the doorway to their room. He ran over and punch Lexi in the face and started going off. I don't know why or how I did it but I got between them and said to him

"If you're going to hit her you have to hit me first" instantly he started to cry and went outside. I was shaking. Lexi didn't say anything. After a while I opened the door to see him sitting out the front by himself crying. I went and talked to him and said

"It will be ok Dad, everything will be ok"

A month or so later I started school at the local high school and we had moved to Long Jetty. We were two streets away from the beach. I made a few friends and I really like this boy called Travis. I spoke to Lexi like she was my friend. She said to bring Travis back to meet her so I did. I hadn't ever done anything before with a boy and I wasn't even thinking about doing that with a boy at this stage. At that age you want to kiss and hug and that is all. Every day I had the same routine when I returned home from school. I went straight to my room put my bag away got a change of clothes, went and had a shower and got changed in the bathroom then I went to play at the saltwater pool with my friends. It was an ocean pool. One day when I came home I went to my bedroom and Lexi was sitting on Corrina's bed. She started talking to me and then said "Get changed in here Emily!"

"I'm just going to have a shower" she got really pushy and I didn't understand why but when I returned from the shower I realised exactly why... She had Travis under my bed and he wanted to see me naked, Travis was about eighteen I think from memory, I was only fourteen. I was so upset but didn't say anything at all. I did tell Travis to get out and Lexi got really angry with me. I didn't tell Dad when he got home as I knew he would lose it.

Every now and then Dad would send Corrina and I out to the video parlor. He would give us money (only when he was drunk) and tell us to go and have fun. Every time this happened the next morning when we woke up we would see Lexi had a black eye or bruising. He didn't want to do it in front of me.

One night Corrina and I were told to go to our room. We did what we were told. We had a bunk bed and because I was bigger I slept on the top bunk as Corrina couldn't get up and down. We went to bed and then I heard the loudest bang I had ever heard it shook the wall. Corrina jump up and started to cry. I got down and just held her as we listened to my Dad beat her Mum. Lexi was screaming and Dad was yelling at her. The evil had come back. I had flashbacks and all I could think is cover Corrina's ears. The screaming continued and then all of a sudden there was silence. I was petrified. The door opened to our room and Dad walked in. He looked at me and Corrina and said "Here kids go to the video parole" (by this stage it was 10pm). We took the money but we just sat around the corner and waited for an hour or so. The whole time I kept telling Corrina it would be ok.

The next morning when we got up Dad had gone to work. Lexi was standing in the kitchen. Both her eyes were black she had blood stains on her head and hair missing. She looked at me and screamed "See what your fucking Father does, your nothing but a fucking slut" I stood frozen and didn't understand why I was getting the blame but I just turned around and walked outside the house and wandered. When I returned Dad was at home sitting on the lounge. As soon as I walked in he looked at me and his eyes were vacant.

"You fucking little slut, you're a whore!"

"Dad what's wrong I haven't done anything wrong" he then proceeded to tell me that I had done a strip in my room for a boy and Lexi had seen it so there was no need to lie. I didn't know what to say I didn't want him to hit Lexi but this was a lie.

"I didn't Dad I would never do that" he proceeded to tell me to fuck off and that my Nan was coming to get me. He called her and said to me whilst pushing the phone in my direction

Emily Reilly

"Tell your Grandmother what a fucking slut you are" I started to cry and Nan said

"Emily listen to me. Do not argue with him. Leave the house and I will call your Mother, don't say anything until I tell you and all you are to say is yes Nanny" I listened while she spoke and she told me if I spoke back he would lose it. When I got off the phone I walked out the front and went around to a friend's house. I stayed there for a very long time then my Mum arrived to pick me up and take me home. Mum called Dad and told him a few choice things then she said she was taking me home.

We got home and Barry was really cold to me. My cousin had taken over my room and things had changed. But I was glad to be with my Mum and Barry again....

Chapter 13: First Date

Well here it is my first date.

Before Mum agreed to my first date she had to meet Dan. She also wanted my friend Pam to go along with me which wasn't a problem as her boyfriend was good friends with Dan. I could see Dan was very nervous when he met my Mum. My Mum stands at a height of four foot nine inches and Dan was at least six foot but my Mum can be very intimidating. She read him the rules and made him promise to get me home no later than 11pm. We were to go straight to the movies and return straight home.

The night of my first date started with Pam arriving at my house, she was staying the night. Wow excitement was in the air. Mum just smiled as she looked in through my door at me getting ready and putting my makeup on. I think she had a tear in her eye and I can only imagine that she was thinking my baby girl is growing up. We were ready extra early so Pam and I just sat listening to music until the boys arrive. Because Dan was eighteen he had his P Plates and he was driving us.

A car pulled up in our driveway and we giggled. We went to go outside and Mum said "Sit down and let them come to the door, if they are gentlemen that is what they will do" she was right Dan and Pam's partner knocked on our glass door and Mum opened it.

"Emily, Dan is here to pick you up" as if we didn't notice they were here. We got up and I couldn't wipe the smile off my face. I was so excited my heart was racing and I must have been blushing. Dan stood there staring at me as he had only ever seen me in my school uniform before this. I was wearing a short black dress that hugged my perfect fourteen-year-old figure. When he finally spoke he said

Emily Reilly
"You look beautiful" all I could manage to say was

"Oh!" not "Thank you" not "You look nice" but "Oh!" as we went down the stairs Mum stood watching just before we got into the car Mum yelled out

"Dan! Don't forget our talk and no later than 11pm" I was so embarrassed as all I could think is great timing Mum. But she is a Mum and this has to be expected but back then wow bad timing.

We starting driving to the cinema which was about a 45 minutes away in the next largest town. All the way there Pam and her partner were talking. They were so comfortable together as they had been going out for about twelve months. I kept looking in the passenger side mirror to make sure my makeup and hair were ok. Dan reached over and grabbed my hand and whispered "You look so beautiful tonight" my heart skipped a beat and this time I said

"Thank you" we were listening to the Guns'n'Roses Song 'Patience' for most of the way there on repeat. We finally arrived at the cinemas and to be honest I can't remember what we watched at the movies but I was only pretending to watch anyway because I was so excited about being on my first date and being with Dan that it didn't matter. Pam and her partner where kissing the whole way through the movie. Dan did not try once. He reached over and put his arm around me and I rested my head on his shoulder. I was so nervous when he first put his arm around me that I jumped in my seat. He must have realised that I was nervous as he didn't try anything else he just kept his arm around me the entire movie.

When the movie had finished as promised to my Mum, Dan drove us home but on the way Pam's partner dared him to drive with no lights on. So Dan switched off the lights and was driving pretty fast. Pam's partner was laughing and tell him to go faster. I didn't want to be a little kid and say anything so for some time I just sat there and every now and then he would look at me and I would smile. Pam's partner egged Dan on to drive on the wrong side with no lights on, I started to get so scared but still wouldn't say anything. We were on a highway going up the wrong side of the road with no lights on approaching a hill. Just as we got to the top of the hill I saw headlights. I reached over and tried to grab the wheel and pull it but by this time Dan had already started to pull over in to the left lane (which happened to be the correct lane to be in) not even a second past when the other car flew past us just missing us. I looked at Dan and the terror was on my face and no one could have missed that look. He quickly turned the lights back on and slowed down. He pulled up not far down the road and got out of the car, he came around to my door and open it. He unbuckled my seat belt and grabbed my hands and pulled me out of the car gently. Holding my hand, he walked me away from the car. After a few meters we stopped and he bent down to look me directly in the eyes and said "Emily, I am so sorry I did that and that I scared you. I promise never to do that again" I didn't know what to say but at that moment I had forgotten what he had done and what nearly happened all I wanted to do was kiss him but I was not going to do it first. Dan pulled me in to his chest and held me. I didn't want it to stop but he then said

"We have to get you home or you will never be let out again" Dan drove us home just before we pulled in to my driveway he turned the lights off so not wake my Mum when he went in to our driveway. He stopped the car and said

"I had a great time tonight Emily"

"Me too" then he put his hand on my left cheek and moved in close and just looked in to my eyes and whispered

"You are so beautiful" I didn't have a chance to respond before his lips touched mine......That night after our first kiss all I could do was smile. My soul was buzzing.

Pam and I went inside via the back door that Mum had left open for us. We tiptoed past Mum's room so as not to wake her but I can guarantee that she would have been waiting and had we been one minute late she would have been waiting on the back veranda. I had a double bed so Pam and I slept in it together. We talked till the sun came up about how we were feeling and about my kiss and about Dan and just about everything really. We planned that we would join Dan and Pam's partner next weekend also on another date. We were so excited.

When we finally woke up Mum had already left for work. She left me a note saying

I hope you had a good night sweetheart,

I will see you when I get home.

Love Mum

Pam and I just hung around all day at my house and Nigel came over as he was living just down the road at the time. We watched movies and just relaxed all together. It was a great day. I told Nigel what had happened and he was happy for me at the same time he was worried and said "If he ever hurts you I will kill him" I thought this was cute as he truly was one of my best mates. It is really hard for me to write about Nigel so I won't go in to him just yet any further. Just know that he was a HUGE part of my life and he would make a huge change in it a little later, but for now I have to leave him as it hurts too much. I will get to his story and his impact on my life though just not now.

Mum got home after Pam had left. She sat down with me on my bed and asked how my night was. I told her but not about the car ride on the way home or she would have lost it. I told her Dan kissed me and being young and naive I thought it was love and I guess back then it was and my first love at that. She was supportive but told me to be cautious, take my time and just have fun. Fun is exactly what I intended on having but I also thought I was so much older than my fourteen years.

When I returned to school all my girlfriends wanted to know how it went. By this stage they had all dated. Trish had a twenty-one-year-old boyfriend and I didn't like him much as he used to hit her. She would come to my house and stay over. Trish and I were very close, she saved me one day, I will go in to this at a later date. We would talk about her relationship and I would tell her she deserved better, then she would leave him and then she would go back over and over. At that time, I didn't understand it but I stood by her as best I could. If he was ever around I would say hi and that was all he was really nice to me but I didn't like how he treated Trish.

I told everyone how it went and they were all so happy for me. During each day we would walk past where Dan and his mates sat. I would say hi and act like it was no big deal when I walked past but we would look at each other and smile with our eyes. Dan's brother was in my year at school and one of my mates so we would pass notes back and forward through him. It was all very exciting. Every time I walked somewhere that Dan had been I could smell his cologne and I would look around but most of the times he had been and gone. Funny how a smell can make you think of someone or something.

Dan invited me out again the next weekend and Pam was going to come and stay at my house. This time we were going to the beachside town that my Pa lived in just for a drive to the beach at night. I asked Mum if we could go out to dinner as I didn't think she would allow me just to go for a drive. She said yes because Pam was also going to be there. Again the preparations had started but I found out that Dan hated people who smoked so I brushed my teeth and washed my hair before going near him (every time). Dan

Emily Reilly

arrived at about 7:30pm and again Mum said be back by 11pm no later. I again sat in the front of Dan's car while Pam, her partner and Shaun sat on the back seat. Shaun was a good friend of Dan's I didn't expect him to be there but he was. Shaun was really good looking and I found it strange that he didn't have a girl friend at the time. He was a super nice guy and treated me like royalty.

On the way out to the beach we listened to Guns N Roses again (they were really popular back then). Pam's partner was drinking in the back and sitting behind me. I noticed bright lights following us, the person behind turned on their high beam and got really close to Dan's car. Dan sped up to try and get away from them but they kept doing it. Pam's partner put the top half of his body out the window and told the guy where to go. That seemed to only upset these people more, they got closer and closer. Then Pam's partner who was a bit drunk threw a bottle at their car. We heard the smash as it hit the front of their car then next (we had no idea he did it until we heard the smash) this caused them to try and run us off the road. They were going to kill us!

I was so scared. As I knew the beachside town so well I told Dan where to drive to try and lose them but it wasn't working. We finally got half way up a hill and couldn't see their lights so Dan turn off his lights and drove in to a drive way and waited for them to pass. Not long after we parked the car sped past us they were still looking for us but this road you couldn't turn around unless you went in to someone's driveway or got to the top where the water tower was. Phew! We had lost them thank god. Dan drove back out of the driveway then he started yelling at Penny's partner about how stupid that was etc. etc. We made our way back down the hill and drove to the beach. We parked the car and got out and walked across the bridge that went over the creek. We walked for ages then we sat on the beach. We were all talking about general stuff, then Dan stood up and took my hand and said "Emily, let's go for a walk" I looked at him and immediately got up and followed. We walked up the beach away from everyone. When we got far enough away he asked me to sit with him. He held me in his arms and started sing me the song "Patience" by Guns'n'Roses. It brought tears to my eyes. When he finished he said to me that he thought he was falling in love with me and that since the day he first saw me he wanted to come up and kiss me. Wow if I didn't cry before I did then. Such beautiful words. All that was going through my mind was '*There are good men out there*' I blurted out

"I love you too Dan" then he leaned in and kissed me. We spoke about us and what future he could see for us. It was all so romantic almost like novels that you read where people live happily ever after. He told me as soon as he left school which was only a month away he would have to go away for his apprenticeship week on and week off for training in a nearby town but that he would call me every night he was away... All the way home he held my hand only taking his away to change gears if required. He kept looking at me and smiling. I was so happy I had tears in my eyes all the way home. By the time I got home I had forgotten all about the car chase and the possibility of being killed. I was on cloud nine....

Chapter 14: Moving Out

I dated Dan for some time. He went away for his apprenticeship training for two weeks at a time and as promised he called every night. I was so in love (or so I thought). When he got back from being away we would go out on dates. A few times he was away he would call and be very distant. He would say to me "Emily, I don't think this will work" and hang up the phone after we talked for a little while longer and my heart would be broken. I would go to my room and cry. Mum would come in to check if I was ok but I wouldn't talk about it. She would say

"Emily! There are plenty of fish in the sea" all I would do is look at her and say

"I don't want anyone else Mum I want Dan" Dan would call again in a week and say sorry and be nice and rope me back in and the next day he would call it off. I had my heart broken over and over again but being young I would always go back for more.

After a few months I had had another fight with Arthur and decided I would move out. Mum was not happy but she knew if she pushed me she would push me away. So she supported me. Dan had moved in to a one-bedroom flat with another couple. I know it sounds funny but in the hallway they built a bed close to the ceiling. It was about 3 feet below the ceiling and the window was blacked out. There was a ladder that you walked up to get to his bedroom (if you could call it that). When you reached the top of the ladder and looked in the whole area was a mattress and to the left was a shelf which he had a radio on and straight ahead was a window that he had painted black so not to be woken by the morning light. I asked if I could move in. He and the other flat mates agreed and I moved in. I had to pay my own way so I kept working at my Mums shop for a while.

I had never had sex with anyone and this scared me so much. The first night Dan just held me all night not pushing me but we made out. That was the first time I had felt his man part against my leg. The next night we had sex. It hurt so much. I was so scared and so young but I thought I was so much older than I was. I hadn't been to karate for so long and I stopped going to hockey. I didn't even turn up to school. Mum spoke to a detective in town about it to try and get me home but he said there was nothing he could do about it so I stayed there.

I had never lived away from a home where meals were cooked for you and I had to fend for myself so my meals consisted of one slice of toast and juice for breakfast and a packet of 2 minute noodles and that was it. Over the months I lost so much weight. I started to eat less and less. I would look in the mirror and see a body size so much bigger than I really was. I got on the scales and thought they were broken I weight 35 kilograms; this is the weight of a small child. I was always cold so wore a thick jumper and long pants most of the time and white hair started to grow on my face and my nails started to go purple. I hadn't seen some of my friends in a long time when they all arrived one day to see how I was and spend some time with me "Oh my God Emily!" one friend said to me.

"You are way too skinny" I thought they were joking.

"No I'm not I have fat everywhere" I remember saying to them. They soon realised that there was something wrong with me so they decided to change the subject when as I got irritated. We spent the day together and it was great to have friends around me again. When they left that day we promised to catch up more often. I thought I was so much older than I was because I had moved out of home. My weight kept dropping and I was getting weaker and weaker by the day. No one in the house said anything, maybe because they saw me every day and didn't realise. My friends on the other hand did notice and were really worried.

One day I decided to go and see Mum at the shop. I had given up working there also when I moved out. When I got there my Uncle, Nan and Pa were there visiting. I honestly didn't realise how much weight I had lost until I was my Pa and Uncle. "Emily! You are skinnier than me" Pa said I looked at him and laughed. Then my Uncle who had always called me chubby as a tease (I was never a chubby child) stated

"You are definitely not my chubby any more, you are way too skinny Miss" well this hit me a little but I didn't react. I just changed the subject. My visit was short when I decided to go back to the flat.

A few days later Mel called and asked me to meet her at the hospital, he excuse was that she was pregnant. Well I was shocked and said I would get there as soon as I could. I would do anything for her and at this time she needed me. I walked all the way to the hospital which took forever. When I arrived at the hospital she was waiting out the front. She opened the door to the Emergency Room and we entered. When we got inside there was a doctor waiting there. She must have already been in. "Emily, we need to go in now" Mel said.

When we entered the room I was shocked as this was a setup. Mel and my Mum had organised for me to see this doctor due to my weight. I felt betrayed and hurt by this. I was poked, prodded and weighted. He brought out a little machine like and etch-a sketch and made me turn the circles until I saw the body size I was then he made me turn them again until I showed him what I wanted to look like. When I got the size I wanted to be he said "The is 35 kilos heavier than you are Emily" I was surprised. I truly did not see this when I looked at myself in the mirror. I was on steroid's and other medication for months in order to get my weight back up. The doctor diagnosed me with Anorexia Nervosa I was supposed to attend counselling etc. but I didn't. It's funny how you can't even see straight when you have this disease. It is a horrible thing to go through especially when you don't see it yourself. I spent some time in hospital getting better. They were worried about my heart as the purple nails are a sign of heart problems not to mention the hair on the face. This was my body trying to keep me warm. My hormones were all over the place.

Back to our flat. Dan would go out more often at night and not come home till late or stay out and not return till the morning. I used to feel so alone in this flat as the people who lived there with us weren't my friends they were Dan's so I didn't feel comfortable going and sitting with them, it was like I was intruding. I knew I could go home but I was stubborn and I didn't want to lose him.

A few months in Dan was sitting at the kitchen table and Shaun had come over to visit. He didn't realise I was in our bed. I heard Shaun say "It take a special kind of someone to have two women at once and have one live with you, how do you do it?" Shaun said this with a bit of distain. I was gutted, I didn't know what to do so I left a note with tears spilt all over it saying

'Dan,

I heard what you and Shaun were talking about, I have gone to Melissa's

Emily'.

When I arrived at Melissa's I was a mess as I had to walk for 45 minutes to get there. She held me and said "Sis you deserve better than this, forget him" I trusted her and loved her so much I decided she was right. I was leaving. I walked all the way back and when I got there Dan's car was not there, so I went inside and walked up the familiar ladder to our bed, I packed what clothes I had then I heard the door open and Dan come in. He was drunk. He climbed the ladder there was nowhere for me to go. When he got up the ladder he started saying how sorry he was and that Shaun was wrong etc. etc. but I knew he was lying.

"It's over Dan, I deserve better" as I said this he grabbed my arms and pinned me to the bed. I struggled and when I looked at his eyes I could see the evil I had seen in my Fathers eyes.

"Dan your hurting me please get off" with one hand pressed down on my arms he undid his pants. At this stage I was really scared and there was no one else in the house so yelling out wouldn't have helped. He then ripped my under pants to the side and I kept saying

"No Dan, No Dan" but this didn't stop him. I started to yell even though no one could hear me I was hoping someone would come and help me. He used one hand to hold two of mine and then he covered my mouth with the other. After some time of my crying and struggling I don't really remember how long he hoped off me and just smiled. I grabbed my clothes and started wandering the streets. By this time, it was dark and I somehow ended up in a park. Crying and screaming. I can still hear it to this day especially when I write this.

I don't know how but I made my way down town to a ladies flat, she was about twenty-two from memory and lived above a shop we will call her Skye. I walked up the stairs that led to her flat I was crying and I didn't realise that my shirt was torn and so were my underwear. I knocked on the door. A guy opened the door he would have been about eighteen and all I said is "Skye" he opened

UNBROKEN

the door and walked with me to where Skye was sitting on her bed. The house smelt of dope (Skye smoked) and incense. When I got to her she was wasted. She looked at me and asked what had happened. It wasn't hard to tell what had happened but she asked. I wouldn't answer her I just stared at her. When Skye and I were alone I told her what had happened. She laid me on her bed, she had crystals under her sheets as she believed they healed. After I had calmed down a bit she walked out. I could hear her talking to the guy that had let me in. He wasn't alone there were other people there as I heard their voices also but didn't realise they were there when I walked in and I walked straight past them. I heard Skye tell them

"She has been raped" I heard them running around and the upset voices of young men ready to go on a rampage. I hadn't told Skye who just what. I would hate to think what would have happened had I told her the name as it was a small town and everyone knew everyone. I stayed there that night and Skye slept beside me. I didn't sleep at all I felt dirty and kept thinking it is my own fault. I had slept with him before and maybe I asked for it. But I know now No Means No and that, that was not ok.

I went home to Mums the next day. I didn't tell her what had happened, I had put up a wall so high that even Mum couldn't get through or over it. She knew what had happened I think as I wouldn't leave the house. I did eventually return to school but again I was reserved. I told Nigel, Trish and Kylie what had happened. Nigel was pissed he went straight up to Dan's brother and told him what he thought of his brother. I asked Kylie and Trish to stop him but nothing and no one was going to stop him. The girls where so supportive and didn't want to leave my side my confidence was gone. Someone told my Mum and next thing I know our detective friend came to visit me at home. We chatted in my room and he started with "Mum told me what happened Emily" I didn't look at him and didn't respond. Eventually he said words I will never forget

"Emily, we can charge him but to be honest it will be your word against his in court and they will put you through hell or we can pay him a visit off the record" this time I responded with

"I just want it to go away" the conversation went on for a while but it was all one way (him talking to me) he left the room and spoke with Mum then he left. Mum only said

"If you want to talk about it Darlin I'm here" she knew me too well.

I had been back at school a few weeks when we had a sports carnival. We were all together walking down town when a car pulled up, it was hotted up. A guy came running out and started yelling at friend of mine (we will call her Alice) The guy was the same guy who had opened the door at Skye's house (we will call him Jay). The girl he was yelling at had been picking on his sister and it seemed he was just protecting his sister. I looked at him I didn't think he was hot but something inside me thought he was ok and being he was the first person I saw when I got to Skye's house that terrible night he seemed to be a protector. He said what he had to say after he threatened her and got in his car and drove away.

Jay   had   entered   my   life   like   a   tornado...

Chapter 15: Returning to The Scene

It was December 1990 when that terrible thing happened to me. I need to tell you this.

Not long after I arrived home that day there was a knock at the door and it was the lady (Jodi) who lived with her partner at the flat with Dan. She asked if we could speak privately. Mum was inside sitting at the table. Mum stood up as she had heard Jodi ask me this "I don't think that is a good idea" Mum stated

"It's OK Mum, Jodi just wants to talk. I'll be fine" We went out the front and she asked me what had happened. It was obvious that Dan's brother had said something to him about what had happened after Nigel confronted him and told him what he thought. I froze and didn't know what to say to her as we weren't friends she just shared the flat and was more Dan's friend than mine. She told me someone wanted to talk to me and asked if I would go for a drive with her. I wasn't thinking anything at that time so I agreed and ran inside to tell Mum we were going for a drive.

She drove me to the flat and before we pulled up I started to hyperventilate. She assured me it would be ok and that she would be there and as soon as they had finished talking to me she would take me home. I honestly didn't think she would take me to the flat but looking back how naive I was. I think it was because I was so messed up, confused and broken that I wasn't thinking straight.

We walked down the side of the flat and jumped the ledge that led into the flat. Dan's car was not out the front so I thought it was just Jodi and her partner that wanted to chat. When I got inside she led me to the kitchen and sitting at the table was Dan and her partner. I turned to run but there was someone in the hall behind me and to this day I don't remember who that was. Dan said "Emily it's ok I just want to talk" I was so scared my legs would not stop trembling. I hadn't seen Dan since that night and here he was. I felt trapped, I knew I couldn't escape.

Jodi's demeanor changed when she told me to "SIT!" She was so nice before we got there then she turned. I sat opposite Dan. She stood behind my chair so I couldn't escape.

"Why did you tell people I raped you?" I tried to talk but words wouldn't come out. I have had dreams about this happening, you know when you can't speak, move or react but at this time it was real. Dan was acting really nice and trying to make me feel like what happened didn't happen. I just listened, well not really listen I zoned out, my mind was flicking back to that night. I was a mess and he knew exactly what he had done but because everyone was there he was trying to make me say it didn't happen but it did and I couldn't say what he wanted me too as what he was trying to do was make me lie. He was trying to make me more confused and blame myself. He got frustrated that I wasn't talking but he didn't yell at me, he was trying to be the good guy. That good guy routine was not working on me. I finally gathered the courage to say the words I hadn't been able too

"I said No! Dan, I asked you to stop you held me down and covered my mouth, then when you were done you smiled" he looked at me and said nothing. I got up from the chair and Jodi told me to sit again this time I pushed past her then ran pass the person in the hallway, jumped the ledge and ran. I didn't stop I just kept running. About ten minutes in Jay's sister saw me and asked if I was OK. We had never really been friends but I thought it was nice that she asked. She asked me to sit with her for a while at a park so I did. Then the hotted up car pulled up and Jay got out. He came over to chat to his sister then he realised that I was there also and asked if I was OK. I didn't say anything I just nodded. He stayed for a few minutes then got in his car and drove away. I told Jay's sister that I had to leave and she checked again that I was OK and then said

"Can I get your number we are going to the beach tomorrow if you want to come" it was school holidays. I gave her my number and said

"I will have to see, call me tomorrow" when I finally got home Mum asked what had happened and I finally told her. She was furious. She went to get in her car and go down to the flat but I begged her to let it go.

"Mum I just want it to all go away, please!! Don't go" Mum turned around and walked back inside with me she must have known that this was all just too much for me to handle.

The next morning, I got a call from Jay's sister asking if I wanted to go with them, I told Mum she had asked if I wanted to go to beach with her and her family. I wasn't sure about going as I had only known her a few months as the family had just moved to town and we didn't hang around each other at school. I found her a bit different. They had moved from the city to our small town. Mum told me it would be good for me to go to the beach and have some fun with a friend. I told Jay's sister I would go "Great! We will pick you up in an hour". I went to my room and got my bikini and my sarong on then waited for them to arrive. I heard a car in the driveway and it was the hotted up car. As I went to walk out Mum yell

"Try and have fun Emily" I got to the car and the back door opened and when I looked in I saw Steven (he was the older brother to a friend of mine at school we will call him Ze). Steven smiled at me

"G'day Emily how are ya mate" I felt a bit of relief as I had known his family almost all my life. In the passenger seat was Jay's sister and Jay was driving the car. I felt a bit embarrassed as I thought it was the family not just Jay, Steven and Jay's sister. My embarrassment came from the fact that Jay knew what had happened to me and so did Steven as I later found out he was in Skye's flat that night also.

This day was the start of another chapter in my life ...

Chapter 16: Enter Jay

We drove out to a secluded part of the beach near my Pa's house. When we arrived we walked down a sandy trail that was also covered in wild flowers. I was so very nervous as I didn't know Jay or his sister very well and as I said she was not part of the normal group that I hung around with. Steven was the familiar person as I did hang around his brother Ze every day. I wasn't scared though just quiet and for me that was strange.

When we arrived Jay and Steven went for a walk up the beach and Jay's sister and I set up our towels ready to sun bake. I really needed to go in to the ocean. To me the ocean was cleansing. I will never forget walking in to the ocean that day, the waves smashing against my legs and it was so very cold in the water. Once I was waist deep I bent down and submersed myself. My mind was cleared. I know it sounds weird but at the time I had tears in my eyes and all I wanted to do was wash away all my tears without anyone seeing them. I think I did on the first swim. It relaxed me a little.

After being there for a while I looked up to see where Jay and Steven had gone. I noticed Jay sitting on a towel, he had set up right next to mine and Steven was walking towards us. Steven yelled out to Jay's sister telling her Jay wanted to talk to her. She left the ocean and Steven came in for a swim. He swam up to me and reach out to give me a hug. I wasn't scared at all as his family and mine had been friends forever, he was kind of like a big brother to me. Steven leaned down and said "Are you ok Emily! Really ok?" I had tears in my eyes as he actually did care if I was ok. I managed to say

"I'll be fine Steven, thanks for asking"

Emily Reilly

"If you needed anything at all call me and you know I will be there for you" Steven's words were truly lovely and heart felt. We mucked around in the ocean for a while and Jay's sister came back in whilst Jay just sat on the towel watching us. She came straight up to me really excited and said

"Emily! Jay really likes you he just told me" I was a bit shocked and didn't know what to say. I honestly didn't think he was that cute. He wasn't ugly but also wasn't the type of guy I would usually like.

A bit about Jay's looks. He was about 5 foot 8 inches with sandy blonde hair, fair skinned and blue/grey eyes. He always wore a singlet or t-shirt with football shorts and thongs or runners. Nothing really stood out about him. He was just plain, nothing extraordinary. I really wasn't picky about people but I need to know they have a good heart as my heart has always ruled me and having someone caring was important. I said to Jay's sister that I really wasn't interested in dating anyone at this time. I didn't explain to her why but Jay knew. She told me it was ok but would I like to spend some time with them over the holidays. I agreed as they seemed nice enough and I had nothing else planned at that stage so we spent quite a lot of time together.

I stayed over at their house and met their Mum and Dad. Their Mum was a lovely soul. She was very quiet and most of the time she kept to herself. Their Dad was different, he was the ruler of the house and you knew it. His Mum cleaned and cooked and their Dad worked. Their Mum did work but was expected to do everything else as well. One night when I was staying over Jay, his sister and I were play fighting and having a great time when Jay leant down and kissed me. OMG! I was shocked I pulled away and was a bit of a mess as I was not expecting that and after everything that had happened I felt a bit scared. He saw my face and pulled away. Jay's sister also saw my face and asked if I was OK. Jay asked if I would

UNBROKEN

mind going for a walk with him and he promised not to try anything. He apologised for scaring me with his kiss. We walked down the road to the park. When we got there we sat on the park bench. Jay again apologised to me then he asked "Are you OK"

"I'm sorry for acting reacting like that but you know what I had been through and I just can't get it out of my head"

"If you talk about it, it might help" I just couldn't do it.

"Maybe one day, but just not now" I didn't want to think about it or talk about it I just wanted it to go away.

"Emily if you tell me who it is I will sort him out, I will make sure he pays for what he has done" I still couldn't bring myself to do it as the tears welled up in my eyes he just said

"Let's drop it, when your ready you will speak out" We just sat there talking for a long time about everything but that. He asked about my family and I told him a bit about them. He wasn't being pushy just trying to be a friend I guess. After a while of these conversations he said

"Emily, I know you've been through a lot and probably don't want to date anyone but I really like you and would love to go out with you" I don't know why, maybe because I was feeling weak but I agreed.

We started dating and this is when my life would change forever...

Chapter 17: Seeing Things That Aren't There

During the Holidays I decided to go with my Mum and Barry to visit my Pa and Nan. I hadn't seen my Pa in such a long time and I missed him dearly. When we pulled up out the front of the house on the lawn I saw my favourite person in the world walk out to greet us, my Pa. We went inside and sat in the lounge room. My Nan was in the kitchen getting some biscuits and tea for us all. I looked out and saw her walking towards us. She stopped at the base of the stairs that led to the second floor. She stood there for a while and I heard her say "No"

Just a little bit more info on me. Believe it or not since I was very little I would see people that were not there. It always happened when something was about to happen to me or if something had happened. My Mum had this happen to her when I was three months old to the day. Mum heard me crying in my cradle and came to my room the check what was wrong. There standing next to my bed was her Brother who lived nowhere near us. She saw him touch my cheek as he did this I calmed down. He didn't say anything at all he just looked at me. She asked what he was doing here and he said

"Goodbye" then just disappeared. Mum didn't know what this was as she knew her brother was nowhere near us. She must have felt it was a dream. Mum told me that she went back to her bed, laid down then the phone rang it was only about five minute later. When she picked up the phone one of her other brothers told her that (Uncle Ron) had passed away five minutes before hand. Mum responded by telling my Uncle that she already knew. Ron had come to visit and say Goodbye. The Uncle on the phone was a bit put back, he didn't believe it. Our family are pretty grounded especially the men but he left it at that. Like I said believe me or not but Mum told me this happened and as similar things have happened to me all my life I can't say it didn't. Now back to Nan.

I walked over to her with my Mum to see if she was ok. Nan's face was white like she had seen a ghost. She looked straight at Mum and said "Ronny and Mum where at the top of the stairs!" we all looked up to the top of the stairs at the same time but couldn't see anyone. Mum looked at Nan with no doubt and said

"What did they say Mum?"

"Mum didn't speak but Ronny said it's alright Mum you can come now we are here for you" Nan replied. Mum walked with Nan to the kitchen and I went back and sat down with Pa in the lounge. They finished making a pot of tea then Mum walked in and sat next to me. She put her finger to her lips and made the shhh sounds. I knew not to say anything while Pa was around. My Pa would have thought that Nan was mad if she had said this to him, or at least I thought anyway so I didn't say a word. I looked out the door and saw Nan walking back towards us. She was carrying the tray of tea and biscuits for us all. As she entered the doorway into the lounge room the tray smashed to the ground and Nan fell. She was unconscious... We rushed to her side.

"Call the ambulance!" Pa called as he leaped to Nan's side. Pa lifted Nan's head and held her in his lap as he tried to wake her up. At this moment I saw my Pa melt, I can imagine that he thought he was going to lose his one true love right there and right then. Mum was crying as she made the call, I remember her not being able to explain herself very well over the phone. I just stared, after what Nan had just told us I was in shock. Uncle Ron had come to take her to the other side.

When the ambulance arrived Pa jumped in the back with Nan and off they went to the hospital. Mum made a few more phone calls to family members before we locked up and followed the ambulance. Our local hospital was not made for life threatening emergencies so as soon as Nan got to the hospital a flight was booked for her to be flown straight to the Royal North Shore in Sydney for specialty treatment. They advised us that Nan had had a massive brain hemorrhage, Nan's chance of survival was one percent. Nan was in hospital for months and none of us expected her to live as a one percent chance is a very low odd, so our family prepared for the worst. Pa however did not believe that she would go anywhere, he was by her side the entire time. She beat the odds and survived. I honestly believe this was due to my Pa's prayers and his love for her. In his mind there was no way she was going anywhere without him. When she woke I was told the first thing she tried to say was "Has Kell had the baby?" Kell was my Aunt via marriage. When Nan was stable they transferred her back to our town where she had a tube in her throat that she had to be fed through. I went there every day. I would have to wash my hands, put on a coat and mask so as not to infect my Nan. I had to unclip the tube and clean it out every hour that I was there and then help feed her. Nan needed to learn to talk and walk again and even years later she still couldn't speak properly or walk without my Pa helping her. He gave up everything to be with her 24/7. He promised her he would never leave her. Their love was something that I strive to have every day. I think in this day and age it is too easy to give up but back then they stuck it out through thick or thin. The words 'Till death do us part' meant exactly that.

Next time I saw Jay I told him all about this, we spoke about everything. We were walking down town to the shops one day and Dan was walking towards us. I squeezed in close to Jay. He looked at me worried then looked up and Dan was the only one on the street. Jay stared at him and Dan just walked past with his head down really quickly. Jay and I went and sat in a small cafe to have some lunch "Emily! Who was that?" I had tears in my eyes but didn't say a word

UNBROKEN

"It's him isn't it, I'm going to fucking kill him!!!" Jay spat

"Please just leave it Jay, enough please" he looked at me and he had a look in his eyes that I didn't like. He was angry but not just a little angry his eyes had changed colour to a dark grey. That scared me because I had seen people's eyes change colour many times before and I didn't know what Jay was capable of. I just wanted it to go away. Jay had no intention of letting this go...

Chapter 18: I Have to Tell Mum

I finally introduced Jay to my Mum. Let's just say she wasn't too happy when we turned up in a hotted up car and she found out I was dating him. Mum was cold towards him but nice enough. Mum knew better than to say she didn't like a friend of mine or a boyfriend because I didn't listen and I also would rebel and become closer to them. I got the distinct feeling though that she didn't really like him. Jay had no idea but I knew my Mum she didn't have to use words with me her body language said it all.

I stayed over at Jay's house quite often and one night when I was there he asked if I would sleep with him. He had a fold out sofa in his room the type where it is a mattress that folds up to a lounge, so when you fold it out it is a very skinny mattress directly on the ground. It was not comfortable at all. That night we did have sex. I was so nervous I actually hid my face and cried (not good tears though). I really didn't want to do it but I felt bad as he was 18 and to me so much older and he made it out like this is what you're supposed to do when you are together without saying those words. The light was out so you couldn't see while my silent tears rolled down my face (I hated sex so much). This happened a few times and after a few weeks I started to feel really sick every day, Jay took me to the doctors. When we arrived at the doctors I didn't want Jay to come in. "Can you please wait out here? I'll be back soon" I asked. I don't know why but I don't like people coming in to the doctors with me even now. The only person I don't mind having with me is my Mum but she wasn't there this day. The doctor asked me a lot of questions then he said

"Are you sexually active?" how embarrassing I went red in the face and couldn't speak. He asked me again

UNBROKEN

"Emily! Are you sexually active?" that word 'Sex' I hated hearing it. I finally managed to say

"Yes Doctor" he told me to take a specimen jar to the toilet and get a sample. I didn't even think about pregnancy at that time, I had been taking the pill for period pain for about six months. When I return he got a dropper and put some of the specimen on a square pregnancy test.

"Now we wait" this waiting was killing me it felt like an eternity since he had told me to wait then all of a sudden I got the courage to look down and I saw a blue cross... It was positive...... He looked at me and all I could do was cry. He gave me a tissue

"Emily, you are going to have to speak with your Mother "So many thoughts were running through my brain.

How was I going to tell Mum?

Mums going to hate me

What am I going to do?

What will I say to Jay?

The only words that came out were "I'm only fifteen" then more crying. I stayed in the doctor's office for at least an hour whilst he tried to calmed me down. I went through so many tissues whilst trying to figure out what this 15-year-old was going to do now that she was pregnant.

"You have options Emily, how about you go and speak with your Mother then come back with her and we can talk it through" I got up and walked to the door. I stopped and look back at him

"You should really take this Emily" and he handed me the test (I still have that test in my memory box to this day).

When I finally opened the door Jay was sitting there "Are you ok?" I couldn't respond

"What took so long?" since I had started to sleep with him he had changed a bit. It was almost like he took me for granted and now this!!!!! I asked if we could go for a drive and we did. We went down a dirt road close to where my horse paddock use to be. He pulled the car over

"Emily, what did he say?" I looked at him and all I managed in a whisper was the word

"Pregnant" he went really quiet then he looked at me and said angrily

"Well what do you want to do?" I told him I didn't really know, that I needed to tell Mum and go back to the doctor for the options. Jay started the car and drove really fast sliding along the back road I was so scared I yelled at him

"Jay!!!! Your scaring me, slow down" he slammed the breaks on and looked over at me

"For fuck sake Emily! You just told me your fucking pregnant and you want me to calm down!" I didn't say a word I just sat there his eyes had turned grey and he was furious.

"Jay I can't do anything about it now. I just have to have time to think. Can you please take me home" we sped off down the track and this time I didn't say anything, I just sat there holding on tight to the seat hoping we wouldn't have an accident. When we got to our driveway Jay leant over close to me

UNBROKEN

"I'm sorry Emily, I didn't mean to get angry with you I was just shocked that's all" he leaned in to kiss me and I kissed him back. He asked if I wanted him to come in

"No I'm fine, I'll call you tomorrow" I walked around the back and walked up the familiar stairs that led inside. Mum's car was there, I walked past the laundry, the kitchen and through the dining room till I got to the lounge room. I looked over at Mum she looked so content sitting on the lounge that I couldn't bring myself to say anything. I sat down and we had a chat about the day and going back to school etc. we had dinner and I went to bed early.

I went back to school the next day it was the first day back after our break. I was not myself all my friends wanted to know what was wrong. I just didn't go in to it. I went into my own little world as they all chatted about their holidays and when they asked what I had gotten up to I spat out "I'm pregnant". There was silence then some of the girls being teenagers and hating school thought it was great

"A baby wow it would be so awesome" one said

"No more school" another said and they went on listing all the great things about being pregnant, like it was a normal thing to be discussing at fifteen years of age but those I was really close to knew me and knew it wasn't great and I was scared. Trish, Kylie, Pam and Nigel took me away. They asked what I was going to do. I had no idea but I knew I had to tell Mum and I told them. They all offered to be with me when I broke the news for support which was nice but they all lived out of town apart from Pam and Nigel. I asked Pam to come with me to Mum's shop that afternoon as I couldn't wait any longer to tell her, she agreed. That day went so quickly. We stayed at school all day that day as I didn't want to go home. When the last bell rang everyone came over and hugged me and said it's going to be ok we are here for you no matter what. They were true friends.

Pam and I walked all the way down to Mums shop that day where Pam's Mum also now worked a couple of days a week. When we got there Mum looked over a bit surprised to see us as it was not my day to be there "What are you two up to? What brings you down here today?" I froze so Pam said

"Emily needs to talk to you Mrs. x" Mum must have known it was serious as she asked Pam's Mum to watch the shop while we went out the back. I sat on a table in the lunchroom and cross my legs (I never did this) and Pam sat next to me, Mum sat on a chair across from us.

"So Emily what do you have to say?" I giggled. Weird reaction I know but that is what happened. I was so nervous and my brain had a stupid reaction and this giggle was it. I shifted my gaze to meet Mum's at this stage my heart was racing I had never been so afraid of a reaction as I had at this very moment

"I 'm Pregnant!" Mum didn't really react she just looked over at me

"You should have done that a while ago" and pointed at my crossed legs.

"Well what are you going to do? Are you having it or getting rid of it?" I looked at her and was so angry, without thinking I said

"I'm having it"

"Whatever you decide it is your decision, but if you have decided to kept it I am not baby sitting and it is your responsibility to raise it. I will be here for you but I will not raise it for you" and I knew from Mum's tone that she meant every word that just came out of her mouth. Wow! not the reaction I expected at all. After breaking the news to Mum Pam and I walked out and just before I left I turned to Mum

"Please don't tell Arthur" Mum agreed and said she wasn't going to tell anyone as that was my responsibility. She also agreed to come back to the doctors with me.

As we walked back to my house there was complete silence as a million thoughts were going through my head. I had just told my Mother that I was pregnant and I told her I was keeping the baby! Pam was obviously also in shock but she managed to blurt out

"My Mum would have killed me and your Mum was so calm and cool" I looked at Pam

"My Mum is disappointed and hurt, I could see it in her eyes" I had just broken my Mum's heart I am sure of it, her baby was having a baby.

"Cool and calm with my Mum is not really cool and calm Pam"

As soon as I got home I called Jay to let him know I had told Mum. He was worried about her reaction and I guess if I was in his shoes I would have been too but I just said "Give me a few days, I'll see you on the weekend and we can go from there"

When Mum got home we went to the doctors and he told me I could keep it, have an abortion or give it up for adoption. I stated firmly "This child didn't asked to be created so I will not abort it and I definitely won't be giving it away" so the decision was made, I was fifteen and having a baby.....

Chapter 19: Telling Pa

On the drive home not much was said between Mum and myself. I remember looking out the window and thinking '*how am I going to do this?*' I was also very angry that someone would think that I could just go and abort my baby or worst still carry it for nine months and give it away. I could not understand how anyone could do that. I know now that there are people that have done this and for good reason, but at the time I couldn't comprehend this or look outside the box as I was so head strong believing I was older than I really was. My mind was racing all over the place. We pulled in to the driveway and I again asked Mum not to say anything to anyone. She agreed "That's up to you Emily, but you are going to have to tell them" I went inside and not another word was said. Barry was in the lounge room, I looked at him as he watched the TV, I wasn't afraid of telling him and I really wanted too so I asked him if he could come with me for a chat and he did.

We sat on my bed and I looked at him "I'm having a baby" Barry didn't have any expression on his face but he smiled and said

"ok" I asked him not to say anything to anyone and he agreed also.

Barry over the years had hardened and he held his emotions close to his chest. Words that never left his mouth are 'Sorry' and 'I love you'. It's a bit sad really but this is how he kept himself together. Barry was now 13 and going through a close the world out stage in his life. I worried about him all the time. He hated Arthur with a passion and at times he didn't like me, I think it may have been that I had moved out before and not really kept in touch all that much and that I left him there to deal with Arthur all by himself. I told Barry that I had thought about moving out and living with Jay now that I was pregnant and he just said "Well that's up to

UNBROKEN

you" so that night I called Jay and asked if we could talk. Jay arrived after we had had some dinner. He knocked at the front door and no one else moved to open it. I opened the door and told Mum we were going for a drive. Mum just said

"Don't be late, you've got school tomorrow" we got out to the car and went for a drive. We ended up at the lookout. The lookout was on top of a hill just outside our town. Right below you was the river then lift your eyes and you see so many lights twinkling. This place used to make me smile. I would think it was magical thousands of fairies twinkling and spreading their fairy dust all over the town. Silly but that's how I felt about this place at the time. When we first arrived we just sat there then Jay turned and looked at me

"Emily, what did the doctor say" I told Jay what he had said.

"What have you decided to do?" I turned side on towards the driver's seat and looked him in the eyes not knowing what to expect

"Jay, I can't abort this baby and I can't carry it for nine months and give it away. I want to keep it" he just looked at me

"Well I guess we are having a baby" he leant in kissed me and smiled. We just sat there for a while not speaking just holding hands. Jay turned to me again

"Now that your pregnant you should move in with me" at this moment I had a tightening and stabbing pain go through my chest. I have had this before it is the feeling I get when I'm scared, I didn't respond. I know I told Barry I was probably going to move in with Jay but until this moment I really didn't know how I would feel. Fear ran through me from my head to my feet. This was real, I was having a baby at fifteen and this guy wanted me to move in with him. My childhood had disappeared in that instant. Jay got angry as

Emily Reilly

I hadn't responded to what he had said. I looked at him and his eyes had turned grey again, I had come to learn when people's eyes change so does their mood and this was not a good thing. He leaned over and grab both my arms and squeezed them so tight

"Emily this is my fucking child and you will be with me while you're pregnant" I started to shake

"Jay you're hurting me, let go of me" he lifted his hand and slapped me across the face so hard I felt my jaw click. I was confused, scared and shocked all at once.

What just happened?

Why had he done this?

What did I do?

What do I do?

I had done karate for so long and at this moment I didn't even block the hit, I didn't respond. *Where was my strength?* I was completely lost and felt so weak. I started to cry and he looked at me "Emily I am so sorry; I don't know why I did that. I promise I will never do it again" My only reaction was to look at him, I just couldn't stop crying. He kept apologising

"It just that I love you so much and now we are having a baby I want to be there 100% and give you both everything you need" I don't know why but I melted after this and thought to myself, '*he didn't mean it he is just scared, I'm sure he won't do it again. Maybe I deserved it because I didn't respond*'. Jay leaned in and kissed me he kept saying

UNBROKEN

"I'm sorry Hon I will never do it again, I just love you so much" over and over again. We had sat there a while and then I responded

"Ok Jay I will move in with you" he smiled and kissed me again

"So when are you moving in?" I told him it would be about a week so I could get my stuff together. He was fine with it and in the meanwhile I had to tell my Mum.

We drove back to my place; it was really late by this stage. I walked inside and everyone was already in bed. I walked to my room and looked at myself in the mirror. My eyes were red and extremely swollen from the tears I had spilt and there was a red hand mark on my face. All I could think at this time was *'I'm glad Mum wasn't up as she just wouldn't understand'*.

I woke up the next morning and got ready for school. My eyes were still swollen from crying the night before. Mum saw me "Emily what's wrong? Why have you been crying?" I looked at Mum and tried to tell her I hadn't been crying. She knew I was lying but she didn't push it. Of all the people in my life she was the one person I could not lie too. Every time I cry my eyes swell and they stay this way over night. I really don't know how I thought she would not notice this.

I went to school and sat with my friends. I felt so out of place, not because they made me feel this way just because I was pregnant and moving out and having to grow up quick. I told them that I was moving in with Jay and that I probably wouldn't be coming back to school as it will just be too hard being pregnant and being at school. They were all upset and said "We will look after you please don't go" but my mind was made up. When I got home that day Jay came over and Arthur was off work, Mum was inside sitting at the kitchen table. Arthur was digging a hole for a pool out the back.

Emily Reilly

Mum told Jay to sit down she wanted to chat. We all sat at the table and Mum began "You have to look after her" Jay agreed though he got a bit annoyed being told what to do.

I don't think Mum realised but I did. Mum then said "Well you have to go and tell Arthur" Jay stood up

"I will do it" then he walked out the back, Mum and I followed. We stood on the veranda and watched as Jay approached Arthur. Arthur had a shovel in his hands Jay must have felt intimidated. I didn't hear how Jay told him all I heard Arthur say was

"Are you fucking kidding me" he was not happy. I don't know why as he wasn't my Dad. Jay and he continued to talk while so Mum and I walked back in to the table. I heard footsteps coming up the back stairs and they both came inside. Jay had told Arthur that he wanted me to move in with him. Arthur got to the table

"Well you better start getting your shit together as your moving in with him, we will be here if you need us though Emily" he wasn't happy but I guess finding out your Step daughter was pregnant at fifteen would be a bit of a shock. I told everyone I would move next week. After a while Jay left and Mum said to me

"Emily you don't have to move out, you can stay here"

"I have too Mum it isn't fair on Jay"

"The door is Always Open Sweetheart; I love You"

The next day my Pa had arrived. Pa came most days for lunch as Mum had started coming home at lunch time to have lunch then go back to work. Pa was coming in to town to go and visit his Mother who was in the hospital due to her age (she was 99). Before Pa arrived Mum told me I had to tell Pa. I told her I didn't want too but knew I had to. This was going to be one of the hardest things I

UNBROKEN

had ever done. My Pa was my hero and what would he think of me being pregnant at fifteen and dropping out of school. The one thing I never wanted to do was disappoint my Pa.

Pa got out of the car and as usual he walked around to my Nan's door and opened it then helped her out. As Nan had not long been out of hospital Pa had to almost carry her as she was learning how to walk again. It didn't both him though he loved her with all his heart. The doctors told Pa if he didn't put Nan in a nursing home he would go before her so he told them "I will never do that, I told her in sickness and in health and that was a promise I will keep" What a man! When they got inside Pa sat Nan on a chair at our kitchen table and Mum poured him his routine cup of tea. Mum then said

"Dad, Emily has something to tell you....Go on Emily"

Oh I was nervous. I looked at him and his old eyes smiled at me. I thought to myself, here we go... "I'm pregnant Pa" I said ever so softly. To my surprise he turned to my Nan

"Mum, Emily has been baking bread" Nan looked at him and managed to say

"What!" with a gargling sound (she was also still learning to speak) she hadn't heard what Pa had said.

"Emily is pregnant" he responded, Nan looked at me and with that same gargling voice said

"What do you want me to knit you?"

Wow not the response I was expecting but believe me I was relieved. I started to cry and Pa stood up and came and gave me a hug. For the first time in a long time I felt safe and ok.

Emily Reilly

"I   love   you   Pa...."

Chapter 20: The Move

I stood in front of my dressing table staring at myself in the mirror. I had my school uniform on. I was contemplating the day I had ahead of me. I had decided it would be my last day at school as I didn't want to be pregnant and around people watching me grow. I think I was also a bit embarrassed. *'What was the point of going to school if you're not going to be able to finish anyway'* I thought to myself *'Well Emily! Time to grow up, you're going to be a Mum and move in with Jay'*. I got my bag that I had packed the day before and walked to the kitchen. Mum was at the kitchen table and had breakfast ready for us as usual. I got a cup and had a cup of tea with Mum as we ate "Mum, I have decided to move in with Jay and I won't be going back to school after today" I stated. Mum looked up from her cup

"You don't have to move out and you should stick with school as long as possible" I explained how I was feeling

"It's your life Emily" she wasn't happy I think a bit more disappointed than unhappy. She had been a teen Mum also and she only wanted the best for Barry and I. I look back now and sometimes think that I should have listened to her more often. I guess we all do that though. Hindsight being 20/20

When I arrive at our usual hangout everyone was there. I told them I was leaving school and that I was keeping the baby. They were all so happy for me. So many of them wanted to be god parents and they all wanted to be the Aunties and Uncles of this baby I was carrying. Wow when I write this down and look at it from an Adults point of view I really was a baby having a baby but back then I didn't think of it that way. School finished and I said my goodbyes and everyone said we will see you soon Emily, we will come and visit, I was so torn. I really was going to miss them all and spending 90% of your waking hours with people like this they were like family.

I got home that night and Jay came over. We talked for ages in my room and he ended up staying the night, it wasn't like Mum or Arthur could have a problem with it I was already pregnant. Mum wasn't happy about it but she didn't say a word to either of us. When we woke the next morning Jay said "Get your stuff, you can move in today" I looked at him, I really didn't want to leave but I had too. I also didn't want to say this to him as I didn't want to upset him again. I got some clothes together and some other things but most of the stuff I left in my room. One of the big issues for me was that we were moving in to Jay's parents' house with his Mum, Dad and Sister. We were going to be sleeping on that fold out mattress. The first time I moved out it was because I didn't get on with Arthur and this time it was because I had too, I was having his baby. Brings tears to my eyes as I write this.

I walked out with my bag and Mum stood up. She came over to me and hugged me she whispered in my ear "The door is Always open Emily, I love You Sweetheart" I had tears in my eyes and held her so tight. I told Mum we would visit all the time and as I said this I looked at Jay.

"We will, She'll be fine I'll look after her" as we left the house I stopped at the door way and turned to look at Mum

"I love you Mum" was all I could say. I saw tears in her eyes and it broke my heart. I was only moving 15 minutes down the road but it felt like I was never going to see my family again.

When we got to Jay's we walked up the winding staircase in through the front doors. When you enter the front door and look to your right there was the lounge room and in front of that an area that had a dining table directly ahead was kitchen. If you turn left you walk down a short hall area first door on the left is Jay's sisters room the door directly ahead was his parents room you then turn right to the next hall first door on your left is Jay's room or now our room. Walk a little further up on the right is the bathroom and straight ahead is the closed in back veranda that adjoined the kitchen. There were also a set of stairs inside that led down to the laundry and the garage. We entered Jay's room. I didn't have anywhere to put my clothes so I just put my bag in the corner. Jay sat on his bed and told me to sit also. I did what I was told. No one was home at the time. We talked for a bit and Jay said "Well I don't know what we're going to do, I'm not working and your pregnant" Wow these are the first words I heard after moving away from my Mum into his house and being pregnant, all I wanted was a hug. Jay started play fighting with me out of the blue. Maybe it was his way of cheering me up at the time then all of a sudden he pinned me down on the fold out mattress.

"See if I wanted to fuck you I could do it any time" What!!! Where did this come from we were play fighting then this!

"Jay get off me! you're hurting me" He just laughed

"I'm in control here" was he joking? Did he think this was funny? I started to cry as thoughts of Dan ran through my head while he sat on top of me laughing... I was petrified all my strength gone.

Did I deserve this?

Is this the way it's always going to be?

He hoped off and started kissing me and as he did I couldn't stop crying. He wiped tears from my eye "I was just joking Emily" I didn't say a word I really didn't want to upset him. My strength had gone. All I could think is '*Emily why didn't you fight back?*'

Emily Reilly

Jay got up and shut his door then came back to the mattress and laid beside me by this time it was early afternoon. He took off his shirt and started drying my tears

"Emily, I'm so sorry, I didn't think. I'll never do it again" he whispered in to my ear as he kissed my neck. All I was thinking is he wants to have sex now; I don't want to do this. He took off my pants as he kissed down my stomach. I was crying and the tears would not stop. I couldn't say no that would upset him, was I being stupid? He had sex with me and when he had finished he rolled over got his shirt and went out to the kitchen to get himself a drink. I laid there still crying silently. I heard him coming back and quickly put my pants back on and wiped my eyes.

"Let's go for a drive to see Steven" I quickly got up and walked out the front and down the stairs towards the car I couldn't wait to get out of that room, away from that house and to see a friendly face. I waiting at the passenger door as he locked the house up.

When we arrived to where Steven was staying he was waiting out the front. They had already made plans by the looks of it. Steven got in the car and Jay started driving. We drove to a back road just out of town, Jay pulled the car over in the middle of nowhere got out and went to the boot of the car. When he got back in the car he had a bong made out of an Orche bottle (I didn't know what it was back then as I had never seen one before) he reached over me to the glovebox and got a bowl and pair of scissors out and started chopping up his dope. The whole time I was thinking, 'OMG! He smokes pot what sort of life is this going to be?'. They started smoking away. I didn't want to look so I stared out the window all I could hear was a bubbling sound. Jay looked over at me

UNBROKEN

"Do you want one Emily?" I yelled at him

"Are you kidding me I'm pregnant" SMACK! I didn't see it coming, he punched me in the face

"Don't ever fucking speak to me like that again" I started to cry and hold my face.

"Don't fucking hit her, what's wrong with you she's your woman and pregnant" Steven yelled at Jay but his reaction was too late. I took my hand away from my face and there was blood on it. Jay saw the blood

"I'm so sorry Hon, I didn't mean it" he tried to touch my face but I pulled away. I opened the door and got out of the car and started running up the road. I don't know where I thought I was going but I was going away from Jay. He got out of the car and chased me till he caught up with me. He grabbed my arm and swung me around. He kept apologising then he started to cry

"Emily, I am truly sorry I don't know what came over me, hit me Emily! Hit me"

"I can't be with someone who hits me"

"I love you Emily, I love you more than you will ever know. I was a fucking idiot, I'm so sorry Hon" then he pulled me in close to him. I felt sorry for him, I hated seeing people cry and I had made him cry.

"I'm sorry Jay don't cry, it's ok I'll stay" we turned and walked back to the car. Jay opened the door for me and I got in to the car. Before Jay got in Steven asked

"Are you ok Emily?" I told him I was fine. I looked down and saw blood all over the front of my shirt. I looked in the rear view mirror and realised Jay had split my lip and it wouldn't stop bleeding. I pulled my shirt up and held it to the cut hoping it would stop. They continued smoking a bit more and then we drove off and dropped Steven at home. By this stage it was early evening and when we pulled up Jay's Mum and Dad were there along with Jay's Sister. I rushed inside still covering my mouth and straight into the bedroom. I quickly took off my shirt and changed so they wouldn't see the blood. When I came out my lip was swollen and split but the bleeding had stopped. Jay's Dad asked what had happened, Jay looked at me and I quickly responded

"I tripped getting in to the car and hit my lip on the car door" this is how Mum did it all those times she was playing games with Dad. Hiding what Jay did was as easy as that. Jay's Dad asked his Mum to get me an ice pack. He asked us all to sit at the table as he had something important to discuss.

I will take you back a bit here. Earlier in my story you will remember the day I was walking down to a sport carnival with my friends and Jay pulled up and got out and started threatening one of my friends (we will call her Alice) as she had been bullying his sister well this discussion was about Alice.

We all sat down, Jay and I on one side of the table. Jay's Sister and Mother on the other side and Jay's Dad at the head of the table. Jay's Dad started "I have a way to fix the Alice situation" we all looked at him and he continued

"I have a guy that is willing to get rid of her and there will be no more problems" my head was racing excuse my language but I was thinking *'Are you fucking kidding me? Did he just insinuate he was going to have Alice killed? what the hell is going on here, is he crazy'* in my world if you had a problem with someone you faced them and dealt with it not organised a hit man to get rid of them. Alice was only fifteen. No one said a word until Jay's Sister said

"No Dad, it's ok I can handle it really" he looked at my face and must have seen the shock. I didn't say a word. Alice was my friend and yes she didn't like Jay's Sister and yes she could be a bully but kill her! No way, how could that enter anyone's mind ever... She's a kid...

Jay's Father stood up and said to us all "Not a word to anyone!" then he walked away.

What should I do?

He was serious?

Should I call her and warn her?

Could I talk him out of it?

Jay and I went back to our room and I flopped on the mattress "Jay was your dad serious?"

"Yep" was his response, I had to be smart here and say the right thing.

"Jay you should talk him out of it, I can talk to Alice and get her to leave your Sister alone, your Dad doesn't need to do this. What if he gets caught and has to go to goal? Is it really worth it? Let me talk to her I promise not to say anything about the talk we just had" I hope I played that right was all I could think. Jay looked at me

"Ok Emily, I'll get him not to do anything for now. I'll tell him to leave it with us and if it doesn't work then he can do what he has to do"

Emily Reilly

Jay did just that and I had to organise to meet Alice.....

Chapter 21: Speaking to Alice

The next morning after everyone had left the house Jay and I got up. Jay wanted to go out and I reminded him I had to speak with Alice. Jay glared at me and raised his voice "Why do you care about Alice anyway, she is scum and deserves what's coming to her" from the look in his eyes I knew not to say a word or he would lose it. He walked away and I walked over the phone. I dialed Alice's number

"Hello" a firm woman's voice answered the phone

"Hi Mrs. X, it's Emily is Alice able to talk?"

"No Emily she's at school, is everything ok?"

"Yep everything is fine" I lied. I couldn't really tell her as I didn't know what to say and god only knows what Jay or his Father would have done if I said what I wanted to. She was my friend and his Father was prepared to have her killed.

"Can you please tell her I'll call her later" we said goodbye and I got off the phone when I turned around Jay was standing right behind me. He had heard the whole conversation.

"You have till this afternoon to sort this out Emily or Dad won't hold off anymore" I freaked out, I needed to go to school and see her and talk to her straight away.

"Can you please drive me to the school" I asked sheepishly, he agreed. We got in the car and drove the 10 minutes to our school. As we got to the front of the school I asked Jay to park away from where everyone was hanging out. I didn't want everyone to see him. I got out of the car and walked towards our hang out. As I got closer I saw everyone chatting and laughing and all that was going through my mind was how am I going to get her to leave Jay's sister only. I knew I would come up with something. As I got closer Nigel recognised me and come running over, Kylie and Trisha followed. They all hugged me. Nigel stood back and looked at me and he was the first to notice my lip.

"What the fuck happened to your lip Emily?" I told the same lie I had told Jay's Dad as it had worked once but he didn't buy it like Jay's Dad did. They all knew I was lying and every one kept asking me questions I didn't want to answer. I told them to drop it I was fine and that I really needed to speak with Alice. Nigel walked off to find Alice they both returned not long after. Alice reached out and hugged me so tight. She asked the same question Nigel had in exactly the same way. I asked everyone if I could talk to Alice in private. They all looked confused as we never spoke in private, we shared everything but this time I was hiding a dangerous secret that I couldn't afford to slip up on and because we were all so close had they asked me a direct question I would not be able to hide it from them. This was killing me. They were like family and I really did want to tell someone, I wanted to protect her and I wanted out of that house and away from those people. They scared me and I had only been there a day in that time I had been hit and been told they were capable of putting a hit on someone it was horrible.

Everyone walked away and as they did I could hear them asking each other why I would want to only speak with Alice. Ok so the time had come for me to tell a big lie and convince my friend to leave someone that she really didn't like alone. Alice interrupted my thoughts "Emily, did Jay do that to you? Honestly, you can tell me anything you know that don't you?" my lip was the last thing on my mind.

"Alice I need to ask you if you could do me a favor" she looked at me and agreed.

UNBROKEN

"Can you please leave Jay's sister alone?" she looked at me oddly

"That whole family is fucked up Emily, why are you with him anyway? and she is a bitch" she was getting frustrated. She must have known this family better than me. I don't know how as they hadn't been in town that long but she really didn't like them and she had to have a reason but I didn't want to ask

"Please Alice for me! I'm pregnant and I don't want my friend and my boyfriend's sister arguing, I just can't handle it" she looked at me and obviously knew this meant something to me.

"Ok for you I will but if she is a smart arse I will not hesitate" she had agreed thank god.

"You know she is scared of you so she won't be I promise"

"I don't know what's behind this Emily but I will take your word for it and leave well enough alone" we hugged and she looked at everyone and they came back over. Everyone looked concerned and they asked what was going on, Alice stepped up

"Nothing it's all good, Emily just wanted a chat" she had saved me from answering. Everyone wanted to catch up one afternoon so I wrote Jay's number down and as I had written down the last digit a horn was blasting behind me; it was Jay he was obviously sick of waiting. I hugged everyone goodbye and walked back to the car. I just wanted to turn around, run back and just breakdown but I couldn't do it. I had a commitment now and I had to stick with it. I got in the car and told Jay what had been said.

"Lucky for her she better stick to it" We drove down town and as we pulled up just outside a shop Alice's Brother came running over to the car. He was about six-foot-tall and he was known as a tough guy in town. We had always got on well but this time he came straight up to the window and started yelling

"Emily what the fuck are you doing with this dickhead? you are so much better than him" Jay was furious... He leant down and opened his boot. He got out of the car and ran to the boot the and next thing I know he is swinging a baseball bat at Alice's Brother. He connected a few times, Jay was screaming at him I don't remember the exact words but I could see if he had a chance he would have killed Alice's Brother. Alice's Brother backed away yelling

"You had better watch yourself Jay and leave my Sister alone or next time I won't back down" Jay kept ranting and I just sat in the car shaking. After I had just had the conversation with Alice at school this had to happen. It would have been done then and there but now the whole issue had been fueled again.

Jay threw the bat in the boot and got back in the car and sped off. I could see he had lost it; his mental state is something I cannot explain. All I can say is he was crazy mad. I was too scared to ask him to slow down as he was driving he was banging the steering wheel and ranting about how he was going to sort him out. I didn't know what to say or do.

Do I answer?

Do I stay silent?

I decided to do the later, all of a sudden the car swerved to the other side of the road and as I looked up I could see Dan walking on a footpath. Jay was going to run him over. I looked at Jay and instinctively grabbed the steering wheel and pushed it away. We just missed him. Dan was yelling at Jay calling him all sorts of names. Jay slammed on the breaks and rushed out of the car he had opened the boot again grabbed the baseball bat again and was heading towards Dan. Dan had just gotten in his car. Jay started smashing the windows and bashing the bonnet. I was crying so much I was a mess. What was going on? I had never had this in my home town. I used to feel safe now my life was chaos. I yelled out to Jay to come back to the car. When he had done enough damage he walked back to the car slammed the boot and got in the car. He was laughing... I was a mess and he was laughing! I hated Dan for what he had done to me but I would have been happier just to never see him again. This violence this I couldn't understand.

After Jay calmed down a little he decided to go and get Steven and we would go to our local pub. I was underage but if I didn't drink it was ok and I had no intention of drinking. We got Steven and headed off Jay told Steven about our day. Steven said "you should just leave it Jay, let it all settle" Jay was having none of it. When we got to the pub we went straight to the poker machines to try and win some money. Jay didn't drink he just smoked pot so before we entered the had smoked a little pot. We went to this pub daily. Not really the place I wanted to be but we did and I didn't really speak up. This is not the life I had dreamt of.

I hadn't seen my Mum for weeks so I asked Jay if he could take me to see my her, he wasn't really happy about it but he agreed to take me to the shop. By this time my lip had healed. When I walked in Mum looked at me and smiled her caring smile "Emily!" she came rushing over to hug me. She had a million questions about how I was and what I have been doing. I just held her so tight. I didn't want to let her go I felt safe at this moment and as I held Mum she realised I was not going to let go. Mum moved me away from her and asked me calmly

"What's wrong Sweetheart?" I couldn't tell her. What would happen to her if I said something? I just looked at her

"Nothing Mum I just really miss you..."

Chapter 22: Leave Her Alone

Over the coming months the beatings got worse but Jay got smart and wouldn't touch my face. I am going to run you through these over the coming pages. I won't go in to all of them as there were so many.

One-day Jay wanted to go to the local pub again so he could try and win some money. We drove over and picked up Steven and headed down to the pub the usual routine. When we got there Jay gave me a dollar coin "Here put this in to the machine" it was a poker machine and I hadn't ever really been around gambling but had spent a lot of time sitting there watching Jay play. I put the dollar in to the machine and press a button. Five cards came up and four of them where the same. I clicked on the four and won twenty dollars I was so happy. The machine started making a noise and Jay came over.

"Well done Emily" he said "keep playing" I just wanted to take out the twenty dollars and buy a cold drink with it as I was so hot and as you ladies who have had children know your body temperature is elevated when your pregnant. A guy came and sat at the machine next to me. He would have been about twenty and I had never seen him before. He looked over and saw that I was hot and offered to buy me a cold drink, I thanked him and asked for water. As he spoke I heard stomping coming towards us, it was Jay.

"What the fuck are you doing Emily?" I looked at him and knew if I said the wrong thing I would pay later.

"He offered to get me a water Jay, that's all I am really hot and thirsty" Jay glared at me and spat back

UNBROKEN

"If you want a fucking drink I will get it" the guy sitting next to me stood up. He must have been over six foot and was really well built. He walked in front of me and stood there

"Are you her man?"

"Yep" Jay spat back

"Well you should take better care of her or you'll lose her and you definitely shouldn't speak to a lady that way" he then turned to me

"Be back in a minute with your water lovely" I hadn't had a guy speak to me so nicely in a long time and I just wanted to walk with him and grab my drink and be safe for a minute but I knew that when we left this place I was in trouble and big time. I didn't say anything back. I turned to my machine and started playing cards again. Jay sat at the machine next to me now. The guy returned and handed me a glass of water. I was so grateful but didn't want to say much because Jay was right there. I think Jay must have been scared of him because of his size, usually he would have lost it if someone spoke to him like that.

"Thank You" I said really quietly.

My twenty dollars seemed to go on forever because before I knew it, it was getting dark outside. The nice guy had left and it was just Jay and I sitting in this room I hadn't seen Steven for a while. I kept hitting buttons not really knowing what to do. Jay looked over (I was on my last dollar) then WHACK! I felt a fist strike me in my side near my ribs, it was hard enough for me to buckle over and I started to cry silently, I was used to it by now, I knew not to react or say it hurt.

"What the fuck did you do you stupid bitch?" I turned with tears rolling down my face, looked and didn't know what to do.

Emily Reilly

"You had a royal flush you fucking idiot that would have been a hundred dollars" Jay pushed his chair back and grabbed my hair so violently. I didn't make a sound he pulled me out through the room by my hair backwards. There was no one in sight. I prayed someone would come and see me and rescue me but I knew I couldn't yell for help. He pulled me out through another room past the room Steven was sitting in. He hadn't seen us. Just as we got past the door I tripped and fell down and Jay ripped some of my hair out, this made me cry out in pain but because there was music playing no one heard or they just didn't want to get involved. He dragged me a good 20 meters by my hair and the whole time I was crying. Someone was walking in the car park but they didn't say anything. All I could do was will someone to do something. My head was numb by this stage. He dragged me to the river and started punching me all over just not in the face and was swearing and calling me all sorts of names. He didn't care I was pregnant he just kept hitting me over and over again. I was struggling to start with but in the end I just resigned myself to the fact that this could be your last minutes on this earth. He was so violent and it was all over me not knowing that I could have won him a hundred dollars. It felt like this had been going on forever when all of a sudden someone jumped over me and pushed Jay backwards. He fell and hit his head, it was Steven. I must have passed out as I don't remember anything after this. The next thing I remember is waking in the back seat of Jay's car. Jay was driving and Steven was looking at me. He had tears in his eyes. Jay stopped the car and opened the door. I cringed, what was he going to do now? He leaned in and started crying saying

"Emily I'm so sorry, I didn't mean it I promise I will never do it again" I was too scared to look away, I must have been a sight. After a while of Jay apologising I said

UNBROKEN

"It's ok Jay I messed up, I'm so sorry. Please don't cry" he leaned down and kissed my forehead and then got in the car and drove to Steven's to drop him off.

After dropping him off he Jay asked if I was ok, I told him I was fine. He told me to get in the front seat and we would go home. I tried to get up but I found it really hard to move. I was so sore and there were cuts everywhere and the bruises were already coming up on my arms and legs. Jay came to the back door and helped me up. He opened the passenger side door and sat me on the seat. Before we pulled up at Jay's house he said

"I'm going to park under the house, stay in the car until I find out where everyone is. Go straight in to the bathroom and I will bring you clothes; you need a shower your so dirty" I sat waiting then I heard Jay running down the stairs.

"Emily, hurry up!" I couldn't move all that fast, firstly I was pregnant and secondly I was extremely sore. I moved as quickly as I could and did what I was told and went straight to the bathroom. I ran the shower then Jay walked in carrying a jumper and a pair of long pants. It was so hot and he wanted me to wear these but I didn't argue for fear of enraging him again. As I washed my hair I realised I had lost a lot of hair but mainly from underneath so it wouldn't be so visible if I wore my hair down. When I had finished showering I looked in the mirror. I had bruises, gravel rash and scratches everywhere. The shirt and skirt I had been wearing had blood on them and were ripped. I couldn't wear them again. I slowly got changed in to the hot clothes Jay had chosen and walked to our room. I was called out for dinner and when I got to the table Jay's Sister asked why I was wearing long clothes. I looked and her and didn't say a word. Looking back, it was pretty obvious what had happened but she just looked at me in a knowing way and didn't make a comment again. Jay's Mum looked and didn't say anything, we ate in silence. Later that night Mum called and asked us to come to dinner the next night. I asked Jay

"Yeah why not" so the next night we headed to Mum's house. I again dressed in long clothes but this time I had a long sleeve cotton shirt on and long skirt. I thought Mum wouldn't recognise. After dinner Mum asked me to help with the dishes.

"You can wash up Emily, I know you hate drying"

"No it's all good Mum I'll dry" I replied, Mum looked at me strangely

"Wash Emily and pull up your sleeves" I started washing the dishes and Mum yanked my sleeves up to my elbows. The look on her face was pure pain.

"Emily, what happened to your arms?" Thinking on my feet I replied

"I ran into a door, I'm so clumsy now that I'm pregnant"

"I have used all the excuses Emily, don't try it on me" I insisted that is what happened and asked Mum to drop it. She didn't speak to Jay much after that at all. She had her worst nightmare confirmed through my lies.

The next day Jay and I were walking down town and a family friend the Detective saw us. He and his partner spoke to each other and the next thing I know the Detective had Jay up against a wall between two shops by the neck. I rushed over to tell our family friend to leave him alone, he just looked back at me still holding Jay off the ground by the neck "Emily, you deserve better than this scumbag" he then looked at Jay and ever so calmly said

"If you ever lay a hand on her again you will have me to deal with... Do you hear what I'm saying?" I looked at the Detective and

UNBROKEN

all I could do was will him to stop. I knew what was going to follow and it wasn't going to be good for me. The Detective didn't let Jay go until he agreed.

All I could think is '*I am going to cop it now...*'

Chapter 23: A Piece of Me Died

Jay woke me mid-morning. I was getting big by this stage. This day Jay decided to take me out "Let's go bowling" this was so strange as we only ever went to visit his friends and he smoked pot while I sat there watching or to the local pub to gamble. I agreed and thought it was awesome that we were doing something together maybe things where turning around.

When we arrived at the bowling alley all of Jays pot mates were there. I should have known there wouldn't be a day he could go without it but I didn't say a word I knew better. Jay parked out the back and smoked from his bottle before we went inside. We got inside the bowling alley that I had been to many times before whilst still at school for sports day, Jay walked up and paid and got shoes. He didn't get me any and didn't pay for me. Well I really shouldn't have been surprised but I was really disappointed that he hadn't meant 'WE will go bowling'. He really meant 'Get out of bed we have to leave, I'm going to smoke pot then go bowling with my mates and you can stay and watch'.

While Jay bowled stoned with his mates they were having a great time. I asked Jay if he could get me a drink and he told me to wait. Whenever he was stoned he never thought about me, that's not really true he did but it was usually to abuse me. I walked over to one of the two pool tables and sat at a chair close by. I felt like I was sitting there forever when one of the doors opened and there before me were two of my school friends (Fred and Nigel). As I was sitting behind the door they hadn't seen me as the door opened towards me. Jay looked over as the door opened and saw me sitting there, he glared at me. Since I had moved in with Jay I hadn't seen any of my friends as he didn't like me seeing them firstly and secondly I was embarrassed to see them as I was always bruised and I couldn't stand to answer their questions and I knew there would be many questions. I watched them as they walked over and got some change and turned around. As soon as they did they saw me and rushed over. The first person to say anything was Nigel "Emily! How are you? Are you OK? Why are you wearing that long shirt you look really pale?" The questions just rolled out of his mouth and I didn't get to answer them as he asked them so quickly. I stood up, Nigel threw his arms around me and I winced. It was completely unexpected, he had hugged me really tightly and it happened to touch my bruises that had been a buildup of bruises from the previous few weeks. I didn't go a day without a new one. Nigel pushed me away a little

"Emily what's wrong?" I told him I was just pretty touchy because of the pregnancy (what an excuse pretty lame I know) I don't think he brought it but he didn't say anything. They asked if I wanted to play a game of pool but I said I'll just watch. I really was feeling funny. Jay wouldn't get me a drink and I was feeling worse by the minute. They started their game all along they were chatting to me about school and what was happening and who was doing what. I was loving being around people who really cared about me. I remember Nigel looking at me as I stood up again to go and ask for a glass of water then I remember waking up in a back room with a fan on me and someone putting water over my head, I had passed out. I was really groggy and couldn't really make out who was there. The first person I saw was Nigel. He was sitting next to where I laid and was wiping my head down with a wet cloth. When he saw my eyes open he lifted my head

"Emily, you're ok just have a sip" and he poured a little water in my mouth. I must have passed out again because the next thing I hear is Nigel and Jay arguing. I heard Nigel extremely angry

Emily Reilly

"What have you done to her you scumbag?" Jay was denying everything as Nigel was getting even more furious. Jay pushed him away from me and I remember him saying

"Are you OK baby? You should have asked me to get you a drink" *REALLY! You think!* Is all that went through my head. When I was able to sit up I realised that my sleeves had been pushed up and my shirt unbuttoned to just under my bra line. I was told afterwards that Nigel did it as the Manager was trying to take my top off to cool me down but Nigel would not let him undress me. Nigel had wet my arms and my tummy and kept moving the fan over me to cool me down. I only then realised why Nigel had been so angry. He had seen all my bruises; they were everywhere but my face. After sitting for a while Nigel wet my back and yet again he saw the bruises. This time he just looked hurt but he didn't say a word. Jay had left the room to go and see his mates in the car park for another smoke. When he returned I had gotten a bit of colour back in my face. He told Nigel to help me up. When I was standing Jay came over and put his arm around me. I winced again but he continued to hold me then he lifted me up and carried me to the car. Nigel and Fred followed closely behind, Nigel opened the back door and told Jay to lay me down. Jay put me in on the hot leather seat, wound down the window and got in the driver's seat and started the car. Nigel leant in and touched my face.

"You'll be fine Emily, I'll call you soon" Nigel smiled at me and watched as we pulled away. All the way home Jay asked if I was ok. I told him I was fine, that I just needed to lay down. We finally got home and I stripped off to just my bra and undies and laid on the horrible mattress in the heat. No fan, no open window and no clothes.

Later that night the door opened and Jay's sister came in. She knew what was going on with Jay and what he was doing to me but was obviously too afraid to say anything. She sat next to me and to

148

UNBROKEN

my surprise she had a wet cloth. She had told Jay she would watch me while he went out to see his mates for a smoke. Jay sister didn't say much she just put the wet cloth on my head "Emily, I think you should tell Jay you want to spend a few days with your Mum until you get better"

"There is no way he will let me do that"

"He will if you say you're really not well and need to spend a little time with your Mum" she replied. She then got up and left the room without saying another word.

When Jay came home he was off his face. I knew not to say anything to him in this state but this time it seemed a bit different. The first thing he said when he walked in was "Are you ok baby? I was so worried about you" it seemed like he actually cared. Weirdly my heart fluttered. If you have ever been in this situation your heart plays games with you and being pregnant your hormones are all over the place. Now was the time to say it, I just had to word it right so his mood didn't change.

"I am not well Jay; I feel really bad. Would you mind if I go and spend a few days with Mum? This way you can also have a bit of time out with your mates and don't have to worry about me because Mum will look after me" to my surprise he agreed and I called Mum and told her I had passed out and that Jay had some stuff to do for about a week and was it ok if I could stay with her. Mum was so happy

"I'll come and get you if you want" I relayed this to Jay and he said

"I'll get some stuff for you baby" he packed some of my clothes just enough for a week and I waited for Mum to arrive.

Emily Reilly

I woke the next morning in a real bed. I had the best night sleep I had had in a while. Mum had Brekky on the table. I remember thinking 'oh how I miss this' I think I actually had a few tears in my eyes. It was a school day (Monday) so Barry was at school he had left before I woke up. Mum had decided to take a bit of time off. Barry got home late from school, when he came home he ran in and said "Hey Emily! I saw Nigel today and he asked me to get you to call him, he said he really needs to talk to you"

"Yeah I'll call him tomorrow" I thought I knew what it would be about after what had happened the day before. Tomorrow came and went and then Wednesday and I still hadn't called Nigel.

Thursday 2nd May 1991 the day I will never forget and probably never get over. I am UNBROKEN now but a piece of me died this day.

Mum and I went down town and on the way back we stopped at the service station to put fuel in the car. I was in the passenger seat. Mum had left the radio on. It was 10am as I heard the familiar sound of the news introduction. I heard an urgent news report come over the radio.

"*A fifteen-year-old school boy had shot himself in a class room full of students*" the school they mentioned was on the other side of town. I knew a few people there but not many. When Mum got back to the car I mentioned it.

"Do you know anyone there?" I told her that I knew a few people and that Nigel had moved there just recently. We drove home and I didn't think any more of it. We went inside and sat at the kitchen table to have a cup of tea when I heard a knock at the door. Mum shouted out

UNBROKEN

"I'll get it" she walked to the door and when she opened it I heard a voice I knew well

"Is she her Mrs. x?" said Ze. Mum started to say where I was but Ze didn't wait for a response he came straight in and straight up to me and held me while I was sitting there.

"Emily" there was a long pause.

"Nigel's gone" I looked at him blankly

"No!" I heard a strained voice say not realising at the time that the voice was mine. The next thing I remember is that there were about thirty people in my house all crying and I couldn't comprehend what was going on. This wasn't real. I would wake up any minute. Then there was another knock at my door. I don't remember doing this but about a year ago I was told by Kylie that this is what happened so this is not from memory but from what I was told. I opened the door and Kylie was at the door, she was crying and I looked at her and said

"What are you doing here Nigel hated you" then I shut the door in her face. I don't remember anyone leaving. I didn't cry I didn't react, I think I must have been in shock, I didn't believe it. The next thing I remember was Mum calling me to come out to the lounge room that night, the 6pm news was on. The story came on the TV a fifteen-year-old boy had walked in to a classroom with his sports bag, he stood up and said to the class

"I've got something to show you" he walked to the front of the room. Before he did this two girls that knew he had the gun had gone to the Principals Office to tell him. As the Principal got to the door Nigel was unzipping his bag, pulled out a sawn off shotgun, held it to his head and pulled the trigger. Nigel's body was left on the floor with no head all day while police investigate. I saw the story and as soon as I saw Nigel's picture on the news it hit me so hard. I burst in to tears and ran to my room. I couldn't stop crying. Mum came in and I just cried and cried (a bit like right now). I remember Mum trying to calm me down. Then my reaction

"It's my fault, I should have called him, he asked me to call and I didn't call, I could have stopped him Mum, I could have stopped him" Mum just kept saying

"It not your fault sweetheart, it will be ok" nothing was going to make this ok. If only I had called maybe just maybe, I could have stopped him. Nigel had been abused by his Mother's Boyfriend's physically and sexually. Nigel and I had spoken about these many times over his short life as you all know I had known him since we move to this town so forever. One time one of his Mother's Boyfriend's who was in a wheel chair put Nigel's penis below the toilet lid and slammed it down really hard on it because he left pee on the seat. This is just one of the things that happened to this wonder friend of mine that he wanted to escape.

RIP Nigel xx

The Day of Nigel's funeral ....

Chapter 24: The Funeral

I stayed with Mum for a few more days and finally Jay decided to call me "When are you coming back?" he didn't ask how I was just when are you coming back. I told him to come and get me, I didn't feel like leaving Mum's but he was not happy and I just didn't have the strength to argue. I called Mum to tell her I was going back to Jay's and that I would call her again soon and come and visit.

"Are you sure? You can stay at home sweetheart" she said. I told her I was fine and that I had to go.

"If you need me just call" she replied

Jay arrived and we went for a drive to see Steven. Steven's brother was Ze the friend who broke the news to me about Nigel so Steven knew Nigel well. Ze was there when we arrived. Jay went inside and left me in the car as usual and Ze came out to the car to see me and check I was ok. "Come in Emily, you'll boil in this car it is too hot"

"No Jay told me to stay here" I replied. Ze stormed off and started yelling at Jay

"What the fuck are you doing you left Emily in the car, she pregnant you idiot" Jay didn't argue with Ze as his family were not the people you messed with.

"Emily what are you doing? I told you to come inside" I was so confused he told me to stay in the car and now he's telling me the opposite. I got out of the car and walked inside. Ze got me a glass of water and we spoke for ages whilst Steven and Jay smoked pot. After a while Jay said we're all going to John's house another friend of Stevens and Jay's I didn't know him very well. We all piled into the car and not much was said. We got to the other side of town and went down a little hill, John lived in a caravan with his girlfriend. This is where Jay disappeared to most nights. It stunk of pot, there were no clean dishes and clothes everywhere. I had to move a heap of clothes to try and find a spot to sit down. I had never lived in a brothel and this is exactly what my Mum would have called this place and exactly what I thought when I first walked in. After being there for hours in a smoke filled caravan I felt really sick. I asked Jay if he could please take me home. He was so smashed that I shouldn't have said anything but I really was feeling unwell and the next day was going to be Nigel's funeral. He finally agreed to take me home to lay down. It may have been that my face turned grey/green and Steven had recognised and said

"Mate she doesn't look good best you take her home and come back" we got in to the car and Jay immediately started yelling at me

"If you didn't want to come you should have just said so and I could have dropped you off before we came, fuck Emily you really shit me" at this stage I had really had enough. I had just lost my best mate and was pregnant to someone who always said they loved me but then in the next move would beat me. I did not think before it came out of my mouth

"Fucking hell Jay, it really is all about you and your bullshit, you haven't asked how I am, if I'm ok and my best mate just killed himself you constantly beat me and I am fucking sick of it, take me to my Mum's house" what the hell got in to me? I should have expected what followed he slammed on the brakes and pulled over to the side of the road. He punched me in the face then grabbed my arms and started shaking me

"Don't ever fucking speak to me like that again" he screamed in my face

UNBROKEN

"Take me to my Mum's now" I spat back at him. Funnily enough he let me got and sped all the way to my Mum's house. He pulled up down a side road

"Well, get the fuck out" I did and he sped off. I sat on my neighbours lawn for about an hour watching my Mum's house and couldn't bring myself to go inside. I picked myself up and started walking at this stage it was nearly midnight. I just kept walking and walking I was on the way to my karate sisters house. As I got just near the lookout that Jay had first hit me I heard his car coming. It was dark and I was trying to hide but he found me. He got out and was chasing me up the road yelling and screaming at me he grabbed my arms and slapped me across the face when a car pulled up it was an older guy he came running over

"Is everything ok here? Are you ok love" even though blind Freddy could see it wasn't I stood in front of this guy battered

"Everything is fine, thanks for caring" I said, he got back in his car and drove away. As soon as the guy left Jay started being nice to me telling me that he was sorry and he only did it because he loved me etc. I told Jay that I wanted to go and see my karate sister

"Ok I'll drive you there" We got in the car and he took me to her house. He said he'd be back in an hour. I walked up to her door and knocked. It was lucky that her Dad didn't answer the door. My Sis got to the door. She saw the state of me and told me to come inside. We spoke for the entire hour. I told her that I loved Jay but I was scared of him. She told me it would be ok and that she could see Jay loved me. I heard Jay's car pull up outside and I said my goodbyes. I felt that I really had no one that I could speak too as no one knew exactly how I was feeling and exactly what was happening behind closed doors.

I got in the car and Jay drove back to his house. We went inside and straight to bed. He didn't try anything that night he was

155

off his face. Before we went to bed I set the alarm and said "I have to go to Nigel's funeral tomorrow"

"Yeah I have to pick up Steven and take him"

I woke before the alarm and got up and dressed in all black. I woke Jay and told him we had to go. He got up and put on his football shorts and singlet. I remember thinking these are not really funeral clothes but he wasn't going to wear anything I asked him too and today I didn't need to be hit before I went and faced a day that I was not looking forward too.

We got in the car and were on our way over to get Steven when I said to Jay "I'm really not feeling well. I can't believe that Nigel is not here and that I can't just give him a call" Jay slammed the breaks on and looked at me

"He fucking deserved to die he was a fuck head" he spat out. I just stared at him in complete shock. I wanted to beat the crap out if him. How could he be so mean? He knew how close I was to Nigel and that he was my best mate since childhood. Why would you say this about anyone? No one deserves this. He pulled away and we went to Steven's and didn't speak any more on the way there. Steven got in the car and we were off to the funeral. We pulled up in front of the church. I remember seeing all these cars everywhere. There were about 300+ people there. As I walked in I saw all my school friends. They all walked over to hug me, then we all walked up the front of the church. We stood to the right of his coffin. In the front row was Nigel's Mum and his beloved Nan. Nigel's Nan was blind so she had her guide dog with her. I walked over and gave her a hug

"I'm so sorry Nan"

"Is that you Emily? He loved you, you were such a good friend to him" she cried. I kissed her cheek and backed away as everyone

156

was trying to get to her. I could see she needed space. I walked back over to the right of his coffin. There were flowers everywhere. Nigel's coffin was white and only about four-foot long. This shocked me as he was at least 5 foot tall when he was alive. I tried not to cry but I could help it

"Jay! Why is his coffin so small? He can't fit in that" I cried

"He blew his head off Emily that is why" he whispered so no one could hear him. I didn't know what to say. I wanted to scream at him and bash him. How dare he. Why couldn't he hold me and say "It's ok baby, he safe now" no not Jay.

I don't remember much more about the service as I was a mess. All I do remember is that they had changed the Lord's Prayer. The words they were saying had changed since I was younger. It was weird I wasn't sure what was going on I was so confused over a prayer and words being changed I just kept going over and over the prayer in my head. Strange I know I think back now and I think I was trying to not think about Nigel in that tiny coffin.

Ze and all my other mates carried the coffin out to the car. I walked beside them along with a lot of our friends. Ze asked me to come to the burial. I couldn't do it. I started shaking and I fell to the ground. Jay told me to get up but I couldn't move. I couldn't control my body. Jay lifted me and got me in to the car. I looked right at him and said "Take me home! I can't go and watch them put him in the ground, take me home please just take me home", he took me home dropped me off then left me there to deal with my emotions by myself. I needed a hug, I couldn't bring myself to go and watch them put Nigel in the ground. I laid down and all I could see was that small coffin and in my mind I was seeing only Nigel's body with no head. I didn't want to close my eyes.....

Chapter 25: It's Bath Time

It was such a hard night I kept seeing Nigel's coffin over and over and over again each time I closed my eyes. My baby would not stop kicking me. Maybe it was telling me to go to sleep or *'it's ok Mum I need you to be happy'*.

The next morning when we got up Jay was in a really bad mood. I didn't want to speak as just one word could have set him off. I remember thinking 'what have I done wrong? was he upset about me being sad about Nigel?' I needn't have bothered.

As bub had not stopped kicking me all night I needed to have a bath. I told Jay I was going to go and have a bath as my back was really sore and my tummy was itchy. I put vitamin E oil in the bath to help stop stretch marks as Mum had said this would help. He didn't respond and just went to the kitchen.

I took myself off and started running the bath. The bath was very deep so it took a while to fill and being pregnant I needed a lot of water to cover my tummy. Just as I reached over and turned off the hot then cold tap I sensed someone behind me. I went to turn around and noticed it was Jay. Jay lunged forward and drove my head into the bath holding it under. I struggled and tried to kick at him but because I was pregnant it was really hard as he was by this stage standing beside me. It felt like forever that I was struggling with him when he pulled my hair back and screamed at me "You are a piece of shit, BITCH"

"Jay what's wrong why are you doing this?" I responded. He didn't respond he just punched me right between my shoulders which jolted my head forward and my chin hit the edge of the bath. He pulled me up by my hair and again pushed my head under the water. I didn't have much strength left after the first struggle but I didn't want to die and I honestly felt like I was going too. After I stopped struggling he pulled me out by my hair and dragged me to the lounge room where he threw me onto my back and sat on my breasts pinning my arms down with his knees. He didn't care this time about leaving marks on my face and this was always one saving grace for me. Every time I had marks on my face I couldn't go out or if I did I had to wear a lot of makeup to cover it up and I certainly couldn't see my Mum. Jay thought by leaving marks in other areas of my body that it would be a reminder to me not to talk back but also that no one would ever see these. I was screaming this time

"SOMEONE HELP ME PLEASE!!!" I pleaded over and over again but as it was mid-morning and everyone was out. To be honest I don't think that any of the neighbours would have heard me or I hope they didn't as I would really like to think someone would come to my rescue when I screamed for help. I never screamed before as it only got worse but this time I wanted to be rescued as I honestly thought he was going to kill me this time.

Jay finally covered my mouth but at the same time he covered my nose so I found it hard to breath. You would have thought after all my years at Karate I would have been able to fend him off. The truth is I had lost my confidence and my strength to this person. He completely controlled me.

Every time Jay removed his hands from my mouth he would hit me over and over again. I gave up screaming and got to the point where I just didn't care anymore. I heard a knock at the door and thought finally someone has come to save me. I screamed out

"PLEASE HELP ME!" I had completely forgot I had made plan with Trisha who I hadn't seen in a long time to go and buy my Mum some flowers and walk up and give them to her at the shop.

Emily Reilly

"Emily!! Are you OK?" Trisha screamed back. By this time Jay had jumped up and told me to stay and don't say a word. He went to the door and opened it

"Hey Trisha, what are you doing here?" Trisha just pushed past him and went to where she had heard the crying coming from (the lounge room) I had moved over behind a wall and was curled up as much as a pregnant girl could be.

"Oh my God Emily!" she said as she touched my face, she quickly stood up and flew over to Jay

"You fucking prick, what have you done?"

"Emily, get up we're going" she said to me. She had to come and help me up. As we got up Jay was standing directly behind her and as she spun around he tried to spin her some crap about me doing something but to be honest I can't remember his words as all I can remember is this girl standing up to him and screaming at him and getting me out of the house. As I got to the bottom of the stairs with Trisha walking closely behind she turned around and looked Jay straight in the face

"If you EVER! touch her again you will pay you piece of scum" she barked at him. Jay looked at me from the top of the stairs and spat

"If you go you will never find anyone else your pregnant and a whore." I know he was just upset that someone had come to help me and I knew what would happen later.

"I'm fine Trisha, really! Jay we will be back soon we are just going to get some flowers for Mum" I really don't know why I said that to Trisha as I was lying she had seen for herself but I was still trying to protect him. Everyone must have thought I was crazy at the time well not everyone because really I didn't socialise as I wasn't allowed to see my friends we were always doing Jay's stuff.

As we got just a little down the road to the park, Trisha sat me down on the park bench and asked me how often this happens. I lied to her again "This was the first time, I really must have done something to upset him, please don't get involved Trisha" she looked at my batter and red face and reached in to her bag and got out her make up

"You can't be seen like this Emily, we can't have your Mum worrying and this is the last thing I will say about Jay. I don't like him, I don't trust him and if he ever does this again call me straight away" at this moment I felt loved and cared for and I cried, Trisha was true to her word and never spoke of it again. She did my makeup ever so gently and we headed down the street. I brought my Mum a beautiful bunch of yellow roses as they are her favourites. We went and saw my Mum. I wasn't dressed the best as I was wearing my around the house clothes and Mum recognised this but Trisha had done such a good job on my makeup that Mum couldn't see the marks. We had a cup of tea with Mum and I headed home to see Jay and hope that he had calmed down....

Chapter 26: On Her Bike

Jay was not there when I got back. It was lucky for me. When he did get home he just looked at me. Jay never usually made a fuss or did anything when his Parents and Sister were home. He took himself off to bed he was so smashed he couldn't have spoken if he wanted too. By the time I went to bed he was snoring.

The next morning, I woke really early. I hadn't slept very well. I remember being sore from the day before and my back was killing me from sleeping on that stupid mattress/bed on the floor. I walked out to the kitchen and I had forgotten about my face from the day before. When I walked out Jay's Sister was sitting at the table "Emily! What happened to your face" she asked obviously she knew what had happened or at least could tell from my face.

"Oh I ran in to the door again, I'm so clumsy now that I'm pregnant" You could see from the look on her face she didn't believe me and before I saw her Mum and Dad I ran to the bathroom and put on make-up. Going into that room gave me shivers. I actually started to shake.

To this day I don't like bathing with anyone. I don't even like people being in the bathroom when I am going to have a bath or shower, this makes it hard for my husband and he doesn't quite understand why. That day has left a scar that I still struggle with. I can swim in a pool but I don't like my face going near the water in the bath and in the shower I fill my hands with water and splash my face before and after washing it.

I digress.

I put on my make up and took myself out to get some breakfast. Jay came out not long after "We're going out today, going to see Steven" he stated. He never even mentioned what had happened the day before. He acted like nothing happened. We went and saw Steven for a little while so he could have a smoke. When he had had enough we went back home. He sat on the lounge and I went and got all our dirty clothes to wash them.

When the washing had finished I got the basket and put all the wet clothes in. The basket was pretty heavy as we had heaps we had to wash. It really was a struggle for me with my tummy so big to pick up the basket and carried it in front of me. If anyone had seen me they firstly would have tried to help but they would have had a giggle at a fat pregnant girl, skinny legs and arms trying to carry this huge load all by herself. Jay must have heard me getting the clothes out. I had to walk downstairs to hang out the clothes. When you walk down the stairs you walked straight in to the garage then there was a door under the stairs that led outside to the clothes line. I heard

Jay walking through the house. As I took the first stair I felt a shove in my back and I tumbled down the stairs. If anyone has fallen down stairs you know that you try to stop yourself falling but when you are this pregnant and trying to carry a basket you have no hope. I ended up sprawled out at the bottom face first. I looked up and saw Jay staring at me from the top of the stairs. He didn't say a word. I was crying and trying to get up. I finally pulled myself up and tried to pull myself together. I looked up again and Jay had gone. I walked out and hung the clothes on the line. I had skin off my knees, elbow, hands and a lump on my head that appear pretty much straight away. I hung the clothes out with tears streaming down my cheeks and I was definitely feeling sorry for myself. I was trying to understand what I had done wrong in this lifetime or the last to deserve this. There was no use. I finished hanging out the clothes and walked back in. I put the clothes basket down on the ground just inside the door. I stood there for a moment breathed in a few times and got the courage up to walk upstairs. All I really

Emily Reilly

wanted to do was run far away as far as I could get and in my state that wouldn't have been very far.

As I climbed the stairs I could hear the television going but couldn't hear Jay. I walked past that dreadful bathroom, past the bedroom around the hallway and in to the lounge room... Jay wasn't there! Where was he? Just as this thought had come to my mind I felt him grabbing me from behind. He covered my mouth and just stared at me with pure evil in his eyes "What the fuck did you tell Trisha?" I couldn't speak and he really didn't want to hear me speak, he spun me around and pushed me onto the familiar floor and again sat on me as he had done the day before. My arms were so bruised from the day before that even touching them lightly hurt so this was excruciating. He was screaming at me, he hit me in the face a few times then a few more times. Then he put his hands around my necks and pushed down while at the same time squeezing. I could hardly breath and every time I tried to scream nothing was coming out, it felt like my throat was on fire. I heard the front door open, I couldn't move. Jay didn't release my throat. I don't think he really heard it or he didn't care more to the point. Jay's Sister walked in and screamed at Jay but that made him even more angry. I think she was as scared of him as I was. I am not sure what or if he ever did anything like this to her when she was growing up but to be honest I think he may have. I remember seeing her face then I remember the door slamming. At this stage I thought I was dead. I stopped struggling and then within seconds everything went black.

The next thing I remember is opening my eyes and seeing Jay's Dad holding him up against a wall screaming at him and Jay's Sister looking at me. She saw me open my eyes "Dad she's alive" I heard the relief in her voice. She honestly thought I was dead. He released Jay and as he did this Jay ran out of the house. Jay's Sister helped me up and sat me on the lounge. I don't remember much of anything else. I don't remember Jay's Dad talking to me. I got up to

164

go to our room and as I got close I sensed Jay's Sister behind me. She helped me lay down.

"Emily you have to get out before he kills you" I will remember those words till I leave this earth. I just laid on the bed and fell asleep felling safe that Jay's Father and Sister were in the house with me. If Jay's Sister had not arrived that day I probably would not be writing this. Just to give you an idea of how long I was out. Jay's Father worked on the other side of town at least 40 km away. Jay's Sister had to ride her bike and it is not a flat ride as you could probably imagine. When I woke up it felt like only seconds she had been gone but it must have been about an hour or more on her bike.

Jay didn't come home that night, he was smart why would he come home when is Dad was furious? He did return the next morning though and what happened then was terrible.....

Chapter 27: Get in The Car

The next morning, I woke to noises coming from the garage below Jay's room. I didn't realise how much I had slept in as it was almost lunch time. I had been up and down all night needing to go to the toilet as the baby was pushing on my bladder and with every noise I heard throughout the night I would jump with fear thinking it was Jay. I pulled myself up slowly and walk to the stairs that I had been pushed down the day before. I wiped away the sleep that was still in my eyes and climb down a few stairs "Jay! Is that you?" There was no response and the noise had stopped. I continued down the stairs tentatively. I know I wasn't dreaming that there were noises coming from down stairs or at least I didn't think I was. I continued making my way down the stairs. Every few steps I would call out to try and get an answer but nothing.

When I got to the bottom of the stairs straight ahead of me was Jay's hotted up car. I couldn't work it out there was a hose of some sort going in through the car window and it was gaffe taped through the window it was then I noticed that the car was running but no one was in the car. I followed the hose to its origin and it was connected to the exhaust. What the hell was this? Then from behind me I felt something hit me in the back of my head. It was that hard I fell to my knees. As I went to turn I saw Jay's face. He had completely lost it! His eyes were so grey and opened wide. He pulled me up by my hair and walk me to the other side of the car opened the door and tried to push me in. I struggled with him using all my strength

"Jay please let me go! What are you doing? Please Jay No!" I pleaded, he over powered me and next thing I know I am in the car and the door was closed behind me. It was so smoky in the car and I was finding it harder and harder to breathe. I tried the other door and it wouldn't open he had put on the child lock. I tried the door

UNBROKEN

where Jay was standing and it too must have had a child lock on. I tried pulling the little piece of hose from the window and pushing the tape but no such luck. I cried and begged Jay to let me out

"Jay!!! Please I don't want to die, think about our baby, Please, Please, Please Jay" I was finding it harder and harder to talk by this stage I was coughing and started to feel really weird and extremely dizzy. Just as I thought to myself 'this is it, I won't see my baby, Mum, Barry or Pa again' Jay opened the door and pulled me out. He looked at me and with a steely voice said

"Make me look like a dick head again and you will not get out next time" I don't know why but I just hugged him and couldn't stop saying

"I'm so sorry Jay, I won't do it again, thank you for letting me out" I don't know why I reacted like this, maybe because I could have died.

Jay started to be nice to me after this for a while. I think he may have been worried I would tell someone what he had done. He got me a juice and told me he was going for a drive and would be back soon. I assumed that he was going to smoke his pot. I just sat around. I wanted to call my Mum but what could I say? I didn't want her worrying. I didn't want to tell my friends because they would hate Jay and if I was going to have a baby with him I wanted them to visit even though they didn't visit now because they all had their own lives I guess. I sat around feeling sorry for myself.

My baby was so very active this day. I could feel bub kicking me and moving a lot. My back was really sore. I sat holding my belly and talking to my baby. I told my baby how sorry I was that I wasn't strong enough to stop what has happened and that it's Daddy didn't mean it he was really sorry too.

Emily Reilly

I told my baby that I couldn't promise I would be the best Mummy or give it everything it wanted. I said I would make mistakes but I would do the best I could to be a good Mummy. It was a very emotional conversation. During this conversation I was rubbing my belly and my baby was going nuts. I listened to a lot of music this day. After my discussion with my baby I felt a little more relaxed.

A few hours later I heard Jay's car coming, that noise is unmistakable. It was a V8 and he never drove it to the speed limit. This day though I knew he was not happy as he skidded the car around the corner then again in to the driveway. He quickly got out if the car, slammed the door and ran up the winding stairs. He rushed in the door and straight in to the lounge room. He threw a bit of paper at me "I have just gotten out of the cop shop" he stated. I looked at him not knowing what to say. Could it have been the drugs? Did someone say something about me?

"Why Jay what happened?"

"I beat the shit out of Dan, he fucking deserved it after what he did to you" I froze, my mind was spinning my thoughts were all over the place. I thought to myself '*what the hell has he done now*'. He looked at me

"I have to go to court next week" he turned and walked away.

Next   week   arrived.....

Chapter 28: Escape

The morning of Jay's court case had arrived. He was in a terrible mood. This morning he beat me again because it was my fault he had to go to court. Did I beat someone? 'No'. It got really bad but my saving grace was that I knew he had to leave. Before Jay had to leave I told him "I hate you! I am leaving" to my surprise he grabbed my clothes and threw them over the top of the stairs (veranda) and they scattered all over the front lawn. He was now out the front screaming at me the exact words I can't remember but he was blaming me for all his problems and the fact that he had to go to court. He kept coming in and screaming in my face and grabbing my shaking me violently. His final act was to throw me across the room.

"You never loved me" he screamed. I was crying and in an instant he changed his tune

"Please don't leave Emily! Everything I do I do for you!"

"Jay you have to go or you will get arrested, I won't leave" I said to try and get him out, I was lying but it was the only way I could see to escape. He kissed me and I did my best not to be sick.

"Good luck today" I said as he walked out and got in the car. I waited till I could no long hear his car and rushed to the phone. I dialed the only number I truly knew of by heart. The phone rang and rang then finally it was answered

"Mum can you come and get me?" were the words that came out between my tears.

"Emily! What's wrong?" she said frantically

Emily Reilly

"Just come and get me please Mum I don't have long" I cried.

"Where are you?" Mum asked.

"I'm at Jay's please hurry" The phone went to the engaged tone; Mum had hung up. I fell to the floor and could not stop crying. Finally, I pulled myself together and went to the bedroom to make sure there was nothing left in there. I then went out the front, closed the door and waddled my way down the stairs. I walked around picking up my clothes and moving them closer to the road so that I could just throw them in Mum's car and get out of there.

Mum arrived and pulled up out the front. She jumped out of the car and ran over to me. She had tears in her eyes and all she could say is "Are you ok sweat heart?"

"Mum we have to go quickly!" she told me to get in the car and threw all my clothes in the back of the car and drove me home. When we arrived home Mum got all my clothes and brought them inside. She went to the kitchen and put the kettle on and made us both a cup of tea. Mum washed all my clothes this day.

"Emily, what happened?" I told her a little and that the only way I could escape was because Jay had to go to court over beating Dan. Mum didn't push me about the rest. She told me to go and have a lay down. I walked in to my room and felt a huge weight lift off my shoulders. I flopped down on my bed and couldn't believe how comfortable my bed was compared to that horrid fold out mattress/ lounge that Jay had.

When I woke I could hear Mum, Arthur and Barry talking. Mum walked in to my room and told me dinner was ready to come out when I was ready. I got myself up and walked out to the table. No one said anything. Mum asked Barry how his day was but apart from that we really didn't talk. After dinner I went to do the dishes but Mum told me to go and sit down and watch some television. I sat on our double sofa that was under our front windows. I heard a noise that sent a chill threw my bones. Jay's car speeding up the road. I was too scared to look out but I had too. When I looked out the front of my house it was dark, parked behind our big jacaranda tree was Jay's car with the driver's lights on and the brake lights were really bright. I could see him standing on the curb staring in. I was so scared as I knew exactly what he was capable of doing. I started to cry as Mum came in and saw me "What's wrong Emily?" she asked.

"He's here Mum" Mum walked to the door and opened it, she was going out to face Jay, she was not happy. I jumped up and grabbed her

"Mum please you don't know what he is capable of"

"I don't care Emily, I am going to sort this out" as Mum went to go down the stairs Jay got in the car and sped off. When we all went to bed that night I heard Jay's car again. This time it sounded like he had parked up the side road. I could hear footsteps coming down the side of the house. I froze in my bed.

I wish I could draw my house for you. I did explain the back of my house a little earlier in my story but I need to give you some more detail.

If you are looking at the back of my house from the yard under our house on the left is a garage on the right are steps that go up to our veranda. At the top of the steps directly to your right is our toilet, straight ahead was the back door. As you get to the top of the stairs and turn left onto our veranda just to your right is Barry's room. He has a window that slides up like all the window in our house to the left of Barry's room was the bathroom with a window and then you walk in to the beer room as you walk in and look right you see my room with a window and a glass door.

I heard someone walking up the stairs out the back then along the veranda. The beer room door opened. I laid very still in my bed. The head of my bed covered the lower part of the window. Someone shone a light in through my window. There was a mirror on the wall at the base of my bed so the light shone straight in and reflected in to my eyes. I dare not move. Everyone was asleep in our house as it was early in the morning. I was petrified, I knew who it was, it was Jay. He tapped on the window but I did not move. Then he walked out and he ran down the back stairs and up the side of our house. I could hear him talking to someone. Then I heard his car drive off.

I didn't sleep that night. I heard everyone out in the dining room the next morning early. Barry was staying home this day as Mum had to go out and she didn't want to leave me. She got in our four-wheel drive and drove off. Not long after she ran inside and called Arthur "The wheel is loose on the car, can you come home and have a look?" Jay had loosened the wheel nuts on Mum's car. She could have been killed if she didn't realise that something didn't feel right when she started to drive it. I knew it was him.

My cousin Layla came to visit this day. Mum had told Layla what had been happening and why I was home. Layla asked if I wanted to come and stay with her for a while. I agreed as Jay had no idea where she lived.

But he would soon find out ...

Chapter 29: Layla

Staying with Layla and her baby girl I felt relaxed for the first time in a very long time. At this stage Jay had no idea where she lived and I was so glad for a little peace. All the turmoil to date had taken its toll.

On the first day of me staying with Layla we decided to down town and have a look at the shops. She wanted me to get out as I hadn't been out of the house in so long through fear. I felt safe with Layla as she didn't take crap from anyone. She had been through similar to me with her ex Stu, though now they were on speaking terms because of their little girl. Layla and I drove down town and had some lunch at one of the only take out places in town. It was really nice to be out of the house, I forgot what it felt like to be with someone other than Jay in public. The whole time I was there I was worried that Jay would walk in cause a fuss and abuse me or worse but this didn't happen.

After going shopping for baby clothes etc. we went back to Layla's little car which was parked in the dark park out the back of the small shopping center. Layla got into the driver side and I had my door opened ready to get in when I felt hands on my shoulders. I got spun around. It was Jay... I screamed as I didn't know what he was going to do and I was really quite petrified. Layla jumped out of the car and within seconds she was around near me. Layla lost it "Get your hands off her" she screamed as she pushed him off me. Jay looked at her, he had tears in his eyes

"I just want to talk to her Layla, she's carrying my baby and left me, I have no idea why" he said calmly which was even more frightening as this was not his normal reaction. This was him trying to get sympathy from someone he thought he could win over with a story. What he didn't know is that she had been there and heard that before. My mind was racing; He didn't know why I left? Really?

Why did I feel sorry for him? I'm not sure but I am a softy at heart and I can't stand seeing people upset even him. Layla kept telling Jay to back off and give me space. "If you want to win her back you have a lot of work to do to prove you deserve her" she said this to calm him. Layla must have realised that was starting to get angry. I could see his eye colour changing and when they hit grey look out... that meant I was going to cop it. Layla told him if he wanted to speak calmly he could see me at her house but there was to be no shit and no yelling. Jay agreed and followed us back to Layla's. I really didn't want him to know where I was and I definitely didn't want him following us. I looked over at Layla still shaking

"I'm scared Layla; he will kill me" Layla kept her eyes on the road

"Not while I'm around Emily, he won't try a thing I promise you" I wanted to believe her and I know she really did mean this but I also knew Jay and no one and I mean no one could stop him if he wanted to kill me.

We arrived at Layla's and as we walked inside I heard Jay coming up behind us. I didn't know where to go, I wanted to hide. Layla told me to sit on her right away from the door. I think she was trying to protect me and she thought this would be safest. Jay knocked on the door and then walked in. I guess the knocking was a good thing as if he was really at the grey eyed stage he would never have knocked. '*Hide me*' is all I could think. "If you want to talk then talk but no shit Jay I'm warning you" Layla stated. She got up and went to make me a warm milk in the microwave. Jay sat down really close to me and touched my leg. I flinched, I didn't want him touching me

"Emily, I miss you, I can't lose you, I am so sorry"

"Jay you have hurt me and tried to kill me; I'm scared of you why would you do this to me?" I think it was because Layla was there that I seemed to get the courage from somewhere to make this response. Jay had tears in his eyes then started to cry.

"Emily I PROMISE I will never hurt you again, I don't know what was wrong with me" he cried harder and I really started to felt sorry for him I put my hand on his

"It ok Jay, please don't cry, I forgive you" at that moment I think I sort of did forgive him but looking back I was just too broken to see past his fake tears and he knew that they always worked on me. Abusers just know what buttons to push and when.

"Emily please come home" he begged with the tears now clearly rolling down his cheeks. I told Jay that I couldn't just now I had to sort some things out but he could come and visit me. He agreed that I could stay with Layla as long as he could come and visit me any time he wanted.

He left not long after and Layla sat with me and made sure I was ok. We played cards and watched movies for the rest of the day. Layla was talking to me about labor and what I could expect during it, let's just say it wouldn't be a barrel of laughs. Layla made me feel comfortable and safe she really did care about me and truly wanted to protect me. I also felt a weight lift from my shoulders because I thought everything was ok with Jay finally.

Emily Reilly

Later that night I heard Jay's car pull up. He came to the door, knocked then walked in. He asked if he could speak to me alone. Layla again warned him and we went to my room upstairs.

Layla had a three story town house. As you got to the top of the carpeted stairs and look straight ahead you will see Layla's bedroom door just a little to the right and straight ahead was the toilet, next to that the bathroom. My room was around to the right at the top of the staircase. We walked in and sat on the single bed Layla had set up for me. As soon as we sat down Jay started raising his voice at me about how much he loved me and how sorry he was. I didn't respond I just let him talk. "I can't live without you Emily, I can't see you with another man" he reached in to his pocket and pulled out a little box.

"Emily this is a promise ring, a ring that says you are mine and you own my heart" I didn't know what to say or do. He reached down and put the heart shaped ring that had several diamonds on my finger. I don't know why but this little gesture made me reach out and hug him. Why is it that something so small can melt your heart? Maybe because all I wanted, all any girl wants is to be loved. At this very moment I heard the words I had wanted to hear for so long and I fell for it hook, line and sinker. Looking back, I see a naive little girl being taking for a foul but in that moment I didn't see this I was blinded. Jay stayed for a while and just held me. He kept telling me he didn't want to see me with anyone else and to be honest at that moment I couldn't see him with anyone else either (again naive). A little while later Jay left as he was leaving he turned to me

"Have a good night and remember I love you" he then kissed me and walked out.

"That looked lovely Emily" Layla said as I made my way over to the vacant spot on the lounge beside her. I smiled and showed her my ring, which I was so very happy about. Maybe just maybe Jay had changed and this tiny ring could be proof. Layla smiled at the ring then looked up at my face it was glowing. She could have said something but she didn't she obviously just wanted me to be happy if even just for a minute.

The next day Jay came over again, he stayed just talking most of the day. He said that he was going out that night so I should have a good night with Layla. He left in the early afternoon.

It was a Friday. I remember this because the nightclub was opened and everyone went there even the under aged. Layla asked if I wanted to come with her so we could dance. I was so excited as I had not been out before and it would be good to get out and dance and forget everything for a while. I dressed in the best clothes I had that fit me being this far pregnant. Layla did my hair and makeup and made me feel like a million dollars. I was feeling fat though; no amount of makeup could cover my growing belly.

You needed identification to get in to the club and because I was only 15 my identity would not work so Layla have me her birth certificate. This was in 1991 so you could use your birth certificate as proof of age back then, no photo ID required you just had to remember the details. Anyone who has been pregnant knows that you do not have the best memory retention so this was going to be hard. Layla schooled me on how to get in. I had to sign in as L. her last name. If anyone asked tell them my name was Layla. We got to the club and when we entered I started to get very nervous. Was I going to remember everything she had told me? I walked up to the sign in desk where they asked me for my ID, I showed them Layla's birth certificate. The burly man quizzed me on her date of birth and Mother's name *'well that's simple she was my Aunty'* I thought to myself as I answered his questions without wavering. The bouncer then opened the door "Have a great night Layla" he said as he eyed me off, I am sure he knew I was not Layla but I went inside before he could change his mind or ask me any questions that could trip me up. When we got inside and I saw the biggest dance floor I had ever seen. The music was pumping; you couldn't hear people speak it was that loud. Everyone seemed to be so happy and free. Layla took me to a table that you stand around and she went to get drinks. She got me a cola as I could not have anything else. We stood around for a while then she asked me to dance. I was having a great time then I spun around and stood facing the other wall and who should I see standing there... DAN!! OMG I wanted to hide... I grabbed Layla's arm and asked if we could leave. She was a bit put back, she had no idea what Dan had done or who he even was.

"Please Layla!" I begged. She walked me back to the table and yelled over the music to me

"What's wrong Emily?" I started to cry as I could feel Dan's eyes on me.

"Let's go Darl, it's ok" maybe it was the shaking that made her realise I was not having fun and that something was seriously wrong. We walked outside and the bouncer asked if I was ok Layla assured the guy I was fine and we went back to her car.

Layla had already gotten in to the driver's side and was leaning across to unlock my door when I felt my feet leave the ground as I went down I hit my head on the road. I was dazed for a minute then I realised Jay was standing over me screaming at me "You fucking whore, I leave you for five minutes and you're off trying to pick up some other guy" he kicked me on my side. Just as he did this Layla realised what was happening and she flew out of the car and within seconds she punched him in the side of the face

"Get away from her you piece of shit! How dare you fucking do that, try it with me big man come on" she screamed. She was

178

not going to let this go. I struggled to get up and just as I was on my haunches I pulled the ring off my finger and threw it away. Jay saw this and tried to reach past Layla to get at me. By this time the bouncer at the door had arrived and he pulled Jay away.

"What's going on here?" the bouncer asked, Jay stood there facing him

"Everything's fine mate" he said as the bouncer looked at me

"Come on Darlin let's get you cleaned up" the bouncer said calmly while helping me up to my feet, he walked me to the stairs. I heard Jay screaming after me

"If I can't have your no one can, do you hear me Emily?" The bouncer turned and walked over towards Jay I heard the bouncer say

"Fuck off mate or I will sort you out" Jay ever the hero with someone twice his size didn't say a word he just got in his car and sped off. I did realise at the time but I had skin off my hands, knees, elbows and side of my face. The bouncers wouldn't let us leave till I was cleaned up and they were sure Jay was long gone.

Layla drove me back to her house and we went inside. I went straight to my room not wanted to say a word. I felt really bad that I had ruined her night.

The next few weeks I would hear Jay's car at night driving past when we went to bed. I'd hear him walk up to the house every night and just stand outside waiting.

One   night   ....

Chapter 30: One Night

Layla and I were sitting watching a movie at her house when I heard Jay's car again. Every time I heard that sound I shivered from the inside out. I couldn't control that overwhelming feeling of dread and fear. It was late and Layla said she was going to bed. I don't know why but this night I had a really bad feeling. "Layla! Can I please sleep in your room? I have a bad feeling" I said with a shaky voice and tears in my eyes.

"Sure Emily, come on we will put a mattress beside my bed" She knew from the look on my face that I was not joking.

Layla carried her little girl up to her room and laid her down to gently as she was already asleep. Layla's daughter had to sleep with her as I had taken the spare room. I have to explain Layla's room to you.

When you looked in to Layla's room straight ahead was a beautiful queen bed behind it was a full length window with long white lace curtains. On the wall to the left was a painting and there was a bed side table just under that. To the right was a built in wardrobe that took up the entire wall and the doors were sliding mirrors. It was a lovely open fresh room.

We put the mattress down on the right hand side of her bed closest to the mirrored doors then we dressed my bed. I went off to have a shower and get changed in to my bed clothes while Layla laid with her baby girl. I came out and laid on my mattress which was quite a bit lower than Layla's bed. You couldn't see it when you stood at the door. We laid talking for a while it must have been past midnight when I finally started to fall asleep. Jay's car had been going past all night so we found it hard to get to sleep. I was woken to Layla tapping me on the arm and whispering "Emily! Did

UNBROKEN

you hear that?" I hadn't heard anything but hearing her words I laid listening then I heard the back door being opened and tapping.

"Layla!! I'm scared" is all I could manage the whisper.

"Emily, move closer to my bed and don't move, don't make a sound pretend to be asleep. I will do the same" she whispered back. My heart was pounding in my chest as I laid up against the side of Layla's bed facing the mirrors if I didn't know better I would assume that she and anyone else in the room could hear it. I had closed the bedroom door when I came in from the shower. I heard footsteps downstairs and they were inside. I followed the sound of the foots steps with my mind as they made their way up the stairs. They seemed to stop at the top. Then I heard them go to the room I had been staying in that Jay knew about. I heard the door open and a voice say

"She's not here" by this stage I was frozen and petrified. Then I heard the footsteps make their way back down towards Layla's door.

It was dark in Layla's room but my eyes had adjusted as I had been too afraid to close them. I needed to see what was coming. I saw and heard the handle to Layla's door turn and the person opened it enough to look in and for me to see that the figure at the door was holding a knife straight up and down. There was a reflection on the knife from the moonlight that snuck through Layla's window. My chest tightened and started to burn. All I could think is '*please don't see me*'. I could then make out the face, it was Jay! I felt sick and my chest started to constrict. I don't know if you have ever been that scared but for me in that moment I was so scared my body was hurting. I was hoping he wouldn't see me because if he did! Well all I can say is he didn't bring that knife for no reason..

181

Emily Reilly

After what felt like forever he must have forgotten that there was someone in the room as he definitely would have seen Layla and her baby in the bed but he slammed the door and started running down the stairs "She not fucking here" he shouted and it was only then that I heard a second set of footsteps. They slammed the back door and I was still frozen. I heard two car doors and the car sped off.

To this day I don't know who the second set of feet belonged too.

After we were sure that the car was gone Layla checked if I was ok. She told me to stay where I was and she went to check the door. I swear we checked the lock before going to bed. There wasn't really a reason for checking as we never used it. Layla came back up and laid down. She told me there was no damage to the door. It was almost like they had a key. I couldn't sleep that night as I was worried he would come back and this time finish what he came to do the first time. Layla finally fell asleep and I guess I should have felt a little safer as he didn't think I was in the house but there was no way.

The next day we went to see Mum at home. Layla told her what happened and Mum told me to come home. I was so torn, if I came home Mum wouldn't be safe and if I stayed with Layla she wouldn't be safe but Layla piped up

"Aunty x, she's fine with me really. He doesn't think she is there. Just make sure you lock up at night and tell Arthur and Barry what happened so they are aware" Mum reluctantly agreed. I went back to Layla's and for the next few nights I couldn't sleep. We hadn't heard Jay's car for a while so I should have felt relieved but I didn't. I know knew he would really kill me using a weapon and this didn't help me sleep or feel safe anywhere with anyone.

UNBROKEN

A couple of weeks later Layla's ex came over and we all went for a drive in his 4WD. I wanted to give them time together but there was no way I was staying anywhere by myself. Layla, her ex, her baby girl and I all got in the front of the 4WD. Layla had her girl on her lap and her legs where laying across mine (this was back in the early 90's so this was allowed back then).

We drove around and then ended up in a secluded back road where Layla and her ex got out of the car and left me there with the baby while they went for a smoke and a talk. After a while they came back so we could go back to Layla's. Layla's ex was driving, Layla got in and lifted her baby and sat next to him and I sat closets to the door. It was really dark outside before we pulled up I leant over and said to Layla "I have a bad feeling that he is here" Layla looked at me quizzically

"No it's all good Emily your just on edge, his car is nowhere around" I sat in that seat and didn't want to get out and most of all I didn't want to get out first but I had no choice being closet to the door. I opened the door and looked around cautiously. Layla's partner said

"You go in I'll bring the baby in"

I stood so close to the door of the car and the fear building up inside me made me be sick physically. I stood as close to Layla as I possibly could. She waited with me to make sure I was ok then she led me inside. She had to stand in front of me because she had the keys so I felt very venerable standing behind her holding the screen door opened. She unlocked the door and turned on the light. We knew her ex wouldn't be far behind us, this gave me a little relief.

Layla checked the house and it all seemed fine. We sat on the lounge waiting for her partner. I heard someone running up the driveway and I thought to myself wow he can run with the baby. Then the door flung opened but it wasn't who I was expecting at that moment at all. Coming towards me really quickly was Jay!!!! (As I write this my heart is pounding, I am home alone and it has freaked me out a bit). He grabbed my arm and started pulling me towards the door. "We have to talk" he demanded. I tried to pull away, then all of a sudden Layla was there pushing him away

"Fuck off! Leave her alone you coward" she screamed at him.

"Layla, I just want to talk to her" he replied calmly. Layla stood between us so he couldn't do anything unless he hurt her first. She then turned around and looked at me for a reaction.

"It's fine Layla, we will just be out the front" I said stuttering a little. Why I agreed I had no idea but I did. Jay promised Layla there would be no trouble

"One noise and you will have to deal with me!" she spat out. I walked down to the end of the driveway and there in the driveway was his car! I hadn't heard it? '*How did he do that?*' was all I could think.

We stood talking for a while and he kept begging me to get back with him. He was telling me he was sorry and that he couldn't understand why I left him? I don't where it came from but I think I had had enough. I finally told him why (he should have known he did it to me). He acted surprised and kept saying

"I'm sorry please come back to me" he tried to put that stupid ring on my finger and I pulled my hand away

"I don't want it and I don't want you" I said in a moment of frustration, BIG mistake. He looked me in the eyes and with his hand he crushed the ring and pushed it in my face, I felt it cut me. Then he pushed me against the car and grabbed my neck and by this time I was laying on the bonnet of the car on my back finding it hard to breath. There is no way I could scream and he knew it. I started to cry silently tears were filling my eyes and rolling down the side of my face. Every time I tried to scream the more he tightened his grip. Then all of a sudden he let go and started say

"I'm sorry Hon, I didn't mean it, I'm just upset"

I slipped off the car and tried to run when I felt his arm go around my neck and he pulled me backwards towards him. He spun me around and then pulled me on the bonnet again he punched me in the face then a flourish of punches followed not just my face but my tummy as well as my baby. I screamed and within seconds he was laying on his back after tripping when Layla had pulled him off me. She started kicking him.

He got up shouting "Your fucking dead Emily! If I can't have you no one will" he got in the car and sped off. Layla walked me inside. During all this time Layla's partner was nowhere to be seen. When I got inside he was sitting on the couch holding their little girl. He had to have walked straight past me when Jay was doing it and I didn't notice and he didn't do anything!! Layla took me upstairs and made me stand in front of the mirror in the bathroom.

"See this Emily? Do you see it? This will get worse and next time you might not be here"

"How can I bring my baby into this life? I have to do something. He can hurt me but not my baby. If he can do this while I'm pregnant imagine what could happen and what he could do to my baby" I said to my bloody face in the mirror. I asked Layla to call the Police and by this stage her partner had left and we sat waiting for the Police to arrive. It took a while for them to arrive and when they did it wasn't anyone I knew. They took my statement and told us to call if anything happened again. They also told me to get to the Police Station the next day and make a formal complaint. They were going to find him.

Emily Reilly

The next morning. We went to Mums and this time she told me to get in the car straight away without us even saying what had happened, she saw it. She took me down to the Police Station to make a complaint and get a restraining order.

Would   it   help?   .....

Chapter 31: Court

We walked in to the Police Station. Mum got to the counter first and said that she wanted to organise a restraining order for me. The Police Officer walked out the back and came back a few minutes later with the Sargent "Follow me please ladies" the Sargent said. The Sargent led us to another room and made his way to a seat behind a desk that had mounds of paperwork piled up on it. Mum, myself and Layla sat in front of the table facing the Sargent.

"What can I do for you today?" he asked. Mum piped up and started telling him what had happened. The Sargent looked at her and told her that he had to hear it from me. I started explaining everything that happened. The Sargent stopped me when I was explaining the drugs

"Is he doing drugs?"

"He smokes a lot of pot and when he does he gets really aggressive" I responded. The Sargent chuckled which seemed strange to me as I was pouring out my heart

"Pot won't make him angry, it will make him calm!" he stated as a matter of fact. I couldn't believe what I was hearing.

"I'm telling you Sir that it does make him aggressive" I responded as I burst in to tears. This was no laughing matter to me, this was serious. Just then another Officer came to the door and asked Layla to follow him to make a statement, she got up and followed him to another room. Back in our room the Sargent asked me to continue providing details of what had happened and when.

"Well love! from experience I must say it will only get harder if you leave, it's probably best to go back" my heart started racing, was I dreaming? Did this Officer just say "Go back?" I thought the police where here to help you but he just wanted me to make it easy. Easy for who? them? so they didn't have to get involved or do anything to help. Mum push her chair back, stood up and leant across the table

"Excuse me but I would like to ensure that you protect my daughter, can you not see what he did? we want a restraining order to stop him coming near her" she demanded. The Sargent then asked me to write down what had happened.

"Why didn't you complain earlier?" he asked. I sat silently then answered almost ashamed

"I don't know why" he didn't say much else apart from telling us we would have to attend court on Monday and sit before the judge to get a AVO (Apprehended Violence Order). We got our paperwork and as we were walking out the young Police Officer that was speaking with Layla spoke up

"We are going to pay this Jay a visit and warn him to stay away from you" I looked up from the ground I had been follow with my eyes, tears still welling, looked him in the eyes and nodded. I couldn't say anything. At this moment I didn't think that there was anyone that could help protect me from Jay. The police were the last resort and the interview with the Sargent gave me no confidence anything was actually going to be done.

"It will be ok" he was trying his best to make me feel like they could actually protect me as we walked out.

As we walked out the front no one said a word. Mum was disgusted in the Sargent and his comment. A single tear rolled down my cheek and I dare not relax or they would all come flowing out. I should have felt safer after walking out of there but I didn't, I didn't feel secure at all. Maybe the Sargent was right, maybe I

UNBROKEN

should go back so Jay doesn't hurt anyone I know. I didn't realise it but at the time I said exactly that out loud. Layla grabbed me "Emily! You're not going back to that lunatic, I'm not scared of him and your Mum and everyone else can help protect you from him" I reached out and hugged Layla without saying anything, she believed her own words but I was not so confident, I had put my family in danger and now they were prepared to protect me from something they could not see coming. Jay was smart, he planned everything down to a tee and if he wanted to get me he would and no one would see it coming.

For the next few days and nights I stayed at Mum's. We didn't leave the house and every now and then I would hear Jay's car drive by. I was constantly frightened and stressed. It wasn't long before my baby was due and this could not be doing my pregnancy any good.

Monday arrived and we went to the court house. We saw someone we had known for years sitting there, he had known Arthur's family forever they had grown up together. We had to sit out the front of the courthouse until we were called in for the case to be heard. The Police Prosecutor came over and had a chat with me before hand, he ran me through everything and told me it would be ok. He was a really lovely guy, so kind hearted and softly spoken but I really wouldn't have liked to be on his bad side. I heard Jay's car before I saw him. He didn't bother getting dressed up for court, he was wearing a Balmain Tigers Jersey and footy shorts. When he got out the front he sat on a bench that was about three meters away from us, directly in front. He kept staring at us the entire time we were outside the court. I couldn't look at him but Layla look straight over at him, when he realised Layla was looking he lifted his hand to his neck and made a cutting movement then said "You and your kid are next" to Layla.

A bit about Layla.

Layla was beautiful long blonde hair, blue eyes and dark skin. She was also a fire cracker. If you threatened her, her friends or family she would lose it. She did not take shit from anyone. When she heard this she raised up from her seat and started yelling at Jay "Did you just threaten my family? You fucking freak!" she was edging closer and closer to him. The Police Prosecutor heard what was happening and came out of the courthouse. Layla explained what Jay had done, the Prosecutor walked over to the Police that were by this stage standing outside the courthouse and asked them to speak with Jay. The Police walked over to where Jay was and told him to behave himself but this didn't stop him. He continued threatening us the entire time we were outside and the Police being in the vicinity did not deter him.

Our names were called and Jay was walked in before me with the Police following closely behind him. He was sat up the front on the left and we had to sit on the right. I looked over at Jay when he made eye contact. He lifted his hand to his throat and made a slashing movement, just as he did this the Judge, Police Prosecutor and Police all saw it. The Judge demanded that Jay stop threatening me and face the front, which he did. The Police Prosecutor told the Judge why we were there "I have read the notes on this case" the Judge stated. I had never been to court before so everything that was happening made no sense to me at all.

"Stand up" the Judge demanded of Jay.

"This is the second time I have seen you in here in the last two months for assault, what do you have to say for yourself?"

"I didn't do anything" Jay lied.

UNBROKEN

"I don't believe a word that comes out of your mouth Mr. x. I saw you with my own eyes threatening Miss x. I find what you have done to be disgusting" the Judge said sternly.

The Judge swore at Jay a few times during the court case but the one I remember the most was when the judge said "I grant the restraining order for two years, you are not to contact or go within 500 metres of Miss X"

"She having my fucking kid, I have to be able to see it" Jay spat, I couldn't believe that he would talk to a judge like that but he did. By this stage I was crying thinking about him coming near me again, he would kill me. I looked at the Judge and tears where streaming down my face, I was shaking uncontrollably at this thought.

"Mr. X, you have beaten this young lady the entire time she has been pregnant. She still holds bruises on her today. You obviously didn't give a fuck about the child when you were doing this. You are not fit to be a parent, I put it to you that you are not a fucking father, the order stands you are not to be within 500 metres of Miss X and no contact" I remember thinking to myself that Judges didn't swear on TV when they were sentencing but I guess Jay again pushed the wrong buttons for the wrong person this day.

My heart lifted, my tears stopped for a minute (as I write this there is a lump in my throat and my heart is racing). Jay screamed out that 'if he couldn't have me no one could' in the middle of the court room. This made me snap out of the relieved feeling and right back to scared again. The Judge told him if he heard one more word out of his mouth he would send him the jail. Jay shut up, jail would not be a place that he could survive that's for sure. When the hearing finished we sat and waited for Jay to leave the Court House before we left, during this time I had to sign paperwork. As we walked out the front Jay was near the door. "I will get you Emily!"

he said to me as I walked out. What he didn't realise was that there were the two Police Officer's standing behind him when he said this. I kept walking but when I looked back I saw the two Officers each holding on to each of Jay's arms and they disappeared behind the Court House.

We went home and I didn't feel any better about the situation '*This bit of paper wouldn't stop him*' is all I could think.

I found out later that those two Officers took Jay out the back of the Court House and beat him whilst using a phone book so not to leave any marks. I smiled when I thought about this. I know that probably sounds bad but just once I would have loved to have been there to see it.

We didn't hear from Jay for a couple of days. I would say that he was a bit sore.

That night while I slept I dreamt of walking in to a pharmacy and a lovely lady said to me "What a beautiful baby girl what's her name?" I told the lady her name and she smiled

"That is beautiful" I walk out of the shop and as I did I woke from my dream. I walked out to dining room where Mum was sitting with her cup of tea "What do you think of this name if I have a girl?"

"That's beautiful Emily" I had picked the name of my baby if it was a girl and if it was a boy he would be Joshua.

The next morning, we went shopping for baby clothes just Mum and I. The entire time I had a bad feeling Jay was following me, usually when I had this feeling he was there somewhere, it's weird how I sensed him. I kept looking over my shoulder my heart filled with dread and fear the entire time. As we were walking back towards the car I saw him. He was standing about ten meters away and followed us to the car "Get away Jay, we have a restraining order, we will call the police" Mum stated to him as she opened my door and helping me in to the car.

"No fucking piece of paper will stop me" he yelled at us. My exact thoughts after leaving court confirmed by Jay himself. When we got home Mum called the Police and told them what had happened. They said they would follow it up. I don't think they did.

The next morning early when I woke I went in to Mum's room. "Mum! I have really bad pain in my tummy" I said as a sharp pain shot through it again.

"Emily, I think you're in labor sweetheart!" ...

Emily Reilly

Chapter 32: You're In Labor

Mum got out of bed and went straight to the phone and frantically dialed a number "Emily is in labor" she said to the person on the end of the phone. Within ten minutes Layla was at our house with her little girl.

"How are you feeling Emily?" Layla asked truly concerned. The contraction had stopped at this stage so Mum went to the kitchen and put the kettle on.

"Do you both want a cup of tea?" Mum called out, just as she said this the contractions where back again. Wow such a pain I hadn't felt before, shooting pains going through my tummy and up my back all at the same time. I was buckled over grasping my tummy silently begging the pain to go away. Layla kept trying to rub my back which I can't say really helped at the time. Nothing! could stop this pain I was sure of it, then all of a sudden the pain had stopped again.

"Aunty, we need to get her to hospital, she's having the baby" Layla called out to my Mum whilst she was still making that cup of tea. Mum knew that the first labor was going to take some time and she was just pottering around trying to buy time.

"What should I wear today?" Mum said to us both like nothing was happening.

"Aunty! Hospital" Layla was panicking. Even though Layla had had a baby her perception of labor was different to my Mum's. Mum's labor with me being the first was eight days on the delivery table Layla's however was only one and a half hours hence her reason for concern. She was worried this baby was going to pop out at any minute.

"She has a while to go yet Layla, You'll be fine Emily" unbeknownst to Layla and I Mum was watching the clock to see how far apart my contractions where but to Layla Mum was being a bit to flippant. This went on for hours. (My labor lasted 17.5 hours, then crowning started). Layla had to leave but said she would be back a little later. Mum changed about four times during this time. She was trying to keep my mind off what was happening or better still what was to come. Finally, Mum took me to the hospital. All the way there Mum found every pot hole and bump in the road. We walked in to the maternity ward, we made our way to the Nurses Station. When we got there we saw a lovely nurse.

"Hi x" the Nurse said to my Mum, she obviously knew her.

"Who's this you have with you?"

"This is my daughter Emily" Mum replied.

"Wow, really? I remember delivering Barry, you were only a baby yourself" the Nurse said to me

Emily Reilly

"You're a baby having a baby, are you giving the baby up after birth?" The Nurse asked me as if this was a normal question to ask someone.

"No!" I stated back not very nicely, just as I said this my contractions started again. I was then guided to a waiting room. The Nurse advised Mum to rub my back if I had the pain again and if I could I was to stand up, hold the end of the bed and sway my hips (like a cow I was told).

The Nurse finally came in and asked me some questions about my contractions and if I had had any blood when going to the toilet. I hadn't... I was so uncomfortable with her questions. Don't get me wrong she was lovely but I was embarrassed. I was at this stage just 16 years of age and my frame was tiny due to the anorexia I had before falling pregnant. The Nurse did an internal '*embarrassing*' was all I could think. "Well she's three centimetres dilated" the nurse said to Mum. I was so confused I had no idea what dilated meant.

"You can stay here or go home, it will be a while off" the Nurse continued this time looking at me. Mum looked at me as if to ask what I wanted to do.

"I'll go home" to be honest I was really scared. I had no idea what to expect. We walked to the car and Mum helped me in.

"Let's go get a video Emily" Mum said as she got in to the car and started it up.

"That would be great" I replied thinking this is exactly what I need, something to take my mind off the pain. We arrived at the video shop and went inside. I was looking around while Mum was at the counter speaking with the lady who owned the shop. The lady behind the counter took Mum over to a shelf then they returned and Mum paid for the video

"Let's go Emily, I've got one" in the middle of the store I had a contraction again. The lady freaked out and panicked running over to me. Mum explained that I was in labor and that I was fine as we walked out the front door and back to the car. I needed a lot of help to get into the car as the contractions had me again buckled over in pain.

When we got back to our house Mum helped me go inside and laid me on the lounge setting up pillows to make me comfortable. She walked over and put the video on. "What is it?" I asked hoping for something funny or a love story.

"You'll see" she responded. I waited for a great movie to start but I was shocked when I heard a woman screaming. When I focused on what this was I realised.. Mum had got me a video of a woman in labor. Funny when I think back I remember Mum telling Barry and I about sex by putting on the video 'where did I come from' and she walked out of the room. I looked at Mum and couldn't believe she had done this.

"Mum! No I don't want to watch this"

"You have to Emily, it will show you what you can expect" I laid there having contraction after contraction watching this poor woman in labor it was almost like I was going out in sympathy. The whole time this woman was screaming I was freaking out thinking '*this is going to be me soon*'. We were home for hour's when Barry came home after school and sat with me waiting for the time we had to go back to the hospital. Arthur arrived home and Mum prepared dinner, I didn't eat as I was feeling sick.

Emily Reilly

At about 7pm we went to the hospital again as the contractions were very close together. When we arrived they immediately walked me in and got me a hospital nightie (so attractive). I was shown how to sway my hips and told to 'walk off the contractions'. Walk off the contractions? Really! they wanted me to walk these off? from where I was standing they were not going anywhere and walking was not going to get rid of them. I remember thinking *'what a stupid thing to say'* I was put in a shower as I was told that it would help with the pain (this was a lie). As I was walking around I heard another lady screaming. I was filled with terror, *'this is going to hurt'* I thought to myself.

Finally, my doctor arrived "Come on Emily, let's bring this baby in to the world" I was set up on a bed in a delivery room. Mum came in with me. Barry and Arthur waited outside. I was given an epidural, yay no pain or so I thought. It only worked from my hip down on the left hand side of my body so I felt every bit of this pain. My feet were restrained in stirrups *'was this normal?'* I thought to myself, *'the lady in the movie didn't have these'*. I didn't care that this man was down there I was in too much pain. They say you forget the pain when you have the baby but that is a lie let me tell you now, it is a pain you cannot explain but you don't forget it. I was told to push

"I want to shit!" is all I could say (classy I know but that is exactly what came out of my mouth).

"That's ok Emily, you shit Darlin, we have two Nurses here to clean it up" my doctor said. He knew I wasn't going to but said it to calm my down. I was crowning for so long it felt like forever and I didn't think I could do it but all of a sudden I pushed really hard and I felt the head release and then was told to push again and the worst pain I had ever felt followed then there was a huge release. I heard a baby cry....

UNBROKEN

"You have a beautiful baby girl; do you want to hold her?" the doctor asked smiling

"Get it away from me" I responded. Mum took my baby in her arms by this time Arthur and Barry had entered the room and they fought over who was going to hold her first, Barry won and Arthur was none too happy.

The night before Arthur had said to me in a drunken state "It's just a grunt and a fart and it's all over" about my labor. I glared at him when remembering his words, I was exhausted.

"I'm sorry Emily I will never say that again" he said I didn't respond. I laid on the bed for a while then it started again... The pain was back 'not again I thought to myself. The doctor explained to me it was the after birth. When everything was finally over Arthur took Barry home and Mum stayed for a while.

"So what's her name?" the Nurse asked me. I looked at this little girl they had since laid in my arms and attached to my breast.

"Her   name   is   Ava"...

Chapter 33: Where Is She?

After some time of feeding Ava, she was taken to the nursery. I was taken to a room that I didn't have to share with anyone. Mum sat with me for a while until I started to fall asleep it had been such a long day and taken its toll on all of us. She kissed my forehead and told me she would be back in the morning before tucking me in and walking out of the room. Because I was so small I had to have stitches.. you know where I won't go in to detail. I was still in pain, my back was aching and down there well let's just say use your imagination but thankfully it was all done now.

I started dosing off but I was really concerned that Jay might turn up. When you have a baby you are supposed to be over the moon but not me. I was happy she was out and in the world but that lingering fear and Jay's final threat kept ringing in my ears. The hospital staff had been warned about the situation but they were all female in the maternity ward so no match for Jay. I must have been really exhausted because I had fallen asleep till I was woken by yelling and a voice I can never forget "WHERE IS SHE?" I heard Jay raw at the Nurse's. I heard one of the Nurse's say (there were four of them on duty this night)

"Calm down, you can't go in it is outside visiting hours and you're not allowed near her"

"Emily! Emily! Where the fuck are you? If you don't come out I'm going to fucking find you and you won't be here to see tomorrow" he screamed past the Nurses. I hopped out of bed and took myself to the little bathroom I had in my room. I closed the door and locked it behind me. I slid down the door, leant back and pulled my knees in to my chest as best I could. My body was

UNBROKEN

shaking so badly that I felt like I was convulsing. I cried so hard but tried to not make a sound so as not to alert him to where I was.

"Calm down!" I heard another voice, male this time and it wasn't Jay.

"Go and call the Police" the voice said again. It was my Doctor he had come out of the birthing sweat. Jay kept yelling out to me, I was under no illusion had he found me I would not have been here to write this. This went on for over an hour then I heard the door slam and the Nurses scurrying around. There was a knock at the bathroom door

"Emily, it's ok the doors are locked and he is gone" said one of the Nurse's from the other side of the door.

"He'll be back" I whispered through my tears and taking in gulps of air. I stayed there for a while then there was another knock at the door

"Emily! It's the police, you can come out" I shimmied my way off the floor to turn and opened the door, as the door opened I fell into the Police Officer's arms. To my surprise it was the one of the Officer's who had taken Jay out the back of the Court House to meet the phone book.

"It's going to be ok; we will deal with him. You're going to be ok"

"My baby! Where's my girl?" I asked, the officer looked at the Nurse for an answer.

"She's sleeping in the nursery; we don't have a name tag on her so he will never know. He also won't be back in this hospital, he's band" the Nurse tried to assure me. The Police Officer's stayed with me for a while.

Emily Reilly

"Let's go see your little girl, that way you can see she's ok" the Officer said and he walked me down to the nursery. This was the first time I had seen her since her birth. My heart ached, she really was beautiful. When we had finished the Officer again walked me back to my room and told me they were going to pay Jay a visit. He had broken the restraining order so he would be arrested. Well this night I can tell you I could definitely not sleep at all.

Mum arrived early the next morning. The nurses had explained to Mum what had happened the night prior. When Mum walked in to my room she leant over and just held me. She didn't say anything as she knew it would upset me again.

A little later the local newspaper came in and took a photo of Ava and I for the paper along with a lot of other women that had had their babies that week. I didn't think much about it but I am sure this set Jay off. "Emily, Pa is next door with Great Nan let's take Ava over to visit" Mum wanted to get me out so I could take my mind off the night before and the one person who ALWAYS made me feel safe was there, my Pa. My great Nan was ninety-nine so not far off a letter from the Queen. On this day we had five generations in one photo I didn't realize that this wasn't normal, that this was very special not many people can have this photo opportunity. When I walked in my Pa hugged me and then held Ava. Great Nan looked at me

"Pass me my Great, Great Granddaughter, she's mine" I had a little giggle at this. Great Nan had lived through a lot so you can probably imagine that he was a hard woman. She was so proud and loved Ava's name. We had to leave after an hour as visiting hours were over. Mum took me back to my room and then Ava to the nursery. Before she left Mum said

"I'll bring you something nice for dinner, hospital food is terrible" I couldn't wait to eat I hadn't eaten in two days.

UNBROKEN

A lot of people came to visit us whilst we were in hospital and a lot of them I hadn't seen for a long time. Kylie brought me some dried flowers from my Drama Teacher with a lovely card I still have   to   this   day....

Chapter 34: You Need to Tell Your Father

I stayed in hospital for a week. Every night Mum would bring me food and the entire time I was there I had very little sleep with feeding Ava and worrying about Jay's return it was very difficult. Jay would constantly get people to call the hospital saying they were one of my friends and then when I had the phone he would threaten me and my family. I was so frightened that the Nurses stopped putting calls through. They were concerned that this could jeopardise my bond with my baby girl.

On the day I was to take Ava home Mum came in and said "We need to tell your Father" I hadn't seen my Dad since the time he had called me a slut and his girlfriend had set me up but I still loved him as he was my Dad.

"You have to tell him about Jay, Emily he may be able to help" I think Mum said this to try and make me feel better. She knew I understood my Father and who better to deal with a lunatic than an even crazier lunatic protecting his family I guess.

When we got home I got Ava settled and picked up the phone. I dialed my Nan's number (Dad's Mum) as I didn't have his contact details she was the only one I could think of that had them or at very least could find them for me. "Hi Nan it's Emily" the call began.

"Emily! How are you sweetie?" Nan hadn't seen me for a very long time so in her eyes I was still that little girl. We chatted for a while about general things then I told her I had had Ava.

"Oh Emily, I'm a Great Grandma, I'm sure she will be beautiful just like her Mummy" she sounded excited but also a little weird as I am not sure she expected this from me.

UNBROKEN

"Nan, do you have a number for Dad?" I continued. Nan gave me a number and we talked for a little while longer and I promised I would see her soon. As I hung up the phone I looked at Mum with trepidation.

"Emily you have to tell him" Mum stated, she knew this was hard for me to do. I picked up the phone and my hand was shaking *'what would he say? Would he think that I was what he had called me when we last saw each other?'* I dialed the number and it rang for quite some time then I heard his voice on the end of the line. I was silent and he kept saying

"Hello" finally I spoke and it must have sounded like I was a teenage boy whose voice had just broken

"Dad! It's me Emily"

"Oh Emily my beautiful girl how are you?" he replied.

"Daddy, I need you right now! there is this boy I have been seeing and he has threatened to kill me and he really would do it" I cried down the phone line like a little girl wanting her Daddy to protect her and make everything better again. This was the first time I had broken down I mean really broken down everything came out all at once.

"Dad, I had a baby girl" I spat out in the middle of him replying. The phone went dead silent.

"Put your Mother on the phone" he barked. I turned and looked at Mum and held the phone out to her, she knew what was coming or so she thought. Mum grabbed the phone. I didn't hear what Dad said to her all I heard was Mum saying

"I'll pick you up. See you then" and she hung up the phone.

Emily Reilly

"He's coming" she said as she looked at me. I knew from the look on her face that he was not going to be happy to see me.

A few hours later we had to go to the train station. Mum, Barry, Ava and myself all drove down to the station, we got out of the car and went and sat in the shelter. Not long after us taking a seat the train arrived. Barry and I stood up and scanned the train up and down. Being a small town the train only came twice a day and not many people traveled on it. At the far end of the station we saw a lone figure step out, it was him.. Barry ran up and hugged him so tight and he patted him on the head then I saw him look down at me. "Hi Dad" is all I could manage to say, he looked me up and down

"I'm discussed and disappointed in you" were the words that came out of his mouth. I was heartbroken but really I shouldn't have expected anything less I was a child that had a child not the little girl he remembered me as. He hugged my Mum and she just patted his back. He swooned over Ava. We drove home and when we got there Dad and I talked I told him EVERYTHING that had happened, as I finished Mum walked in and he looked straight at her then back at me

"A leopard never changes its spots" he said while he looked over at Mum

"Ask your Mother" she didn't say a word but I knew exactly what he was meaning at least he was admitting it. I just looked at Mum and a tear welled in her eyes. You could tell she used to really love him.

"Where is he now?" Dad asked

"Probably at home" I replied

UNBROKEN

"Well get the car, I'm going to pay him a visit" he said never looking me in the eyes, he was too busy looking at Mum and then Ava. Mum got the car out again and I went to get in.

"Stay here Emily" he said firmly. I was not game not to do what I was told. Mum drove Dad down to Jay's house. The next bit was told to me when they got back.

They arrived at Jay's house. Mum pointed it out as she parked directly out the front. Dad told her to stay in the car. He walked up the stairs and knocked on the door. Jay's Father answered the door. Dad asked to speak with Jay and Jay's Dad looked out and saw Mum sitting in the car he obviously knew the man standing in front of him was not there to just talk. Jay's Dad swore at Dad and told him that Jay wasn't there. When Dad asked where he was Jay's Dad replied "Even if I knew where he was I wouldn't tell you" then he continued to swear and call Dad names. Little did Jay's Dad know my Father had a short temper and as much as he hit my Mum he also wouldn't stand down to anyone. He was a hard arse through and through and not someone to push past his limit. Dad's limit was not very high. Dad grabbed Jay's Father and threw him over the balcony. He then ran down the stairs to were Jay's Dad was now sprawled out on the yard

"If he ever goes near my daughter again, if he ever lays a hand on her or any of my family I WILL be back and he will be six foot under" Jay's Father didn't move and didn't respond I think he would have been too scared. I wouldn't like to be on the receiving end of my Father that's for sure and at this stage Jay's Dad knew that he didn't want to be on that side either. He made a smart move not saying anything more to enrage my Father further.

When they arrived home Dad sat down at the table and asked to hold Ava. He was swooning over her. The entire time he was there all he wanted was that she should have his last name 'that is who she is' he kept saying. Dad stayed for a few nights and these nights I had the best sleep ever knowing my Dad was there and if Jay did come he wouldn't be around for long, my Dad would give his life to protect me.

The day he left he just said "Goodbye" no hug, no kiss nothing. He gave Barry a lot of affection and of course Ava and he held Mum for a while.

"If he comes near you again just call me and I will be here in a few hours" My heart sank as his train slowly edged away as much as Dad was ignoring me I felt truly safe. This is the one man I knew did not care about going to goal to protect me.

Jay did not leave us alone, it was like he knew when my Dad was here and when he left. It was getting worse. Phone calls threatening me, Mum, Barry, my Grand Parents and just about everyone I knew.

Not long after was Mum and Arthur's Anniversary. On the day Mum said to him "What's today?" he looked down at his watch and said

"Oh no, I completely forgot, it's garbage day" he got up from the table and walked out to take out the garbage bin. Mum and Arthur had not been good for a while and this was the last straw for Mum she walked off. When he got back inside I told him

"It's your Anniversary" he looked at me surprised

"I completely forgot, what should I get her?" he left the house not long after and came home with diamond earrings. Arthur apologised but Mum knew he had forgotten completely it truly was the last straw.

A couple of weeks later with Jay still coming around and scaring me he would not give up and Arthur being Arthur Mum

UNBROKEN

said "Let's move away from here, somewhere we will be safe and hopefully happy" Barry and I agreed so Mum got to planning, she kept trying to tell Arthur that it was over but he was always drunk and wouldn't accept it. He thought Mum would get over it eventually. What he didn't know is that that was never going to happen.

The day before we left I called all my friends and told them we had to talk. This was one of the hardest conversations I had to have..

Chapter 35: Say Goodbye

Every morning my Mum would wake up then got and light the fires in both of our fire places so that Ava was warm when we got her out of bed. It was winter by this stage and could get very cold.

The day before we left we sat at the table and had breakfast as normal then Arthur left for work. He had not been told what was happening as Mum just wanted to get as far away from this life as possible. A little later the door was being knocked on and a constant stream of my friends filled our house. Barry's friends had also arrived at around the same time. He went to his room with all his friends. My heart sank as I saw him walk away his head was hung lower and I knew he wanted to cry but there was no way he would. My situation had brought us here to this point. It wasn't Barry's or Mums fault it was mine. I had gotten involved with the wrong person and now everyone had to lose something all because of me. This day was the day we were losing all contact with everyone and everything we knew. We were leaving the house we had grown up in and everyone we cared about. To this day I hold this in my heart. I did this! and my family were prepared to drop everything just to make sure I was safe.

I sat with all of my friends and there were a lot of tears and beautiful words spoken. Kylie was there and she cried so much "I will never forget you Emily, you are my best friend, what am I going to do without you" she cried. I didn't know how to respond I couldn't speak my heart was breaking, I reached out and held her tight. Trisha gave me a silver charm bracelet and said

"No matter what happens wear this and remember I will always be here for you" I still have this bracelet to this day. This was not like a normal farewell and see you later this was forever. Talk continued for hours and I told them all we had to leave so I could protect my family and them. Jay had threatened them through me and also made threats to some of them directly as I found out that day. They said they could protect me but they really had no idea who Jay was and what he was capable of and as much as I wanted to retreat into a world where my friends were all I needed I couldn't. They stayed for hours but had to leave before school finished so they could catch their buses. I didn't want to let them go, I held on so tight and for as long as I possibly could. This was the moment I realised that I was losing everything, my life would never be the same. I was falling to pieces and so were they but at least I knew they would look after each other as they always did.

After everyone left I went straight to my room. I stood looking at myself in the mirror where I had questioned myself many times before '*What have you done? Why? You have messed up some many people's lives*' I turned to my bed and flopped faced down and the tears wouldn't stop flowing. Then I heard a little cry coming from the lounge room. I pulled myself together and walked out and picked up my beautiful baby girl then I walked back to my room and sat on my bed. I looked down at her and made a promise "I will always try my best to protect you and a tear fell on her little face" Arthur arrived home later that afternoon, we had dinner as usual and as usual it was quiet and not a word spoken. He then got up got himself a beer and drank until he was drunk and unable to hold a conversation. He got up and went to bed after snoring on the lounge for what seemed like a long time. Mum stayed up and we talked for a while. She was almost please to be getting out of this town but she was truly going to miss a few people and Pa was one. We had told Pa about the move and he supported us as he always did.

The next morning after Arthur left for work Pam's Mum arrived with a truck. Layla came over to help pack it up, Mum only took what was ours. We said long goodbyes to Layla and Pam's Mum. There was a knock at the door and some of my friends had arrived to say a final goodbye. I couldn't tell them where we were going as at this stage we were going to stay with my Great Uncle while we looked for a place to live. We said our goodbyes and we got into the two cabin truck and we started off down the road. As we passed over the bridge to leave our town my heart was breaking. This was where I had grown up, were I had my first kiss, where I played sports, it was the only place I had ever called home. It felt like a million tiny little hands where reaching out and grabbing my heart trying to pull me back and as they pulled it was ripping it in two. This was my heart breaking. My mind was playing tricks on me. I could hear my friends over and over in my head asking me not to leave. I looked over at Barry and he had tears in his eyes that he wasn't going to let fall out and Mum! Well she was not crying and not really showing any emotion at all. She looked a little relieved to be honest but I knew this was killing her.

I made my friends promise not to tell Jay but I knew he would find out soon but by then we should be safe and far away or so I thought..

Chapter 36: The Tap

We arrived in Sydney to stay with my Great Uncle (Uncle J). When Mum was growing up she lived with Uncle J for some time he was also her god father. His house was on a large block and over the years this area was built out by developers but my Uncle refused to sell. One day a private school approached him to use his land. They offered to build flats that he would own and he would be the caretaker. He agreed as he always had a soft spot for kids and this way he had a legacy. We used to go visit him each Christmas and it was always so much fun. We went to the markets and got to eat takeaway food which we didn't have in my home town.

Uncle J was handicap. When he was born the doctor was drunk and broke his spine. The fingers on his right hand curled and he couldn't walk without his trolley, due to this he had meals on wheels visit every day, three times a day and we always got the juice and jelly. He had someone come and tidy his house but it always had a funny smell so when we arrived the first thing we would do was clean his flat from top to bottom.

Uncle J sat in the same seat all day and watched out the window for people driving in to the school. He either let them in or tell them to go away. He couldn't lock the window due to his hands/disability. I had taken Jay here one year to introduce him to Uncle J. Uncle J was pleasant but he didn't really like him and like Mum and Pa he just didn't say much when he didn't like someone.

Finally, I felt safe. The first few days I slept like a baby. I hadn't slept an entire night for so very long that when I woke and it was after 9am I jumped up with a fright. We were looking for a place to live but because Mum had to look for a job we couldn't afford to live on this side of town. We had to go west for cheaper accommodation. We finally found a house out west of Sydney. It was about 45 minutes' train ride to get there from Uncle J's.

The day we went to move in it was so hot. The house was very old and fibro so extremely hot. It was located on a main bus route; this was good as we didn't have a car as Mum left our car with Arthur. We had all our worldly possessions in the back of a truck and spent days unpacking.

Day to day we would walk about 5 kilometres to get to the closest train station in order to get in to the closest city/shop. We couldn't afford to travel on the bus and then the train it was either one or the other. We had enough food to get us by and Ava always had everything she needed. We would always go without to ensure that she had everything. On pay day we would catch the bus to the shops this was a real treat. Mum finally got herself a job at the local hospital and she felt so much better once she had this. She is not the sort of person who can sit around and do nothing. Us and feeling useful was Mum's life.

I told my closest friends my address and I constantly received letters from them. Once a week we would speak on the phone. They would mostly call me after 6pm because it was cheaper.

We had been in our house for a few months when I decided to go and stay with my cousin over in the northern suburbs for a weekend. We will call her Viv. Viv was engaged to a submariner. She worked at the local pub where all submariners drank when they were docked. I had Ava with me and Viv asked me to come straight to the pub and we could sit at the lower bar (it was like a beer garden but inside). I went there and I met so many people they were all so very nice to me and they loved Ava. I would stay at Viv and her fiancées unit. They had people over and we played cards and talked. Finally, I was feeling almost normal again.

UNBROKEN

When I returned home I told Mum how much fun I had she was so glad to see me come out of my shell a little more every day. Barry had started school at the local high school and as expected he made friends quickly, he was a likeable guy. Viv would ask me over each weekend and I would jump at the chance. I would leave at about 4pm and be there by 6pm. One weekend when I was away Viv's phone rang in the morning "Emily, it's your Mum" Viv said

"Hi Mum, what's wrong?"

"Jay's called Emily, he is going to call back soon he said he won't stop till he speaks with you, I'm sorry sweetheart"

"I'll be there soon" I told Viv what had happened

"Let's go" we got a taxi and travelled across the city. She paid and it cost her so much money but she wasn't letting me go by myself and she didn't do public transport. When we arrived home the phone rang. I answered with trepidation

"Hello" I whispered

"I know where you are you fucking bitch and you won't be there for long if I have anything to do with it" in the background Mum told Barry to go and ring the Police from the phone booth up the road and let them know what was happening. Barry did this and when he returned he said to Mum very quietly

"Emily needs to keep him on the line they are going to trace the call, I have to go and ring them every fifteen minutes to see if they have found him" Mum wrote this down on a piece of paper and handed it to me. I was on the phone for about three hours in total. I had to keep him talking and every now and then there would be a tap on the line it sounded a little like clicking a pen. The entire time Jay threatened my Grand Parent, Uncle J, my friends and other family members. I asked him how did he get my number, he told me Layla gave it to him and Kylie gave him my address.

My heart felt like it had been ripped from my chest. I thought to myself '*How could they do this to me?*' Jay asked if that noise he was hearing on the phone line was a tap

"No, how could I get a tap" Barry kept going to the phone booth and after three hours and his last trip to there he came back and told us that they couldn't trace the number as it was old machinery that Jay was calling from a fax line. The last words Jay spoke on the phone were

"I am bringing some people to deal with your mother this weekend" then he hung up. I was freaking out '*what did he mean?*'. Viv wouldn't leave us she called her fiancé he and a few of the boys came and stayed with us for the next few days, we had someone different there every night as all the boys took turns watching out.

That weekend arrived and I heard that familiar sound that sent shivers through my very soul. It was Jay's car ....

Chapter 37: Deal with Your Mother

Mum walked out as she had heard the same familiar sound of Jay's car. I pulled the curtain to the side and peeked out being careful not to be spotted by anyone on the outside. There parked out the front of our home was Jay. He had pulled up on the road directly in front of our house. Jay obviously didn't care if we knew he was there or if you had seen him. He must have loved knowing he terrorised me and my family, that he had this much control over someone.

The car windows were tinted so I couldn't see who he had brought with him to deal with my Mum. I pulled back away from the curtain and looked at Mum, I was extremely concerned, my entire body was on fire and my chest tightened as I told Mum to hide. I heard the car door close then another door close, there were two people. *'Who's coming'* was all I had running through my head "Mum take Ava" I managed to say. She just looked at me. Viv and the boys had left so it was Mum, Barry, Ava and me all alone. Mum picked up the phone and called Viv. Viv said she would be right over with the boys. They were at least 45 minutes away. I was really freaking out but trying to stay strong. I finally got the courage to pull the curtain aside again. I couldn't see anyone; Jay's car was running so I knew he was still in it as he never left his keys in his car. As I was still peeking out behind the curtain I heard loud knocking on the door. Mum walked to the kitchen and peaked out from behind the curtain in there

"It's Arthur and Heff" she whispered from the doorway to the lounge room.

"Barry take Ava and hide, please!!" I said in a desperate whisper. He took her to his room, pulled his blind down so no one could see in. then closed his door behind him ever so quietly so as not to alert Arthur and Heff (my Step Brother) to the fact there was someone else in the house. Usually you could hear everything through the fibro walls of the house. The banging continued then I heard Arthur yelling

"Open the door" I wasn't so much frightened of Arthur or Heff to me Arthur was a drunk and no matter what I knew he wouldn't hurt Mum. I opened the door slowly with the chain still attached as a little protection so I could peer through but no one could come in. I wanted to make sure Jay wasn't there.

"What do you want?" I said to them. Arthur looked at me with those eyes.

"Just get your Mother" he spat at me. I looked at Heff and I could see he wasn't angry at me. We had always gotten on well. I closed the door making sure to re-lock it and went to get Mum. Mum repeated my steps when opening the door checking again to see Jay wasn't there. She opened the door and they pushed past her. As soon as they were inside I grabbed the door, pushed it shut and locked it followed by put the chain back on. Mum and Arthur went to the kitchen and Heff just sat on our lounge. He couldn't look me in the eyes.

"Why did you come here?" he didn't answer and he didn't look at me.

"You just pissed off and left Dad, why do you think we are here" he replied. I asked why he had come with Jay and what a stupid question that was.

"He knew where you were and he said he would bring us to you so Dad could sort out your Mum" Heff stated. We spoke for ages and Mum spoke with Arthur. Heff told me to watch Jay as he was going to kill me. Jay thought that Arthur would do something to hurt Mum but Jay didn't know him well. Arthur being a drunk

218

can say anything to get what he wants and he wanted to see Mum but he wouldn't hurt her. I heard another car door then yelling. Jay's car started sped off. I looked out the front just as I moved towards the door I heard Viv

"Emily! Let me in" I opened the door and hugged her.

"Where Mum?" She asked I pointed towards the kitchen. The boys where following her. They moved straight in and walked toward Heff and they were not happy. I had run over and stand in front of Heff. I explained that they were just here to talk to Mum. I heard Mum saying the same thing to Viv. A few hours later the phone rang. I was afraid to answer but I had some courage because Viv and the boys were there. I picked up the phone, there on the end of the line was Jay

"Put Heff on the phone" Jay said to me. I handed the phone over. I only heard one side of the conversation but it really was just to say where Jay was going to pick them up from. Heff handed me the phone back

"He wants you!" Heff said. I really didn't want to take this call but I did

"I will be watching you and when you least expect it, I WILL DEAL WITH YOU" he threatened. I didn't respond but the tears welled in my eyes and started to run down my cheeks uncontrollable. I hung up the phone.

I don't know what Mum and Arthur said to one another but when Arthur and Heff left Mum and Arthur hugged. This was their goodbye. Mum looked relieved when she came back in.

Everyone stayed that night just in case. I wasn't surprised I didn't hear Jay's car again as he had to drive Arthur and Heff back to my beloved home town. After Arthur and Heff left I called Layla "Did you tell Jay where I am?" I paused waiting for a response.

"He told me you did" she was quiet Layla was not happy

"If that's what you think you can get fucked!" then she hung up before I could say anything. I was so upset but dare not call her back. It wasn't the reaction I was expecting and to be honest I didn't know what to think at this time as I felt so unsafe and didn't know who to trust. I should have known better though Layla was my cousin and had been there for me so many times, she had stood in front of me protecting me and I accused her of this! Jay had a way of turning people against me. He would tell me things about people that I would stupidly believe and then I would react. He isolated me from everyone doing this. I believed at this time I could not trust anyone...

That weekend Viv called and invited us all over to stay. "Emily, I've got someone that wants to meet you" she said to me. We agreed to go to Viv's and stay the night, after everything that had happened this was a perfect time to escape the madness and meet some new people. We arrived at Viv's unit and got ready to go out and have some fun. When we got to her pub we went straight to the indoor beer garden. Viv stood up and waved at someone to come over. The beer garden was full of sailors. I didn't pay attention to who it was Viv waved over as I was busy rocking Ava after her feed. She was always a good baby.

"Grant, this is Emily! Emily this is Grant" There standing next to me was a dark skinned, dark hair, dark eyed guy. I didn't know what to say so I managed a

"Hi" Viv asked Mum and Barry to go with her to order a meal. She was trying to leave us alone to set me up....

Chapter 38: Grant

Sitting there at that table with this stranger I felt a little uncomfortable. The one thing I could think was *'Viv would not let anyone hurt me, so he must be ok'*. He did most of the talking and flirting. He was twenty-four and I was going to be seventeen soon. Grant was a Submariner and worked with Viv's fiancé. He seemed to be really nice. His family owned a beef cattle farm on the North Coast so he was a country boy also. We spoke for about an hour before Mum came back. It was nice to know there was someone showing me some attention after all the times Jay had told me I would never find anyone after having a baby but to be honest finding someone was the last thing I had on my mind but every now and then I would think to myself *'No one is going to want to take on me and a baby'*

We all went back to Viv's after eating dinner and Grant and I continued to talk. When everyone was in bed asleep we were still talking about everything and anything. I didn't speak of Jay but he had been told by Viv a little of what had been happening. The next day Mum, Barry and I returned home. We were planning Ava's naming day ceremony that would be held in a few months.

I haven't mentioned this but on Ava's birth certificate she did not have Jay's name listed. I did not declare the Father. So in that spot it was blank. It may sound bad to you but if he could do what he did when I was pregnant what would he do when she was born. He told me many times that he would kill me and her if he couldn't have us no one could.

The weeks passed and I had a call from Viv "Emily, Grant really likes you" she said. I was a little excited by this as when we

Emily Reilly

had met a few weeks ago and talked all night he seemed like a really good guy.

"You need to call a cab and come over" she continued.

"I can't catch a cab Viv it's too expensive"

"No Emily, you have to come over Grant is going to pay for it, he wants to see you again" I covered the phone and asked Mum if she would be ok. Even though I was a Mother I still always asked Mum as I respected her and because I was still just her little girl.

"Go, and have fun" Mum said with a smile on her face. I told Viv I had to pack some things for Ava and I and that I would be there soon. As soon as I got off the phone I skipped into my room and changed about four times, I wanted to look my best. I did my hair and makeup, got Ava's clothes ready and bundled her in to her baby capsule. The taxi arrived and Mum gave us a big hug

"Stay safe and have fun" she said before we walked out of the door. Whenever we walked out that door we would look around, you just never could tell if Jay would be there or not.

The drive seemed to take forever as it was during peak hour traffic. When we arrived Grant was standing out the front of the units. He had been waiting and I'm sure he would have been there a while. While I was getting Ava out of the taxi Grant went and paid the taxi driver. He then rushed over to help me with Ava. Instead of grabbing her bag he grabbed her capsule. This made me smile because if anyone ever wanted to be more than friends they had to accept Ava as we came as a package.

That night he paid for dinner and we talked again. Viv and her fiancé went out and left us to talk. This was defiantly a setup. Grant was really nice and saying all the right things. He reached out and held my hand, I pulled away the first time due to being cautious.

UNBROKEN

We talked all night, Ava laid beside me in a bassinet as we spoke. Viv had pulled out a mattress for me to sleep on and Grant was to sleep on the lounge. In the early hours of the morning Grant came and laid down beside me. He touched my hand and I felt a chill but this time I didn't move it away. We just talked and talked until I fell asleep. I woke with him holding me in his arms. I didn't move I just laid there.

The next morning, I decided to go home to be with Mum just in case Jay came back. Grant asked if he could spend the day with us, so we all got in another taxi and drove home. Mum was waiting and she rushed out and grabbed Ava. She was so happy to see her. Mum and Ava have a bond that can never be broken. Ava was always her favourite she would lay down her life for Ava. Ava always came first no matter what. I admired this love. Mum, Barry and I all had a bond as well but the first grandchild is always special and the fact that we lived with Mum helped this bond develop further.

That day we just watched movies all day and Grant offered to pay for dinner so again we ordered in. He left late that night in a taxi. I didn't want him to go but he didn't want to disrespect my Mum. I have to give it to him he seemed to be the perfect gentleman. I started to think that maybe there are some good guys out there.

The next day he called and we spoke for ages. He said he had to go to sea for two months but would really like to see me before he went he wanted to take us all out. He told us to get in a taxi and he would pay and meet him near Viv's pub. We all got in the cab with no idea where we were going this day.

When we arrived Grant was nowhere to be seen so we sat and waiting. After about an hour I saw him walking up the road.

Emily Reilly

"Emily!" he yelled as he ran towards me. He reached out and held me.

"Let's go" he said with a smile. We got in another taxi and went to Circular Quay. There we got on a ferry and crossed the Harbour. This was one of the most amazing things I had ever done. Going past the grand mansions that kissed the Harbour all the while the is water splashing up on the side of the ferry. When you turn and look back to where you started from you see the Harbour Bridge, the Opera House and the famous Luna Park smiling face truly an amazing sight from the water. The breeze on my face, every now and then you would get a spray of water. I hadn't felt so free in a long time. It was truly wonderful.

When we got to our destination I smiled. Grant was taking is to Taronga Zoo. We spent the entire day there walking around seeing all of the amazing animals. Barry was in his glory as like me we had never been to a Zoo. Even though we were older it was like being a little kid seeing things for the first time through fresh eyes. Grant pushed the pram and took my hand I was amazed at this, someone was willing to date me but most of all he realised that Ava was a part of me and accepted it wholly. During the day we had many photos taken together so we could always remember this. All in all, it was a really nice day. The sun started to go down so we knew it was time to leave as the zoo had closed. We got back on the ferry for that wonderful, peaceful return trip as we were about to dock Grant lent in and whispered in my ear "I really like you Emily" then he kissed me on the cheek. A little butterfly crept up inside me... This is a feeling I had not felt in a very long time. Fear was all I knew at this stage in my life so having butterflies made for a massive change.

We returned home that night and I was buzzing from the day. It really was a lovely day, the best I had had in a while. Grant stayed for as long as he could but he had to go by midnight in order

to be ready to sail the next morning. As he left I thought to my
'Two months is such a long time, I wish he didn't have to go'

Chapter 39: Pap Smear

I had been having terrible pain in my tummy since having Ava and Mum decided it was time to take me to the doctors to check it out. So started the familiar walk to the train station in order to go to town. I was in pain this day and found the walk excruciating but we really couldn't afford to catch a bus or a cab to the doctors. I was pushing Ava's pram and this was helping a little as I could take some of my weight on the pram.

When we arrived at the doctors he asked if I had ever had a Pap smear. My answer was no I was only sixteen nearly seventeen by this stage. He called the nurse in and they gave me a Pap smear. Well wasn't I in for a shock! what a horrible feeling at that age it feels like you are being invaded. Any woman who has had this done (which should be all of us) will know it is extremely uncomfortable.

After they had finished the doctor said he should have the results back by the end of the week. He didn't do any blood tests or much else but I'm sure he knew what he was doing.

We left the doctors and went across the road the Westfield's Shopping Centre. It is a massive shopping center three stories high and it would take you almost all day to look around. We decided to go and have an ice coffee before catching the train home. I was not looking forward to the return walk but we had no choice. We decided to have a look around the shops before heading off and I wanted to go and look at the baby clothes in Best & Less for Ava. They always had pretty clothes. I found a really cute jumpsuit for her and it was on sale so I decided to buy it. Yes, I know we didn't have enough money for the bus but I could buy a jumpsuit for Ava. Well she never went without ever. The lady at the counter looked down "She is beautiful" as Ava smiled her magical smile that always brought people in. The lady looked at me

"She's not yours is she?" I said yes and she responded

"You are just a baby; you shouldn't have a baby" I glared at her

"Obviously I could she here, well dressed and loved" the lady just scanned my item and looked away. It made me feel about two inches tall.

To this day I get frustrated when people say stupid things about Teen Mothers. Yes, it's true if I had known what I know now back then I would have delayed having a baby but I didn't and I couldn't. I would never take back having Ava. When I look at Teen Mothers I see myself back then. I only get upset when I see that they don't care about their babies. In most cases they do but there are some that don't. I would love to be able to talk to them before they get sexually active and tell them how hard life is being a Teen Mum and what you would miss out on but if they are anything like me back then it would have made no difference. I was head strong.

We finally got home and after the walk home we didn't do much at all. We just watched some TV, had dinner and went to bed.

The next day the phone rang quite early. It was the doctor's surgery. They wanted me to come straight in. The doctor had been concerned and rushed my results through. He didn't show it the day before though.

So again we walked to the station, rode the train to the doctors, as we walked into the surgery we didn't even get to sit down. He called me and Mum in, Barry waited with Ava "We got the results back and they found something Emily" the doctor said. Mum asked some questions then he leant in and touched my leg

"You have to go to the hospital, I have scheduled you in. You have to have a colposcopy (this is an examination of the cervix) and a biopsy"

"Cancer" Mum blurted out before she thought. The doctor hadn't said this but Mum knew that if you have a biopsy it is to determine if you have cancer or not. I had no idea. When we walked out of the surgery I was numb, I didn't know what to think. Mum hailed a cab, we couldn't afford it but there was no way she was going to let me walk to the hospital after being told this. We got to the hospital and as the doctor had said he had organised everything, a nurse walked me in to a theatre room. If I thought the pap smear was bad it had nothing on this. The only benefit was that it was a lady who did the procedure. I was put in stirrups again then the nurse used the clamp she poked around inside and put some sort of dye in and a scope that looked around. She told me the dye would show and problems. She then took a biopsy of the affected area. I didn't have a local and to be honest it must be numb in there because I just felt uncomfortable it didn't really hurt. When she had finished I got my dignity back, dressed and walked out to Mum. The nurse said they would rush the results and call us as soon as they have them.

Again we went home and did nothing. I couldn't really do anything I didn't know how to feel, I was confused and that word rang in my head like alarm bells 'cancer' over and over. I didn't sleep well that night. Again the next morning the phone rang and I froze. I couldn't answer it. Mum walked past me and grabbed the phone, it was the hospital I had to get back again. We travelled on the bus directly to the hospital. We got there and the same nurse came out to great me. She called me in to a little room and I wanted Mum to come also so she did. A doctor came in just as we sat down. "Hello Emily, we have found something. You have cervical cancer" he said. As these words hit my ears my eyes started to water and all I could think is *'no what's going to happen to Ava, Mum and Barry'* I didn't hear what Mum was asking the doctor as my mind was not in that room. Then the doctor tapped my knee

"Emily, the cancer is stage two, this means we need to do a diathermy (this is burning tissue) we will be doing it today as if we don't it could go further at the moment it is in two areas so we should get be able to get it all and there shouldn't have to be any more treatment"

"Ok let's do it" I said as I stood up, the doctor smiled and took me to a theatre that he already had prepared. I got on the bed and followed the same procedure as I had the day before. He rapped a band around my leg and without a local he started the procedure. It was so uncomfortable I didn't feel pain I just smelt burning flesh. It was horrible. I don't remember how long it took because my mind was elsewhere. I was preparing for the worst. Thoughts of Mum and Barry having to raise Ava without me

Would she know who I was when she grew up?

Would they be safe from Jay without me?

Who would look after Mum?

When the procedure was finished the doctor order me to come back the next week and they would check that they got it all. He said I needed time to heal.

"I'm pretty sure we got it all Emily but we need to be sure" he then said I had to have Pap smears every six months for the next few years.

When we got home that day I took Ava to our room laid on the bed and cried holding her. A million questions running through my mind. It's weird but I was laying there and in my mind I was asking Ava

What are you like when your older?

Do you have children?

Are you happy?

Do you have a career?

Is   Nanny   OK?

Chapter 40: Daddy's Back

A few months had passed and Grant was due back in only one week. During the time he was away so much had happened. Jay had been driving past and calling and harassing us constantly. I had found out that he had been harassing my Pa and this was killing me. The worst thing is he knew how close I was to my Pa and he knew this would hurt me badly.

Pa was the sort of man who would not stand down to a fight being an ex-soldier as you all know. He was extremely protective of his family. He was our protector that's for sure. He told Mum about the calls but Jay changed tactics when Pa told him to come and face him and not hide behind a phone. Jay told Pa that the next time he saw me it would be at my funeral. This is the only reason Pa called and spoke to me and told me what had happened. I hated that my Pa was hurting and I felt like it was all my fault for bringing this person in to our lives. I didn't realise then but now when I look back I can't blame myself for this. I really wasn't aware he was psychotic. It scared me so much that I called my Dad. He lived out west of where we were living. When I told him about everything and told him we had moved here he said he would be over as soon as he could.

Dad arrived within two hours. I hadn't seen him for a few months and the last time I didn't feel loved or cared for. I felt like a piece of garbage and he made me feel that way. I was almost invisible to him back then.

This time he was so much different. As soon as I opened the door he picked me up and spun me around "I'm here now baby, no one is going to hurt you. Where's Mum, Barry and Ava?" were the first words out of his mouth. I couldn't stop smiling at this stage as he seemed so different. I felt like I was his little girl again his

Emily Reilly

"SLAM" the was the nickname he used for me, no this won't give me away only to my direct family members if they ever get to read this book. I don't know where this nickname came from but he had called me this for my entire little life. I loved that name when he said it as it always reminded me of the good times with him as we did have some when we were little and visited him, when he was sober.

Dad and Mum sat at the table whilst Dad held Ava. They talked for hours about all sorts of things. They laughed together and everything seemed perfect. This is what I had dreamed of as a young girl that my family would be like, it's just a shame it never was. If you can imagine everything that I saw when I was little what my Dad did to my Mum, you could probably feel what I felt that day. I felt peaceful and couldn't stop thinking 'if only he had changed' but I knew in my heart of hearts he never would or could be because as soon as he had a drink this bubble would burst. Dad stayed for hours then Mum offered that he could sleep on the lounge as it was too late to travel back now. So this is what he did. I went to bed and thought to myself. We are safe now Dad's here. I could hear Mum and Dad talking to the early hours of the morning. It was a lovely feeling knowing that this is how it should have been all along for Mum.

When I woke up Dad was asleep on the lounge and Mum was up getting some breakfast ready. When Dad woke up he said "Do you all want to have a BBQ this afternoon? I'll go to the shop and get some meat" we all agreed this was a great idea. We hadn't had a BBQ for such a long time. Barry was a bit funny with Dad, he stood back and took everything in and didn't really say much, maybe he was afraid that Dad would flip a switch and go nuts.

Later that day the phone rang I answered it not thinking. I was happy till I heard that voice. "I'm going to fucking kill you, you better not close your eyes for too long, I know which room you sleep in and I have watched you at night. Don't look out the window at night you just don't know who might be there!" a tear rolled down my cheek. My choices were about to interrupt our happiness again. I didn't want anyone to see but I didn't realise that Dad had been standing behind me he grabbed the phone

"If you ever call my girl again, you won't have to worry about police coming and getting you because they will be coming to get me after I do what I am going to do to you" Dad said and he hung up the phone. Jay wouldn't have been expecting that! Dad put his arm around me and whispered

"It's going to be ok SLAM" he made me feel safe again even just for a little while.

Jay was never far from my mind. I was shaken and I definitely couldn't sleep even with the blind down, all I could think is 'he's out there'. Luckily Dad stayed for a few more night, when he was in the house I knew that a maniac like Jay didn't stand a chance against my Dad as he was the biggest maniac out there. He had done what Jay has done and knew all the tricks. Don't try and trick a trickster. I knew my father had been to goal and was not afraid to go back. He definitely would have put Jay in the ground with no second thought about it. The day Dad left was a sad one because I did feel safer having him there but we knew he was only a call and a couple of hours away.

About a week later the phone rang early in the morning. I was shaking before I answered and heard that voice on the end of the line "Emily! I'm back and on my way over, I've missed you so much!" It was Grant and within the hour he would be here. I ran around getting myself ready...

Chapter 41: Name Giving

Grant and I had been dating for months. It was nice to have someone around who cared about you and that you could talk too. Mum is the only person in my life that knows absolutely everything about me. She knows me better than I know me. I didn't tell Grant much of my past as I didn't want to taint what we had and I have never been able to say out loud what had happened to me. I always thought that I brought this life on myself. I did it all, it was my fault. Anyone who has been in an abusive relationship will know exactly what I mean. You are not a victim; you feel like you deserve everything you get because you brought it on yourself. When you are told this enough you believe it. Sometimes you even feel sorry for the abuser, sick I know but this is exactly how I felt. Deep down I knew Jay was crazy but I also thought everything that my family and friends had to go through was because of me and me alone. If I hadn't dated him in the first place none of this would have happened.

When Grant and I went on dates we always had Ava with us. If you remember back to when I told my Mum I was pregnant she said "I will not be a babysitter" well Mum meant that and I knew that Ava was my responsibility and mine alone. I am sure that Mum wouldn't have minded looking after her once in a while but I wouldn't do that. Mum was big on taking your responsibilities seriously and me going on dates did not and should not give me the right to forget that.

The day of Ava's name giving arrived. I had chosen two God Mothers and a God Father. Ava's first God Mother was Melissa my karate sister and the one person I thought I could trust. Ava's second God Mother was Viv and her God Father was Viv's husband. We had quite a few people coming most of them where friends I had made after I moved and the only person from my home town was Melissa. My Nan and Pa also came and he was so proud. I have a wonderful picture of my Nan and Pa holding Ava in her Naming Day Gown. The smile on my Pa's face says it all.

That morning before everyone arrived I heard the familiar sound of Jay's car. He had pulled up across the road from our house. Viv, her husband, Grant, Barry and Mum were all inside. I had had enough at this stage, I was sick of being afraid, I was sick of him threatening my family. All that was going through my mind at the time was '*if he's going to do it he can do it now*'. So stupidly I opened the door. Mum tried to pull me back inside and Grant, Viv and her husband yelled at me "Emily! Let us deal with it" I was having none of it. I pushed them all away

"This is up to me, it's my responsibility I have to deal with this once and for all. If he tries anything call the cops" Jay was standing behind the car on the other side of the road. As I crossed the road he said

"Takes some balls to come out here" I just walked straight up to him

"If you're going to do it, do it now" by this stage I was yelling. I was so scared but I really had had enough. He pushed me and I fell backwards. He was calling me every name under the sun. I told him he was being extremely immature and that he needed to get a life. This CHAT if you can call it that went on for about ten minutes. Finally, I decided I had had enough of his insults and I don't know where it came from but I punched him in the face. I was furious this had been building up for ages. He had blood coming from his noise and I felt a small weight lift of my shoulders I thought to myself '*if this is the last thing I do I will be happy*' as he moved forward and believe me he was not happy and I knew I was in trouble, I heard a police siren. Mum had called the police. They pulled up beside us. Jay started shouting how he wanted to charge me for assault

"Look what she did to my face" he spat at the police. I just stood there. The first Officer just said

"I can't see anything" whilst the second asked his full name so he could check the database. He walked to the car and radioed in Jay's details when he returned the Officer asked why he was breaking his restraining order. The first Officer grabbed Jay by the back of his shirt whilst the second grabbed the back of his pants. They lifted him off the ground and went to throw him in the back of the paddy wagon.

"Oops" the first Officer said as Jay's head collided with the doors of the paddy wagon. They hadn't opened them and when they threw him in it was with a bit of force and the top of his head collided badly. Jay started screaming at them and swearing. The first officer held Jay whilst this time the second officer opened the back doors. They again grabbed him and threw him in the back, this time his head hit the front wall. They slammed the doors behind him and then came to talk with me. They asked what had happened and I told them everything. They were aware of Jay due to past complaints by my family, me and also from our Detective friend in our home town, they told me that we would have to go to court and under no circumstance was I to admit I hit him. He fell when he was resisting arrest. I truly am not good at lying though I would try in this instance. They drove off and Jay's car stayed parked outside.

All of my family and friends arrived and the naming day continued without any further interruptions. Ava was in a beautiful white and gold gown that Mum had made. I still have it to this day and hope that she will use it if she ever has children.

UNBROKEN

My Pa cried during the ceremony he was so proud; it truly was beautiful. Grant was also very happy to be there; he had grown close to Ava. Not a word was spoken about Jay that day it really wasn't the right time. I was so happy with how the day went. Everyone had gone home by about 10pm. Viv, her husband and Grant stayed over as they didn't want to go anywhere whilst Jay's car was parked outside. They knew he wouldn't put up with what I had done and I knew it also. He moved his car early in the morning I know because the police escorted him away.

A few days later we went to court. Jay was dressed really well, he wore a suit and tie, I couldn't believe it I had never seen him outside his footy shorts or jeans. I attended with Mum, Barry and Viv. The Police Prosecutor was a lovely man and the Police Chief from the station also came along with the other Officer's from the station who had arrested him. We went in to court and I had to sit up and tell the Judge what had happened. I explained everything and just omitted the fact I had hit him until the Judge asked me directly. I couldn't lie so I said "He pushed me and I hit him, I have never done that before for fear of him killing me"

"What was different this time" the Judge asked.

"I wanted it to stop, if he was going to kill me I wanted it done and to be honest if it was the last thing I did on this earth I would be happy, knowing I stood up to him even for just for a second" the Judge didn't comment he just got me to go and sit with my family.

Jay lied through his teeth the entire time he was there. He said I have never threatened her or her family etc., etc. the judge saw straight through him. He extended the AVO for another two years and put him on a two-year good behavior bond. Well I knew this wouldn't stop him.

Emily Reilly

That afternoon the Police Chief drove us home. He came in and had a cup of tea. He told me he only needed ten minutes alone with Jay and he would never annoy us again. I wish this could have happened so we could be safe but I knew it couldn't.

Grant came and stayed over for about a week. One night we went out for a lovely dinner and Mum said she would watch Ava which I thought was strange as I didn't ask her too but don't look a gift horse in the mouth. This was the very first time Mum "baby sat" Ava.

We went to a steak house restaurant where you could throw peanut shells on the ground (funny you couldn't do that today with all the allergies around) it had a fantastic vibe. Whilst we were eating Grant said "Emily, I know you're young and you probably would say no but will you marry me?" I was in shock. I just looked at him as he opened a little ring box. Inside that box was a single diamond ring. The diamond was set high atop of the gold setting. I was later to find out it was 1 carat. I looked over still in shock "You'll have to ask my Mum and Dad"

"I already have Emily. They said that they will support you no matter what you decide, so it's totally up to you" They both seemed to like Grant which was good for me as this was a first when it came to my boyfriends. I thought to myself that if they like him then he has to be OK because my other boyfriends Mum didn't like and there was a very good reason for that (Dan & Jay). Well I guess that was it I was going to marry Grant...

Chapter 42: Meeting The Parents

The excitement of getting engaged was taking over by the pressure of organising a wedding. We had set a date for the first weekend in October of the next year. I would then be eighteen so legal age to marry here in Australia. Mum was excited for us and we spend copious hours looking at wedding dresses and everything needed for a wedding.

Grant came back from sea one day and asked if I would like to move out with him. This sent me into a state of confusion, I knew I wanted to move in with him and knew we were getting married so eventually we would have to live together but I didn't want to rush in to it. I didn't want to leave Mum and Barry. I was scared the last time I moved out it didn't turn out well as you all know. My mind was racing while he stood waiting for me to get excited and say yes.

How would Mum cope being the only person bringing in any money? As Barry was still at school she would be the only one to feed them both. Mum's wage wasn't that high so she may have had enough to pay rent, food, school fees and bills but that was it. If they stayed in this house who would protect them from Jay? I couldn't get excited, I couldn't leave them. Just as my brain was trying to process this Mum walked in "What's going on here then" she said with a smile.

"Grant just asked me to move in with him" I said with a tear in my eye.

"That's fantastic, you have to do it sooner or later" Mum replied. I thought to myself *'Are you crazy? You can't do all this yourself. Who's going to protect you and Barry?'* Grant had a huge smile on his face as Mum said this. I just wanted to run to her and hold her. I looked at Grant with a look that said

"Can you give me time with my Mum" and he read it well.

"I'll leave you to talk" he said as he walked out of the room. I sat on my bed with Mum, Grant closed the door behind him.

"What's wrong sweetheart?" Mum said concerned as she put her arm around me. I couldn't respond I just cried in her arms.

"Emily! We will be fine Uncle J is going to move in with us, he can't stay in his flat he's getting too old and this way we can move to a nicer house and I can look after him" Mum said while rubbing my back. Mum knew me better than anyone, she always knew what was on my mind before the words came out of my mouth.

"Are you sure Mum? I'm really scared" I responded

"Emily you have grown so much, Grant really loves you and you are getting married so it is better to do it now so you can see what it is like to live with him before you marry" Mum was always right in my eyes she is such a wonderful person. So then and there I made the decision to agree to move in with Grant. I walked out and told him yes. He smiled and hugged me.

It only took us a couple of weeks to find a place not far from Mum. Mum also found a lovely house for her Barry and Uncle J. It made me feel so much better knowing that Uncle J was moving in with Mum this would take the financial burden off her a little.

The house we moved in to was a red brick three-bedroom house and the last people that lived in the house obviously liked Indian as it really smelt of curry. I had to steam clean the carpets it was that bad. When the house got hot that smell came out and it

UNBROKEN

was extremely strong. It was a nice house for the first one as an engaged couple. We had some good times there.

I hadn't met Grant's Parents or Brother so he organised that we would go in and see them when they brought the cattle down for the Royal Easter Show. Leading up to this meeting I wanted to pull out. I was so nervous. I got a really nice pair of jeans and boots to wear to the cattle show. I had been there when I was younger and Mum took us to the show but I had never known anyone at the show. I made sure that Ava was dressed beautifully as I wanted us both the make a good first impression.

We parked the car and walked through the show. Grant wanted to push the pram and I just wanted to take it off him so I could hide behind it. It was my protection like a baby and a dummy. No such luck. We arrived and as we went to walk in to the shed Grant walked ahead of me not stopping to look back. Now I was going to stand out... I saw a larger lady step out and run up to Grant and give him a hug. It was his Mum, following closely behind was a larger man with a grey beard. I finally caught up and stood behind him. All of a sudden Grant's Mum came over and hugged me really tightly. To say I felt awkward was an understatement. I didn't know if I should hug her back or just stand there. I put my arms around her and patted her on the side. It was hard to wrap my arms around her as she was holding them down. Then followed Grant's Dad he just patted my arm "Welcome to the family Emily" he said. Grant's Mum then moved swiftly back to the pram and grabbed Ava saying

"Come to Grandma beautiful Ava" as she picked her up, I wanted to grab Ava and hold her, I felt a bit protective at this stage, this strange woman just picked up my baby. Ava didn't cry she just smiled her little smile. Ava rarely cried and this time was no different.

Emily Reilly

I know this may sound strange but I didn't know these people and they were treating us like they had known us forever and when Grant's Mum picked up my child I wanted to grab her back. It felt really invasive but in the back if my mind I knew that these people would soon be family it was just really strange that people took to people so quickly. I was to learn that they were country people and this was their way.

We stayed there all night, we slept in a loft. All the times we had gone to this show with Mum I never knew there were lofts. As a child you don't see all the people with the cattle and if you do you don't think that they are staying with them. I never remember thinking *'someone owns these cows, they must be staying here'* I used to just think the cows were all by themselves, like it was a normal thing for cows just to be at the show alone. This night one of Australia's top actors was there with his cattle. He was a whiskey drinker, he and Grant drank a lot that night. I was star struck he was so cute and one of my favourite Australian Actors (he has just left Home and Away but at the time he was in E Street). I went up to the loft at about midnight and Ava was already asleep in her pram. which had been lifted up to the loft area and locked. The next morning at about 4am I was woken by Grant and his Dad "Come on Emily, time to get the cattle ready" well I didn't know then but I know now there is a lot of work that goes in to getting cattle prepared to be shown. We shampooed them, blow dried and sprayed the with hairspray. Grant's Mum kept taking Ava for walks and showed her the other animals but Ava really didn't understand what she was being shown. Then Grant's Dad said

"Well you best do your hair Emily, you have to walk one of the bulls out and show him"

"No! I can't do that" I replied nervously.

UNBROKEN

He showed me how and made me practice. Then I had to do it for real. Well the funny thing is I did really well and he won first place for beef cattle but when we walked out he stood on my foot. I was so embarrassed I wanted to scream but instead I kept walking as best I could and when we got back I took off my shoe and the top of my foot was so bruised. I felt like a real idiot. Those few days went pretty quickly and I felt a little more comfortable after this with Grant's parents.

They had decided that we would marry at the property that they and Grant owned up in Northern NSW (not the best place for beef cattle). I had no choice the decision had been made and I didn't want to argue.

When we got home Grant spoke about the wedding and what we could do and where we could get married he tried to explain it to me but I couldn't picture it I just nodded in agreement.

A few days later my Dad brought his girlfriend over for a BBQ we will call her Tracey. She was lovely and had six children all living at home with her. She looked really frail. After a while we both went to the kitchen to get the salad ready. I asked her if she was ok and she said yes but she was nervous I could tell. "If you ever need to talk please call me, I promise I won't tell anyone we have spoken" she looked at me with tears in her eyes but words would not come out of her mouth.

"He's hit you hasn't he" I said to her but before she could answer Dad walked in to check what was happening. I just carried on and didn't say a word. I knew the look that she had given me as I had seen it and given it too many times.

The   evil   was   back...

Chapter 43: Here We Go Again

Standing in the kitchen with a man I remembered from childhood, his eyes were grey as he asked "What are you two talking about?" I didn't look at Tracey, I just continued washing up as I answered so as not to give away that I was about to lie. He would never have picked it anyway he wasn't my Mum and hadn't been there when I was growing up.

"Just chatting about your house and the kids Dad. How's that BBQ coming along" he seemed to accept this and walked outside. Tracey just looked at me with a look that was crossed between relief and fear for what lay ahead when she got home. I walked over to her when I knew he was well and truly outside

"It's OK if you ever need to talk I'm here"

We walked out the back and joined the boys and the kids. Just over my back fence lived Nicole Dickson (Bobby from the Australian TV show Home and Away). Dad said to Tracey's oldest child "Go over there and yell out to Bobby. Tell her I like Home and Away but Neighbours is better" everyone laughed but I had to step in before this actually happened as Nicole was always nice to us and I didn't want her being disturbed. The rest of the BBQ went well. Dad drank a lot of heavy beer so it started to go downhill. His act of Mr. nice guy disappears when he has a drink yes just one does it. He yelled at Tracey because she didn't do something he wanted her too even though she didn't even get asked, she was just expected to know what he wanted her to do. Later that afternoon Tracey's youngest got a little upset and it was time to get her home to bed. Dad was not happy about going and he pointed that out clearly by yelling at Tracey and the kids.

UNBROKEN

"It'll be ok Dad; we can catch up again soon. Ava is tired I am going to put her to bed anyway and I need to go and have a rest also" this seemed calm him. He hugged Ava, shook Grant's hand then came to me and hugged me tight. We walked them to the car and they drove off. Grant must have been thinking to himself *what sort of family is this?* but if he was he didn't say anything to his credit.

A few weeks later I had a call from Tracey "Emily, your Dad has locked me and the kids out of the house. He is throwing things everywhere and is smashing everything, he's crazy!" Were the first words I heard. Tracey had gone to my Aunties house to keep herself and the kids safe. I told her to call the police and not go back till they got him out.

A few hours later I heard a knock at the door. When I looked through the peep hole to see who it was I saw it was Dad. Grant had taken Ava over to Mum's to help her with something around her house, Mum loved having Ava there and we knew it so I stayed back to tidy up while they were out. It was easier to do when Ava was not there to help by putting everything everywhere. I opened the door and didn't let on that Tracey had called me "She's kicked me out Emily" Dad said as he walked through the door *'of course it was all her fault'* I thought to myself. He was sober which was a surprise being that it was midafternoon. I asked what had happened and he told me that Tracey called the Police for no reason, that she was lazy and her kids were terrible little brats. What he didn't know was that Tracey had called and told me the truth. I told him it would be ok then I went and made him a coffee. Not long after I had given him his coffee he asked if I could take him to the shop because he wanted to get smokes and a six pack.

Emily Reilly

"Dad you don't need to drink" he saw the look in my eyes as he had seen it before, it told him I didn't want him to do anything stupid. He leant over and touched my knee

"Slam, it's ok I'll only get a six pack" he finished his coffee then went outside got in the car and he started saying he had nowhere to go.

"You can stay with us for a couple of weeks until you get on your feet" I said to him hoping this would make him feel better. No matter what he was my Dad and he needed help so I wouldn't ignore that. He looked at me and out of the blue he said

"I don't think we are going to get on" well this should have been a warning sign. Who in their right mind would say this to their child? especially when she is trying the help you.

"Don't be silly it's only a couple of weeks Dad we'll be fine" I replied. We didn't talk for the rest of the drive to the bottle shop or on the way back. I just kept thinking to myself that this was a very strange thing for him to say out of the blue. When we finally arrived back at the house we walked inside Dad took a beer out of the six pack and took a seat on the lounge while I put the rest of the beer in the fridge.

"Slam!" he yelled out to me. I walked into the lounge room and looked over at him he patted the lounge next to him encouraging me to sit. I took a seat next to him

"Now it's time you hear about your Mother" he said menacingly. I immediately stood up and looked down at him

"No you don't" I said sternly

"Yes! you are going to hear what she is REALLY like!" These words cut me like a knife.

UNBROKEN

"Don't even think about it! She has been my Mum and Dad all my life. She cared when you didn't, she held me when I hurt, she supported Barry and I and struggled all her life giving us the best she could" I paused and stared at him. I raised my arm and pointed to the door

"There the door, leave and never ever come back again" I stood there pointed for some time before he started crying and got up and walked out. I walked behind him and closed the door and locked it behind him. I fell back against the door and crumbled to the ground.

"Why! Why does this always happen? Why can't things be normal?" I said to myself through my tears. I sat there a while then picked myself up, wiped my eyes and looked through my front blind. There he was sitting on our brick fence, his head in the palm of his hands crying. Well I wasn't that little girl that ran to her Daddy all those years and put her arms around him and comforted him. This time I would not go out, I would not chase him. He had no right at all to say that. He sat there for hours waiting for me to come out as this is what I always did when I was younger. I walked in to my room and stayed there until I heard our car. I looked out the front and he wasn't there anymore.

I didn't tell Grant what had happened with my Dad. I didn't want to ruin his mood and me being me I always bottle up my feelings especially pain.

A few weeks later when Grant was out when I heard a car pull up across the road. I looked through the blind and saw a familiar face it was Steven in the driver's seat. I couldn't see Jay. My heart raced, I didn't know which way to turn. I ran around locking all the windows and the back door. Since we had been in this house I hadn't really thought about Jay, I had let my guard down. It was just Ava and I at home. I picked up the phone and called Mum. She told me to hang up and call the Police and she would try and get hold of Grant. I walked over to the window again and peaked outside. I saw Jay he was walking down the passenger side of Grants 4WD back towards Stevens car. He stopped at the footpath and spun around, he smiled and ran to the car and they drove off.

I called Grant's work and told him what happened. He told me he was on his way home now. I went in and grabbed Ava and held her until Grant arrived home, he had a couple of the boys with him. I told him exactly what had happened and he went out and quickly checked his 4WD. He came back and told me it was all ok "Emily we have to call the police" Grant said as he picked up the phone and dialed the police station. They told us to come in straight away as the Sargent wanted to talk to us the Sargent was aware of the situation with Jay. We drove to the Police Station and the officer behind the desk took us straight to the Sargent office as he was expecting us. He had my file on his desk and it was not small. I told him what had happened every detail I could remember. When I had finished he looked straight at Grant

"Do you have a gun?" he asked, Grant looked down

"No" Grant responded but he really did.

"Off the record, do you have a gun?" the Sargent asked again. This time Grant admitted it.

"Do you know how to use a gun?" he asked me.

"No I hate guns" I said. Whenever I thought of a gun I thought of what Nigel had done. Guns scare me, I know it's not the gun that kills people, people who have guns do but I am still scared of them.

"You need to teach her how to use it" the Sargent said whilst looking at me.

UNBROKEN

"Now listen carefully to me Emily" he paused making sure that I was listening

"If he comes again let him inside, when he is inside yell out "stop or I'll shoot!" then straight away shoot him then shoot the ceiling" I was shocked how could I hold a gun let alone use it.

"Ballistics cannot tell the difference between shots if they are that close together. Make sure that the neighbours hear you, yell it out as loud as you can" I didn't know what to say but I knew if it came down to it he would take my life and god knows what he would do to Ava.

We went home and Grant started teaching me how to put the gun together, load and unload it. I was crying a lot and must have looked a right mess but I couldn't help it. I was holding a weapon similar to what Nigel had that day. That night I didn't sleep.

Grant had to go I work the next morning so Ava and I were going to be home alone. There was a knock at the door, I jumped up freaking out that it may be Jay but when I looked out it was Grant's mate. It was Grant's day to drive in to work. I kissed him goodbye and locked the door behind him. I walked in to our room and looked up in to the top shelf of our cupboard where that gun was hidden. I turned and walked out knowing that if anything happened I had to get in to my room with Ava and put that thing together and be prepared to use it. A few hours later I had a call "Emily" I heard a shaken voice on the end of the phone, it was Grant.

"What's wrong? you're scaring me" I had never heard him like this. My mind raced

"We were driving and the passenger side tire came off in peak hour traffic, I lost control of the car. We could have been killed!"

Emily Reilly

Grant said. I froze and remembered what had happened to Mum's car. I was shaking thinking to myself '*here we go again*'

"I'm so sorry, it's all my fault" Grant told me they were ok and not to blame myself.

"Emily, let's go away for a little while. We can go and visit Mum and Dad on the farm" I answered yes straight away. Grant was coming home as soon as he could. He had called his work and told them the situation and they agreed to give him leave.

I called Mum and told her what had happened and that we were going up the coast for a few weeks. I asked if she could just check my mail and when she did she had to bring Barry. I told her I would drop the keys over soon....

Chapter 44: A Trip North

We arrived at Mums to dropped off the keys. I reiterated to her that she could not go to our house without Barry for fear that Jay might arrive, he hated Mum. She agreed, I held her tight and told her loved her. I felt she would be safe whilst I was away because she had move house and no one knew where she was, not our family or my friends so there was no chance Jay could find her there. She still lived with Barry and my Great Uncle J. We said our goodbyes and Grant, Ava and I all got in the car and headed off on the long drive north.

We drove north for hours and finally arrived at Grants parents' house. They had a huge property and a lovely big house with an in ground pool. By the time we arrived I needed to go to bed I was exhausted. It's funny how stress and worry affect you. When I get stressed I become exhausted. It truly drains me and all I want to do is sleep.

The next morning, we got up and as I went to walk out of the bedroom and down the veranda to the kitchen I stopped in my tracks and screamed out to Grant. He came running out from the main house "What's wrong Emily, are you ok" I just pointed down. Grant laughed at me

"It's just a cane toad Emily, it won't hurt you" I wouldn't move until Grant scared them away. Stupid I know but these are the ugliest things I had ever seen and they spit, my logic was if they spit they are dangerous. They paralyse animals with their spit and the slime on their backs 'YUCK!'

Ava was just walking by this stage and she loved the farm. She use to chase the peacocks and loved riding on the ride on lawn mower with the maintenance man that lived there. She called him

Emily Reilly

'Oh Oh' not sure why but she did. Ava loved to walk around the front paddock. It was fenced and one fence was electrified. That afternoon we all sat out the front having a cup of tea while Ava walked around the front paddock. I walked inside and heard Ava yell out "Ouch!" It wasn't a cry just the word. Then I heard

"Ouch!" Nothing

"Ouch!" Nothing

"Ouch!" I ran out the front again and saw Ava at the fence as I was running towards her I saw that she had her finger in the hole where the electrical fence joined.

"Ouch!" as she said this she jumped off the ground. I finally reached her and pulled her finger out. She ran up to the house and all I heard was

"Shit, Shit, Shit" this was coming from this little girl who just started walking and now she was running. The only words she could say before this was Nanny, Bar, Dad and Mum and Oh Oh. She wasn't hurt and later that night I had a giggle to myself not that she was hurt but because of the sight of her running up the paddock saying Shit.

During our time there we went to Dreamworld. I was so excited about going and when the day arrived and it was raining. Grant didn't want to go but I had my heart set on it so we went. What I didn't know at the time was that there was a cyclone off the coast and the rain was not going to let up. We had a great day., there was almost no one there only one bus load of tourist so we had the park to our self. I went on every ride and had an amazing day rain and all.

When we arrived back at the farm Mum called "Emily did you leave bread on the kitchen bench?"

UNBROKEN

"No Mum I threw it out before we left and the house was spotless" my house was always clean as I didn't work.

"Mum check the rest of the house"

"Did you leave a wet towel on your bed?" she said as she went in to our room.

"No!" my heart was racing by this stage.

"Where is Ava's Baby monitor?" Mum asked.

"I left the handset on her bedside table with the fixed microphone"

"It's not here Emily and the Monitor is on!"

"Mum get out now, get Barry and leave the house NOW! He's been there and he has the baby monitor Mum he's waiting to hear when you or we come and go, call me as soon as you get home" I was so shaken but I didn't say anything to Grant while we were with his parents. I asked Grant to come with me for a minute and took him out the back and explained what was going on.

"That's it when we get back down south you stay with your Mum and we are moving house" Grant said. I cried and cried that night. When was this going to stop. This had really ruined a good trip and I really wasn't looking forward to going back. When we returned to Sydney I decided to go back with Grant to the house, he had a mate come over and stay with us also while we looked for a new place.

Don't think I'm crazy but what follows DID! happen.

A couple of nights after we got back we were in bed asleep when I felt a pressure on my leg. I thought it must have been Grant putting his leg on me so I turned over and realised he was laying on his side nowhere near me and there was nothing there, I went back to sleep. I again felt this pressure on my leg like someone was sitting on it. This time when I look down I saw Nigel! (Right now I have goosebumps and my heart is palpitating) I wasn't scared at all. He said "I've come to say goodbye" Nigel wasn't see through or Smokey it was him sitting there on my leg clear as day. All I could say is

"Why did you do it?"

"She told me too, I love you Emily goodbye" then he was gone. I had a tear in my eye as I woke Grant and told him what had happened.

"You were dreaming Emily go back to sleep" he said half asleep then rolled over. I could not get back to sleep those words rang in my ears "She told me too".

The next morning Grant had to go to work and organise some time off. I called Kylie, if anyone knew what happened and what he meant by this she would. I told Kylie what had happened and she went silent then she said "That day Nigel got on the bus with the gun in his bag, he had a girlfriend that was also on the bus. He showed her the gun and told her what he was going to do and she told him 'well just do it'" I was shocked I had never heard this before and now his words made sense. This was the last visit I had from Nigel when he said goodbye he meant it and I fell really blessed that he came to say goodbye it was the closure that I needed. Whether you believe it or not this happened and I will never not believe it. He loved me enough to say goodbye.

Grant got back from work and decided that we would go looking at houses so we could move ASAP. We looked all day and finally found a beautiful two story split level house with a saltwater in ground pool. On one side of us lived the Police Commissioner and the other the big boss of IBM so it was a lovely area. We got approved and move in that weekend. This time I could tell no one where I was apart from the closest people to me. I didn't want to keep running. I wanted to be safe and secure just like a normal person.

I loved this house it was truly beautiful. I had a ducted vacuum system so I thought I was special. My eighteenth birthday was not far away and I was miserable as you are supposed to have your 18th with close friends and family. When I called my friends and spoke to them they couldn't get my number as it was a silent number so I didn't have to worry about it. Grant and Mum saw how miserable I was and they spoke then came to me and said "Let's get a couple of your trusted friends to come down for your birthday" I hugged them and cried so much I had had to close off from everyone I knew and I missed having friends, real friends that I had grown up with. This made feel like it was going to be the best birthday ever. I call Alice, Kylie, Trisha and my Karate Sis and invited them. I made them promise not to give out my details or tell anyone what was happening. They were all excited and a few weeks later they all arrived.

The party was not massive but I had the best possible time as I had all my friends and my close family there to celebrate with me. You cannot imagine how good it was to see these girls. I missed them so very much. We had grown up together and they were more like family to me than friends. They stayed for a few days and we just sat around chatting, swimming and doing girlie stuff. The day they left I cried so much it hurt, my heart ached as I saw them drive off. Now it was back to just me, Ava, Grant, Mum and Barry. It should have been enough but when you are ripped away from everything, segregated you have to live like a recluse and you are far from a recluse it is like cutting out your soul. I had asked Trish and Alice to be my Bridesmaids and told them we were getting married in just three months. They were so excited. We talked every day on the phone and Mum made their dresses.

Grant took me to his cousin's house one day and he and his wife were lovely. She asked if I had picked my dress out. I told her that I hadn't and she said "That's fantastic! You can borrow mine if you like, it was made by the same designer that made Lady Di's dress" what you all probably don't know about me is that I love the Royals always have and always will, so when I heard this I was excited. I went and had a looked at this dress. It was almost the same as Lady Di's dress only more frills. I was so excited I wanted to show Grant.

"It's bad luck to let him see the dress before you marry" she said to me. Well there I was standing in the dress I was to wear on my   wedding   day....

Chapter 45: What Your Back

In the months leading up to our wedding day I was so busy running around trying to organise everything between raising a child and running a business. What you all don't know is that since I had left school I had completed my Higher School Certificate by correspondence, studied to become a Hairdresser and became a Nail Technician. I had just started my first business sharing a Salon with another lady. Between my studies, work and having Ava I was really busy.

On the weekends Mum and I would go shopping for materials for the girl's dresses and organise all of my accessories. Mum and I did a calligraphy course so we could do our own invites. Finally, it was all ready and we were going to get married on the farm. The wedding was only two weeks away.

I told you all about Nigel coming to visit, well like I said before this stuff happens to me and one night not long before we were to get married I went to bed as usual and was really tired from everything we had going on. I woke in the middle of the night and sat straight up in my bed. Standing at the end of my bed were about seven to ten people. I wasn't scared but I was a bit shocked. I couldn't recognise anyone until I looked to the right and saw a dark haired man in a red checkered flannel shirt, it was my Uncle who had passed when I was a baby. The same one that visited Mum and I all those years ago when I was a baby. Standing right at the front was an old lady. She was wearing a black dress with a lace collar. She was a larger lady with her hair in a bun and she was very stern looking. "Watch your back!" this lady said. Nothing more was said and then I turned over and shook Grant

Emily Reilly

"Grant! Wake up there are people here" he sat up his eyes still closed as he was in a deep sleep. When I turned around to point at them they were all gone.

"There's no one here Emily, go back to sleep" he said as his head hit his pillow again. He immediately started to snore. I couldn't sleep for the rest of the night as I wanted to call Mum and tell her. I had been having back pain and the doctors where checking that I didn't have kidney problems so I thought this is what the lady was talking about.

Finally, daylight came and I went straight to the phone and called Mum to tell her. Mum asked me to come over so I got Ava ready to go and see Nanny. When we arrived Mum had a cup of tea ready for me and some toast for Ava. I explained to her again the faces that I saw. "Follow me Emily" she said as we walked out the back door towards her garage. In the back corner there was a lot of old pictures in really old frames. Mum flicked through them

"Stop! Mum that's her, that's the lady that told me to watch my back" Mum picked up the large frame and carried it back inside to my Great Uncle J.

"Uncle J who is this?" Mum asked

"That's my Great Grand Mother" he stated as a matter of fact. Well that hit me. I understood Nigel but my Great, Great, Great Grandmother I couldn't understand being so far removed from her that she would come and say this to me.

Mum, Uncle J and I talked for ages then I decided to go home as I had some tidying to do before Grant came home. When I arrived home the phone was ringing.

"Hello" I said, the phone was silent

UNBROKEN

"Hello" I asked again after no one responded I hung up the phone and went to put Ava in for a nap. The phone rang again this time there was a voice that I knew well

"I will be there in five hours you better watch your back bitch this time I'm not playing; I know where you live" I was so put back by this call I couldn't speak. He then told me my address so I knew he actually did know where I was. I hung up the phone and called Grant straight away

"He's coming Grant; I'm going to Mum's. I only have a few hours and he will be here" I was so panicked. Grant told me to call Mum to come over because he was at least three hours away before he could be here. I got off the phone with Grant and dialed Mum's number straight away.

"She didn't mean my kidneys Mum she meant Jay's coming, that's why I have to watch my back" were the first words out of my mouth

"Emily slowdown"

"Mum can you come over and help me pack, Jay's going to be here in five hours and Grant can't be here for three hours" Mum said she would be over soon and in the mean time I was packing Ava's clothes and everything she would need. I got my clothes and everything I needed for the wedding.

When Mum arrived I had pretty much gotten everything I needed. We put it all in the car and sped off. Grant came straight to Mum's after work. We only had a few days before our wedding so he decided that we should head up early. He had some boys with him and they decided that they would all go and stay at the house that night and see if Jay arrived. If Jay arrived they would be ready and waiting. Grant said we would head off the next morning.

Jay drove past a few times but he must have seen all the cars at our house so he didn't bother going in though he did manage to at some time in the night slash most of the car tires. He must have been disturbed as he didn't get to our car. New tires were required all round. We offered to pay for them but the boys would not accept the money. They just wanted us to head off and they would see us in a few days a couple of the boys decided to stay at or place to keep an eye on it and I was so grateful for this. These boys truly were good guys and treated us like their extended family.

Well again we were off to the farm and the big day was closing in   very   quickly...

Chapter 46: The Wedding

The day before our wedding day all my friends and family arrived. Right next door was a new Resort so many of them stayed there or they pitched a tent and stayed on the house yard. Grant went out with the boy for his buck's night to the local pub. I stayed at the house trying on my dress and the girls were trying on theirs. We were having a glass of champagne. The weirdest thing happened, my breasts were really sore and I told Mum as she was the only one I felt comfortable talking to about this. She then called in Grant's Mum who was a nurse. Well long story short they took me to the hospital for a blood test and a pregnancy test. This was not how I expected to spend the last night before I got married.

Alice, Trisha, Mum, Aunties, Cousins and Ava were all there waiting for the results. We had to wait for hours. Finally, the doctor arrived and he said I wasn't pregnant and that the soreness and swelling was caused due to fluid retention so nothing to worry about. We left the hospital after 1am. I was exhausted and to be honest a bit disappointed about not really having a hen's night. Mum and my friends could see my disappointment but there was nothing they could do. I didn't see Grant that night or the next morning.

I woke in the morning and everyone was in the kitchen cooking a big breakfast with bacon, eggs, hash browns, toast and juice. When I walked in Mum told me to go back to bed and she would bring me breakfast in bed, so I promptly spun around and headed back to my room. Not long after that everyone came bouncing in to the room. They were all so excited. Mum handed me my breakfast on a platter and kissed my forehead and told me she loved me. Whilst eating my breakfast Alice and Trisha were sitting with me talking about how excited I must be and how beautiful my dress was and how much they were looking forward to the wedding. I got an empty feeling in the pit of my stomach. I couldn't understand what this feeling was so I wasn't going to say anything. I just smiled and nodded. After breakfast we went swimming in the pool and just lazed around until lunch time. It was now time to get ready. Grant's Mum had given us her room in order to get ready. The girls had their showers and started to get dressed everyone was fussing around me. I walked in to the shower as the beads of water hit my skin they felt like little needles even though the shower was cool I felt my body temperature rise, my face got really hot and the tears fell freely. I didn't make a sound as I didn't want people to know I was crying.

What would they think?

Why would I be crying on my special day?

There was an emptiness in the pit of my stomach that would not go away. I started to have a burning in my throat it felt like it was going to close over and I was finding it hard to breath. I stayed in the shower until I heard Mum call out "Emily! You have to get out sweetheart and get ready it's not long now"

"Coming" I whispered over the sound of the shower running. I got out of the shower and wrapped myself in a large white towel that wrapped around me almost twice. I remember the towel being very soft and fluffy. Mum and the girls guided me over to a chair so they could do my hair and makeup. I had my hair half up and half down. After I had my makeup done the girls got their dresses on and Mum brought me a bottle of champagne. The girls all left the room for a few minute and left Mum and I alone.

"Mum, I don't want to do this" I said as the tear welled up again.

UNBROKEN

"Emily you just have nerves sweet heart, you will be fine it has just been a busy few days and your probably tired also after not having much sleep" she replied. A single tear slid down my cheek. Mum realised and leaned in and gently wiped it away.

"You will be fine sweet heart, if you cry you will ruin your make up. Come on get up and I'll help you get in your dress" she said trying to comfort me. I stood up and put my hand on Mum's shoulder as I lifted my first leg into the dress with the other following close behind. Mum pulled the dress up and I put my arms in to the sleeves. She slowly buttoned the back of the dress and when finished she lent down and grabbed the white hat I had chosen with the veil connected and placed it carefully on my head, she placed bobby pins through the hat into my hair so it wouldn't move. Mum spun me around when she had finished, she took to steps backwards and smiled then I saw a tear roll down her cheek.

"You look beautiful Emily, truly beautiful!" she said this as she wiped the tear from her own cheek. The girls entered the room just as we had finished and they squealed.

"Oh my god you look beautiful" Alice said. Trisha could see that I had a concerned looked on my face as much as I tried to hide it.

"You ok Emily?" she asked and as she said this I had to turn away. Mum walked over and placed a hand on my shoulder

"She'll be fine girls she is just nervous" I heard the door open and I turned to see who had entered the room, there standing in front of me was my Pa.

Pa was dressed in his grey suit and looked amazing. My heart raced. Here was my favourite person in the world, the one who I called my protector, my hero standing in front of me all dressed to give me away. For his age he was so very handsome in his suit. His age was showing but he still looked perfect to me. I smiled a real smile for the first time that day. Seeing him I felt safe and relaxed. I knew no matter what he would be there for me. The only man that had never hurt me in any way, never let me down, picked me up when I fell, put brown stuff on me when I hurt myself and held me when I cried. Pa had little hair on the top of his head actually he had 3 hairs only on top. I knew he had had his hair cut especially for today and I know he would have said to the hair dresser "short back and sides and don't take too much off the top" or "I'll have to give you a finder's fee for the hair on top" as he always had. Pa looked at Mum and the girls and said

"It's nearly time you had better get out there" they all gave me a final hug and made their way out.

I stood staring at my Pa with a slight smile on my face. "What's wrong Emily" he said as he walked closer.

"I don't want to do this Pa"

"Well then... You don't have too. If you don't want too" he said softly then he reached out and held me.

"But everyone has come so far Pa, so much money had been spent, how am I to get out of this?"

"Emily, we are all here for you! If you don't want to do this and really truly don't think it's right I will walk out there with you and we can tell them all together, it's not a problem as long as you are happy with your decision" he said looking me in the eyes. I knew he meant it, he would have done anything for me. Pa had a way of making you feel like you were the only person in the world even in a room full of people. We stood there for some time when I heard the music playing. It was the start of the song Unchained Melody that had been chosen for me to walk down the aisle too.

UNBROKEN

"I'm ready Pa, Mum was right it's probably just nervous" We walked out arm in arm to the veranda and then to the base of the limestone stairs leading up to the top garden. As we walked I stopped and looked at Pa

"You are my hero Pa; I truly love you" I said then he kissed my forehead through my veil. Pa didn't respond but I saw his eyes swell but no tears fell. I needed to say that to him at that exact moment. We got to the top of the stairs and there in front of me was Grant. I wanted to turn and run, run as fast as I could but I then looked to the right and saw all of my family and friends. There was no turning back now. We reached Grant and the Minister asked who was giving this woman away

"I do" said my Pa ever so proudly. He then leaned down and whispered in my ear

"I will never give you away, he can marry you though" I looked at him and smiled, he gave me a wink. Another reason I loved this man so very much. Pa gave my hand to Grant

"You look after her" he said. The rest of the vowels I don't really remember. I just remember a great feast and drinks (I didn't have too many) then the waltz. As we waltzed Grant told me loved me but I couldn't say the words. I just smiled. I saw my Pa across the veranda then he walked towards Grant and I.

"Can I have this dance" he said and Grant agreed. Pa waltzed with me. He made me feel like a princess by spinning me around. I had the feeling that I was that little girl again that he use to sit on his lap and burn with a spoon. That was the best dance I had ever had or ever will again. I danced with all my uncles then as the night went on I danced with my friends and cousins. Speeches where done by my uncles and Grant's side. Funny ones and lovely ones.

Emily Reilly

We were supposed to have a room at the resort for our wedding night but they had double booked it so we had to stay in a caravan....

Chapter 47: Goodbye

The night of your wedding is supposed to be romantic. My dream night would have been rose petals on a bed in a hotel room. Champagne would have been poured and romance would have been in the air. Well my night was far from it. Because the resort had double booked we had to stay in the old caravan up the back of the property. There was no flower, champagne or candles. The light didn't work and the bed smelt, we had been having a bit of rain so it was a damp smell. Grant did not try and carry me over the threshold as all girls dream. I walked up the rusty old stairs with Grant behind me. Grant was a bit drunk so our night was spent with me laying watching the ceiling and Grant snoring. I cried that night and not tears of happiness all my emotions had built up. I was asking myself;

Did I get married so Ava could have a Dad?

Did I do this so I wasn't alone and felt safe?

I'm too young for this.

To be honest you are supposed to have your heart sing when you are happy and mine wasn't. It had been crying for years. Broken in to pieces and I was hoping it would be glued back together. Then it dawned on me to pull myself together I was now a married woman and I had to look after my husband and daughter. I finally fell asleep.

When we woke the next day all our family and friends were out cooking a breakfast BBQ. I spent time with them all, Mum was so happy this day. You could see her beaming as she was proud of me and she really liked Grant. Everyone loved Grant so why was I not feeling it? Pa walked over to me and put his arm around me

"How are you feeling today sweetheart" he said quietly as he leant down closer to my ear.

"Not bad Pa, I think it must have been all the planning and having all our family here, I must have been nervous" I replied. Pa looked at me and smiled. The look in his eyes told me he knew I was lying but he didn't say anything more about it.

"You will always be welcome at Pa's you know that don't you Emily"

"I do Pa; I love you" his words actual made me melt. As I write this I have the same feeling I had that day. I have tears in my eyes and I can hear his words exactly as he said them.

"I love you too Emily and I always will" he leant over and kissed my cheek so very gently. He always, always knew how to make you feel like you were the only one that mattered. I am pretty sure he made the rest of my cousins feel the same but I saw Pa as my hero and I always will.

Later that day everyone started to leave and we had to pack to get ready to go home. After everything was packed we said our goodbyes to Grant's parents, put Ava in the car and started our long trip home. The one thing this entire time I didn't have to think about was Jay. As we neared our home all the fears rushed back.

What if he had been there?

What if he came whilst we were unpacking?

As I was thinking this Grant interrupted me by touched my leg "We're nearly home, don't worry about Jay Emily we will make sure he never comes near you again" I just smiled a fake smile. I know he was trying to make me feel better and it truly was nice that he realised what was going through my head but no one could every stop Jay. If Jay wanted to get me he would.

The next day Grant went back to work and I left with Ava early in the morning to go and spend time with some of my cousins as they lived about 45 minutes away. I couldn't have stayed in that house by myself. These daily trips happened every day for months until one-day Grant came home and told me that he had been posted to Western Australia "I can't move all the way to Western Australia and leave my Mum and Barry and everyone that I know" I said to Grant. I felt like he was trying to ripe my life apart. Take me and Ava away from everyone we knew and loved to a place we wouldn't know anyone. I started to have separation anxiety.

"Emily let's go chat to your Mum and see what she thinks. At least this way you won't have to worry about hiding from Jay. We will be on the other side of Australia and I'm sure he won't come there" I walked in and woke Ava from her sleep

"We're going to see Nanny baby girl" I said to her quietly as she was still half asleep.

"Nanny" she said excitedly then fell back asleep. Ava had the same look on her face when I mentioned Nanny as I did when I saw or spoke of my Pa.

We got in the car and took the short drive to Mum's. Mum was a little surprised to see us but as always she took Ava and hugged her tight then kissed my cheek and said hi to Grant. We spoke for ages and Grant pleaded his case. Not so much to Mum but to me. Mum looked at me

"Emily it's only for a couple of years' sweetheart, then you will be back by that time Jay would be long gone and you could live a life without worry" I had tears in my eyes that I would not let fall. I

Emily Reilly

wouldn't speak up because I didn't really know how. Maybe what they were saying was actually the best thing for Ava and I. We stayed for dinner then we went back to our house.

The move was organised quickly. We only had three weeks left in this town then we were off to the other side of the country. We were driving there so it was going to take a week. Grant said "It will be like a holiday" I was not so sure but as the days passed I tried looking for the light that was being drowned out by the clouds. I started to get a little excited, a new life maybe this is exactly what we needed. I had Grant and Ava so I would be fine.

The day before we left we had a removalist come and pack up our house ready to go. Our final night we stayed in a hotel. I had a cat named Silvester that I had to give away as he wouldn't travel well. The time had come to leave this house, Ava was put in her car seat, Silvester was in a box ready to take to my friend's house and our bags for the long trip were placed in the boot. As we were driving to take Silvester to his new home he pee'd in the box and it got all over the back seat. Well let me tell you the smell of male cat urine is disgusting and if you have a male cat you will know this smell all too well. We had to wind the windows down in the car as it was so strong I was going to be sick. We pulled in to a service station and Grant ran in and got some Nil Odor. He put it in the air conditioning vents and turned the air-conditioning on high so the Nil Odor could fill the car and take away that terrible urine smell. That smell and Silvester urine in one did not mix, it made the car smell worst. Oh well nothing we could do now. We eventually dropped off Silvester and I cried as he had also been a protector. I haven't spoken of him or what he got up to but he used to lay behind me on the couch and when Grant would come near me he would growl then jump at him with his claws out. He connected a few times and Grant wanted to get rid of him but I would always

UNBROKEN

say he is just trying to look after me. He was good with everyone else just not Grant for some reason, I think he was jealous.

When we first drove in to the hotel driveway Grant said to me "Watch this Emily, this is going to make you laugh" we all got out of the car and a valet driver came over to us.

"Would you like me to park your car for you" he asked every so nicely. I looked at Grant knowing what that car smelt like and was a little embarrassed when I heard Grant say

"Of course, thanks for that" and handed the keys over, we turned to watch as this young guy get into the driver's side door and went to put the keys in to start the engine. He wound the windows down and started coughing. The poor guy it really did stink and I beat you a million dollars he wasn't expecting that smell when he got in. When he started the car he looked over at us and there were tears in his eyes. I lost it completely and started laughing the heartiest belly laugh I had ever done, tears rolled down my face and I couldn't stop. It was so hard I almost pee'd myself and my belly really did hurt as I watch him disappear underground in to the parking bays. We turned and walked inside.

The hotel was so very beautiful. I had never really stayed in a place so nice. I was a little embarrassed I wasn't dressed up and wearing makeup. Grant however looked like he was right at home. He got the keys to the room and ensures everything was ready for us. As soon as we got to the room I wanted to call Mum and Barry and get them over. I knew I wouldn't see them for such a long time and my heart was being torn in two.

Mum arrived with Barry and we all went and had a meal. Mum held Ava the entire time. "You look after my girl's" she warned Grant. He promised he would. We didn't talk all that much during dinner. We had to head out really early the next morning so this was to be the last time I saw Mum or Barry for years as I didn't think at the time about holidays. We got back to the hotel, Mum and Barry came in for a short time then they had to leave.

"I'll miss you sweetheart but I will just be a call away and you can come back on holidays any time" she said with tears rolling down her cheek. I couldn't hold the tears back. My heart started to race and it felt like it was going to break out of my chest. I was aching inside my throat started to burn and close up and my chest was sore. This is what it feels like when you are heart broken, well it does for me anyway. Tears were rolling down my face and I felt they would never stop. I was huffing trying to breath and talk.

"Mum, I don't want to go!" I was begging her in my head to tell me to stay but she didn't.

"You'll be fine sweetheart, you're a wife now and Grant will look after you and Ava" she held me for so long, I didn't want to let her go. Ava started crying

"Nanny, no go Nanny" Barry picked her up. Ava didn't realise we were going for a long time; she knew something was happening though.

"Bar, no go Bar" she said to Barry through her own little tears. Well at this stage my heart felt like it had exploded as I hated seeing Ava upset.

"Uncle Bar will see you soon Ava you be good for Mummy and Daddy" he said as he kissed her head. Barry didn't cry but this pulled on his heart strings and a single tear came down his cheek. Barry walked over and by this stage he was quite a bit taller than me

"I love you Sis, I'll see you soon" he said softly but firmly. He knew how long we would be gone and I think it was hurting him also as I had never been that far away from him before and we were so very close but he was going to be strong for Mum and me right at this moment.

"You look after Mum and yourself, I love you too" I gave him a kiss on the cheek.

"Come on Mar we have to go" Barry said as he put his arm around her shoulders. Grant put his arm around mine at the same time.

"I love you Mum" I yelled after her.

"I love you too sweetheart, take care of my girls" were her final words as she got in to the lift. I turned around and Grant pulled me in to his chest as I sunk down. I have a lump on my throat as I write this and tears rolling down my cheeks. I grabbed Ava and held her and tried to calm her down as she was crying out for Nanny and Bar. I realised I needed to pull myself together and be strong for her. I finally got her to sleep a few hours later.

I walked into the room where Grant and I were staying and he just wanted to have sex. I did not feel like this at all. My heart was breaking. I thought to myself what is it with men and wanting to have sex all the time can't they just hold you. We had sex or I should say he did as I was crying the entire time. Not out loud and not so he could see but I was as I really just wanted to be held.....

Chapter 48: The Big Trip

The next morning, we packed our things that we had unpacked the night before. I remember walking in to the bathroom and standing in front of the mirror for a long time. I was staring at myself and thinking '*have I made the right decision?*' Tears fell down my face again. As you can probably tell all through my life a mirror is not just used for my physical reflection but my personal reflection place. I have ever since I can remember look at myself and ask any question to me that I need too. Weird for some but this is my place to reflect on life in general.

I was moving to the other side of Australia and wouldn't see Mum or Barry for a long time, years maybe. Grant yelled out and broke my reflection time "Emily! we have to get going before it gets too late".

I walked out the lounge area and scanned the room for the phone as soon as I found it I walked over picked it up and dialed Mum's phone number. It rang and rang until it rang out. I had forgotten that Mum had to go to work and Barry would have been at school. I couldn't say goodbye. To say I was heartbroken is an understatement. I walked over to were Ava was playing with her teddy. I picked her up

"Nanny" she said holding her hand out towards the door as she had done many times before when we were going in the car to see Mum.

"Not today baby girl, we are going for a big drive" I said struggling to hold back my own tears. We walked out the front and the car was waiting for us. When we got in I had completely forgotten about Silvester peeing in the car and it stunk so badly. This did make me giggle a little as I remembered the day before when the poor guy got in thinking he was great and then seeing his face, well it was priceless.

We headed off in the direction of the Blue Mountains, the scenery was so beautiful, luscious and green. It was a few months before the fires were to come as they did every year, the fires would go through this bush land and the landscape would be blackened. We drove for hours until we got the Nullarbor. The Nullarbor is the arid land in the middle of Australia. Australia is a vast country, the coasts are green and lush but in the middle is red dirt, cactus, wild emus, kangaroos, wombats and not much else. There is 500 km between service stations or towns. The towns may only consist of one family and they live above the service stations.

We travelled for two days. We had air-conditioning in the car but the temperature was so high that we couldn't turn it on while driving as our car couldn't handle it and it would over heat. The last thing we wanted was to break down on this vast road, there could be hours between cars or trucks passing you and in the meantime you might pass out from the heat. It is not easy traveling across the Nullarbor as you cannot travel before the sun comes up or when the sun goes down. You always needed to start driving after dawn and stop before dusk or you could hit a Kangaroo, Emu or Wombat. It is really dangerous. Hitting any of these animals could ruin your car they have been known to stop trucks. When trucks travel they straddle kangaroos (hit them in the middle of the truck) so they don't ruin the truck. Your probably think you should try not to hit them well this is almost impossible as they jump in to the headlights and it blinds them then they just stand there unable to move a bit like that movie 'A Bug's Life' "Don't look at the lights", "I can't help".

During this trip I got a lot of photos of Ava. This was the first time she got to drive a car she got to sit on Grant's lap and hold the steering wheel. She was so happy and kept clapping her hands it was really cute. The best part of the trip was stopping at the Great Australian Bight. There is a chain that is set as a fence, it is there to deter people from going to close the edge. The stupid thing about this stop was the sign. The sign was so far away from the fence (on the inside closest to the edge) this sign explained the Bight. There was another sign saying "Please do not pass chain, high winds can be dangerous". Well I wanted to read the sign with information about the Great Australian Bight so I got Grant to hold Ava while I climbed over the chain fence. When I got to the sign it was only about five meters away from the edge. As I stood there I looked over the edge, the sign was not wrong the winds were so strong I had to hold on to the edge of the sign.

The Bights is right at the bottom of Australia, when you looked down there is a 60-meter drop. The waves crash against the base of the Bight. What a wonderful sight and the feeling that you are at the very edge of your country is amazing after taking in the ocean and being completely amazed by this great natural feature I made my way back to Ava and Grant and we started off on the next leg of the trip.

I think deep down I was blaming Grant for taking me away from my family and to top it off I was still thinking did I do the right thing? At this stage I was eighteen, married and a Mum of an eighteen month old at the time I thought I was so much older than I really was. Looking at my child now I realise how young I really was. I didn't want to make love to Grant or even be held but I did it because I felt I had too. I was his wife and this is what wives should do.

We continued traveling for days then we stopped at Port Augusta. I will never forget this place it stunk of Sulphur. If you have never smelt, it before it was like breathing in rotten egg. It is disgusting. I do not to this day know how anyone can live with it.

UNBROKEN

There are 13500 people living in this town. I didn't want to stop but we had to as it was getting late and we needed to eat and sleep.

The next morning, we headed out really early as I did nothing but complain about the stench (I have always had a sensitive nose). Grant was not happy but it was great to get out of there. I promised myself that if I ever had to travel this way again I would flight over Port Augusta at any cost. We travelled 2650 km this day and got the beautiful Margaret River. The roads where paved in pine trees and when we got the little old town I was so happy. We had made it to Western Australia and we were on the other side of Australia right on the beach. Beautiful golden beaches and massive waves. Margaret River is known for its surf world wife but let me tell you if you ever get to go to Western Australia you cannot miss this place. We went down to the beach with Ava and she ran up and down in the sand. The sun was setting. You have not seen a sunset if you haven't been to Western Australia. This is the place that made me fall in love with sunsets. I will explain further the sunsets in Western Australia as my story goes on.

The next morning, we made our way up the coast for the last leg of our trip it would take three hours to get to Rockingham. When we finally arrived in Rockingham the first stop had to be Garden Island (the Navy Base) so we could organise a house. We got given one set of keys to look at a house. The house was a three-bedroom house nothing great but a military house. We took it and moved in a few days later. Hopefully this new house could become a   home....

Chapter 49: Winnie

We had been in Western Australia for about four months and Grant had just come back from a trip to sea. I asked him to get me a dog for protection. We searched high and low for the right dog but I had always loved the English Mastiff. They are extremely loyal and would scare anyone off if required. We had lost hope of finding anything when I looked in the paper and found a ten month old pure bred English Mastiff. I ran out to Grant and told him I was so excited and jumping around like a little kid. He agreed and we got in to a Ute that we had hired and drove to the house of the current owner.

When we arrived I got out of the car and went to the door. Just as I knocked I heard an almighty bark from the other side of the door. This was going to be a big dog!

When the door was opened a lovely guy invited us in. The dog was a cream colour with a black mussel. She was beautiful but did not leave the side of her owner. I patted her and she licked my hand. The owner told us that he had to move interstate for work and he couldn't take her with him. You could tell that he loved this dog and that she had been very well looked after. She was beautiful and fat.

After about two hours we had decided that she was perfect for us. We paid for her and put her in the back of the Ute. She was extremely calm the entire drive home. We reversed into the drive way and I got out and opened the gate so we could take her straight out the back to her new home. I got hold of her lead and led her through the gate then I disconnected the leash and closed the gate behind her. Ava was so excited. My dogs name was Winston well that was her show name but she was Winnie to us and this is what she answered too.

We walked inside and I went straight to the back door as I went to open it Winnie ran at the door growling and barking, she was not happy. What I didn't realise was that her old owner had a white Ute so she was calm because she thought it was him in the Ute but when I went to the back door she wanted to eat me. It was extremely scary.

For the next month I would sit at the back door most of the day with Ava and look through and talk to her. When I fed her I would tell her to sit and I would push the food out without letting her get too close to me. After a month she would come to the door and cry for me. I finally got to the point where I felt comfortable enough to go out the back and let her come up to me. She was definitely going to be my dog. It took a long time for her to settle in.

Three months had passed and it was like we had had her forever. Winnie would lay beside me on the floor when I went to bed then when I fell asleep she would walk around the house keeping an eye out. Ava and I would walk her every day whilst Grant was at the base. We would get to a road and I would say. "What do we do at roads Winnie" and she would sit, look both ways and then stand and look at me when the traffic was clear we would walk cross the road. She was extremely intelligent and very protective. She walked well on a lead and not many people wanted to come near us as she was 110 kilos of dog (MASSIVE) just what I wanted.

One-day Grant came home and walked out the back and up the shed. Winnie watched him go as she was still a little weary of him as he didn't spend that much time with her. I was in the lounge with Ava when I heard someone yelling from the backyard. I ran out to the kitchen and peered out the window. It was Grant, Winnie had let he go to the shed but she was not letting him out. "Emily! Get your fucking dog away from me" he yelled. I giggled to myself as I knew she wasn't going to bight him but he thought she was. She was very intimidating that's for sure. I called Winnie back and she came straight over to me and sat down. I patted her as Grant ran past us and inside.

We decided that we would try and get Grant a little better acquainted with Winnie so one afternoon we went for our walk we ended up going to the local park so he could walk her with me by his side. Winnie was extremely well behaved and did everything that she was asked. Winnie loved Ava and every time we went to cross a road Winnie would give her a big kiss. It was very cute the only problem was the drool that she always left behind.

We got to the park and Grant and I started wrestling when I stupidly squealed as he was tickling me (I hate being tickled). Winnie ran over and pushed Grant off me started growling then she put her entire mouth around his throat whilst still growling. She applied a little pressure. Grant managed to whispered to me though throat was being squeezed, "Get your fucking dog off me" I said to Winnie calmly

"Winnie release, come here" she did exactly what I said. She sat down beside me and I patted her on the head then I walked over to make sure Grant was OK. He was fine no punctures or marks. He was shaken up though. We decided then it was time to go back home.

Months passed and Grant started to get on well with Winnie. He didn't try and wrestle me again though. Not long after Grant had to go to sea on the submarine and this meant me and Ava being home alone but at least we had Winnie.

UNBROKEN

This trip was a four-month trip around Australia or so they said. They weren't really allowed to tell us where they were going and if the submarine ever went down the Government would tell the families that the submarine went missing off Sydney Harbour.

I had made a friend since moving there but it was really a neighbour type relationship as I didn't like getting close to people. Her husband was on a ship. Our whole street was a Navy street (well 90 %). I was told that when the boys went away there were some guys who knew this and they sometimes tried to break in. This was a little frightening as I had no family or real friends to visit or lean on whilst Grant was away.

I was looking for a job the entire time Grant had been away but everyone was turning me down as I didn't come from Western Australia. It was weird as I hadn't really known that Western Australia existed before I moved there but a lot of the people that I had interviews with didn't like people from the East Coast so it was hard. I started a job at the Sheraton in Perth a week before Grant came back from sea and Ava was in daycare during the time I worked. I only worked casually though as I didn't want to leave Ava too long.

The night before Grant was to come home I went to bed as usual. I had tucked Ava in to her bed and kissed her good night. Ava was about three years old now. I walked in to my bed and laid down. Winnie got up on the bed next to me as usual and just as I started to dose off I felt her get off and walk around and lay on the floor beside me. During the middle of the night I was woken to the sound of Winnie growling. I got out of bed and checked Ava then I heard a noise in the lounge room like someone was trying to open the window. I tiptoed down the hallway and slowly opened the front door then I flung the screen door opened "Sic em" I said to Winnie and she took off out the front. There was a guy trying to get in to our house as he ran down the road he was yelling out something with Winnie right behind him. She took a big leap with her mouth wide opened and took a bite at his backside when she pulled away she had a chunk of his pants and a bit of his bum but this did not stop him he kept going. I looked down the road and there where at least six other guys trying to break in to other houses. Lights where coming on all down the street because of the commotion. I called out to Winnie and threw the piece she had in her mouth in the bin. She came inside and I felt so very safe. With her by my side Ava and I would never have to worry.

Grant arrived home the next day and I told him what had happened. He decided to go and see if we could move house. Well he was allowed to so we went looking at houses and Warnbro and we found a beautiful one that was perfect for us. We moved again not long after and hopefully this was to be the last time until the day we move back East.

Chapter 50: Flying Home

Grant came home one day and told me that he had to go on a six month around Australia trip. I was devastated as I really hadn't made any real friends and my family where so far away. He had organised for Ava and I to go back and see Mum. We were going for three weeks this made my day it also made Grant having to leave a little easier. Being alone in a remote location with no family or friends was hard enough when your Husband was there let alone when he wasn't.

The day before Grant was to sail I took Ava over so I could do some fishing on the wharf at Garden Island, just down from where the Submarine was.

This day I caught a huge Snapper and I didn't want to take it off the hook so Ava and I walked to Grants submarine and were greeted by all the boys. "Ha! while Grant is hard at work this is what you're doing?" laughed a guy called Jamie. Jamie was so handsome. He was over six-foot-tall dark skin and brown eyes and he loved Ava and treated me like a sister.

"I can't take it off" I replied with a giggle. Funny I could catch fish and gut them but taking them off the hook was another thing all together. Jamie called down to Grant and he surfaced not long after. Here I was holding on to a fishing rod and the fish was flapping everywhere. Grant walked over and laughed at me then laid the fish on the top of the submarine put his foot on it and pulled out the hook.

"It's fish tonight and for a month" Grant joked. It was no joke though I really couldn't have eaten all of this fish in a month it was huge. I told Grant to give it to the chef and he could cook it for them when they sailed. I kissed him goodbye and said

"I'll see you later"

The day Grant left was a bit emotional as I knew it would be six months before I saw him again and even though we were going home to see Mum I would come back to an empty house apart from Winnie. I organised with Chantelle (my old neighbour) to house Winnie for me whilst I was away. She had got to know Winnie and Winnie was comfortable with her. Chantelle was excited as she still lived in the same street I had moved away from and was worried as her husband would be away too. Ava and I took Grant to the base and stayed on the wharf to wave them all off as we had many times before. Now it was time to go and pack our bags ready to see Mum and Barry. We were flying home on a free flight from RAAF Base Pearce. It was a Hercules that we would flight on. We drove up to just outside the RAAF Base and stayed with one of Chantelle's friends for the night as we had to be at the base early. The house was an old fibro house. The guy was an SAS Soldier and his wife worked on the base. This house was an Army house and to be honest should have been pulled down a long time ago. It's funny how the Navy have awesome homes and the Army get given the shitty ones. They are on the front line whilst the Navy are safer at sea.

The next morning carrying our bags and holding Ava's hand we walked over to a hanger, just outside the hanger was the massive Hercules. We were handed a white box each and inside this box was a meal and a popper. This flight was going to be at minimum of ten hours as we had to stop off at Adelaide. I had never been inside a Hercules before, they are massive. There are no actual seats inside this plane there are nets set as chairs. Everyone was handed ear muffs as the noise was obviously going to be bad. Ava and I took a seat on the nets hung as seats and she cuddled up close. It must have been overwhelming for her as she had never flown before and this was not a normal plane. We did have seat belts though a fat lot of good they would do if you had an accident as you would be flung out of the nets. The safety talk was something I hope I never to hear again and I will never forget.

The flight crew were all males and not used to having women and children on board I would say. "Ladies and Gentlemen" one I of the flight crew started off

"If we go down on land then kiss your arse goodbye, however if we crash into the ocean and by some miracle do not break up in too little pieces, behind me you will see a life raft, make your way too it" he finished. I was glad to say that I had already put Ava's ear muffs on so she didn't hear this but I did hear this and it did not fill me with confidence. We finally took off and to be honest the flight was pretty smooth, though it felt like the plane was flapping its wings up and down. The noise was unbearable without the ear muffs. Windy and noisy, best to kept them on if you ever find yourself in a Hercules. The ear phones I was give had a micro phone thing on them and I could hear the banter between the flight crew. It was quiet amusing. They were picking on a larger lady on the plane and I said out loud to myself

"That's terrible, how rude" what I didn't realise was that they could hear me if I spoke also.

"Who's that?" someone said then I had a person tap me on the shoulder and then I hear the voice inside my head phones say

"I'm sorry madam we didn't think anyone was listening" I didn't say anything for the rest of the trip. Ava slept for a lot of the trip so that was good for her as there are only so many things to do on this sort of aircraft and trying to read her a book was not one of them it was completely useless as she couldn't hear a word I said. She was so very well behaved.

We finally landed just outside Sydney at a RAAF Base. Mum was there to greet us. Grant had organised a pass for her so she could come on to the base. As soon as Ava saw Mum she took off "Nannyyyy! Nannyyyy!" she was screaming and crying. She had missed Mum so much. You can probably imagine how emotional it was.

A few days after we landed it was Barry's eighteenth birthday. Mum had organised a huge party with a lot of our friends and family coming. The big night arrived and Barry's new girlfriend Rhonda was there. I had never met her before but instantly fell in love with her. Rhonda was Lebanese with beautiful dark skin, dark hair and dark eyes. The moment Ava saw Barry she ran to him and hugged his legs "Happy Birthday Uncle Bar" Ava said. Barry introduced her to Rhonda.

"Aunty Rhonda" Ava said. We all laughed and I went to say

"No Ava" but Rhonda leant down to Ava's level and said

"Yep! you can call me Aunty Rhonda beautiful" this is the moment I fell in love with Rhonda such a beautiful soul. That night was fantastic seeing most of my family and some of Barry's friends was amazing. We had a BBQ and lots of drinks then when everyone had gone home we decided we would go out to Penrith with friends we had known forever.

Richard was born one year exactly to the same minute before me and he, his brother and sisters where like my own and his Mum was like a second Mum to me and she happened to be Mum's best friend in the entire world. I asked Mum if it was ok if I went and she watched Ava. She agreed and for the first time in a long time I got to go out. We all piled in a taxi as we had had way too much to drink and went on the long trip to Richards. When we arrived it was early in the morning and the boys brought out more alcohol. I wasn't a big drinker but they made me blue lagoons and wow they were nice. Before I knew it the entire bottle of Blue Vok was gone and I was in the toilet being extremely ill. The toilet bowl was blue almost like they had used blue loo but this time it was just the Blue Vok. I finally got it all out and by this stage my second Mum was looking after me and put me in the spare bed to sleep it off. Wow what a night.

The whole time we were with Mum was so relaxing. Mum fussed over us and my Great Uncle J was there as well. We shopped at the markets and spent a lot of time together. The day had come for us to leave and I was devastated and so was Ava. Mum drove us back to the RAAF Base and we had to say our good byes. You can only imagine how hard this was. Ava cried for hours after we left and so did I.

When we arrived back in Western Australia we got in the car and drove straight over to Chantelle's to pick up Winnie. Winnie was so excited to see us she ran at me and knocked me over then drooled all over me. This made me laugh so hard as Ava tried to push Winnie off me. I told Ava to go for a ride on Winnie so she climbed up in her back and Winnie walked around as she had many times before with this little girl straddled over her back.

We finally got back to our house and I bathed Ava gave her dinner and put her to bed. Then I sat down on the lounge feeling very lonely. Grant called a few times from the different ports he stopped in and once he called and told me he was in Cairns and was going diving the next day with a few people he had met. I knew this meant he had met them at the pub with the other boys.

I had started working at a bank so my work was full time and meant that Ava was in daycare a lot. I would drop her off at daycare then travel the hour to work, finish up go and pick her up, go home fed, bathe and put her to bed. This was my boring existence.

I had won a glamour shoot experience and was so excited. I booked in for the Friday afternoon. I was treated like a star, someone did my make-up and my hair and styled me for four different looks, I felt so glamorous. Ava was with Chantelle whilst I had the shoot. This is where I met Kelly. Kelly had strawberry blonde hair and pale skin, she was quiet beautiful. "Hi! What's your name?" she said

"Emily, nice to meet you"

"What are you doing tonight" she asked

"Nothing I have my little girl at home and my husband is away"

"So is mine, let's go out" Kelly said.

"Sorry I don't know many people and wouldn't be able to get a sitter" I responded though this girl seemed like she would be fun to go out with even though I really had never been out before.

"I've got a sitter I've been using forever and I'm sure our kids would get on really well, you can use mine and that's final. You can't go home looking like THAT you have to show it off and make the most of it". She wasn't taking no for an answer so I decided that I would take Ava to meet the kids and the sitter and if I felt comfortable I would go out for a little bit.

Ava loved Kelly's children and the sitter so I decided I would go out with Kelly for just a little while. When we got to the local club everyone knew her and she introduced me to everyone. I was a little put out as I didn't really like being around strangers and I didn't like leaving Ava, this was the first time I had ever left her with a sitter. I stayed for a few hours then thanked Kelly and went back to get Ava to take her home. I did have a good night thought being out with people my age and just having fun.

The Day Grant arrived home...

Chapter 51: Cairns

The day Grant was to arrive home I rose early. Winnie knew something was going on as she wouldn't leave my side. I walked into Ava's room and stood there for a little while taking in the peace that was on her tiny face as she slept. I remember thinking how beautiful she was and that I wished for her to grow up happy and most of all loved. I finally woke from my thoughts and walked over to her, kiss her little forehead and told her it was time to go and get Grant. She sat up quickly and pulled her covers back "Now!" she said excitedly.

"Yes sweetheart now"

We got dressed and took the twenty-minute drive to Garden Island, pulled up at the gate and showed the person on guard duty our pass then travelled across the bridge to the submarine wharf. When we pulled up there were other wives and girlfriends waiting patiently to see their men. Finally, they started to come ashore. Ava was jumping up and down and would not stand still, I knelt down to pick her up. She was so excited as I had been telling her all week that Grant was coming home. Ava called him Daddy. As I looked up I saw Grant walking towards us. My heart jumped a little as it had been such a long time since I had seen him. He went straight to Ava and picked her up and kissed her on the cheek then he came over and hugged me and kissed my forehead. "I've missed you both" Grant said and we responded the same. We all got in the car and drove home.

If you don't know the Oberon Class Submarine is a diesel submarine so you can imagine what Grant smelt like, that's right diesel and it was really strong. You only have to go in the submarine for a minute and you will come out smelling this way so for him being at sea for such a long time everything in his bag also smelt strongly of diesel.

When we got home Grant just wanted to sit down. Ava needed a nap so I took her to her room so she could have a rest, all the excitement and being up so early had tuckered her out. While Grant had been away I had been spending a lot of time with Kelly. We would go out on Saturday nights and I had made a lot of friends. As I worked at the bank I couldn't really go out during the week and also I didn't like to leave Ava, however Kelly had no problem leaving her children. "Emily! Come I want to show you the video of my trip" Grant called out to me, I had made my way to the kitchen so I could get us a cup of tea. When I got to the lounge room Grant had the video set up and as I sat down he pressed play. I snuggled up to him and watch as his trip passed by. He had been around Australia and stopped at most of the ports along the way.

"This is Cairns" Grant told me as we got to scenery of Palm trees and surf. The video continued for some time with both Grant and all the boys featuring saying stupid things as boys do along the way. Then it jumped to a boat trip, during the entire video so far Grant had filmed it himself but on this one part there was footage of Grant and he was sitting next to some girl, at first I didn't think anything of it.

"Don't film..." Grant said to the person filming the video then it jumped to a part of him going in to the water. This is when I saw that he had a major look of concern on his face. I felt Grant looking at me but as I looked over he moved his head as if to not recognise my movement. Then there was underwater footage filmed by someone else. This footage showed Grant in diving gear and swimming along then all of a sudden it shows him holding hands with that girl! I jumped up

"Who was that and what was that?" I yelled a bit heart broken.

"No one Emily it was just a girl one of the boys met over in cairns, I was helping her"

"Bullshit, the look on your face says it all. You didn't think this was going to be filmed, maybe you should have checked it before you showed me you idiot!" I retaliated. Grant tried to tell me lies so I called Jamie one of the boys on the submarine. Jamie said he didn't want to say anything and I took the tone in his voice as saying

"Yes he cheated on you Emily" Jamie never said the words but it was definitely in his tone. I grabbed Ava and went to visit Kelly. I told her what had happened and she said we could stay there. Later that night I went to visit Grant and have it out but he continued to lie and kept changing his story. I was not having any of it. I told him I wanted a divorce. He started to cry and say sorry but he had done the wrong thing and now the trust was gone. If he had just flirted it may have been different but this was more than that and after everything I had been through I definitely was not putting up with this.

We stayed with Kelly for a few weeks while I got myself and Ava a house. Two of my new found friends said they would rent a room as they were a couple and it would definitely help me out. The day we were to move in I called Grant and told him I was coming to get my things. He wasn't happy and said he wanted to be there. When we arrived he was standing inside. I had three boys with me all friends and partners of my girlfriends. I walked past Grant in to Ava's room. I packed all her clothes and undid her bed so the boys could take it out to the truck I had hired. Everything in Ava's room was taken as I had purchased it all and it belonged to Ava. I then walked in to what was our room and packed my clothes and shoes etc. I left everything else. Grant started yelling at me

"Which one of these guys are you fucking?" I looked him in the eyes and said calmly

"I'm not the one who cheated Grant, you did this not me, don't make me out to be the bad one" as I looked out the door one of the boys was watching quietly from just behind the wall. I went to walk out carrying the bag I had packed when Grant grabbed the bag and ripped it from my hand then he grabbed my arms and pushed me up against the wall with force and I hit my head. I had tears well up in my eyes, just then one of the boys walked in and pushed him off me

"Don't touch her again" he said very calmly. Grant was furious but he didn't respond. I was guided out of the room and the guy grabbed my bag for me. I walked out the front with the boys following closely behind

"Leave the fucking keys here" Grant yelled at me so I turned and handed him the keys.

As I got in the first car and closed the door I broke down. This was the worst feeling, if I had been there alone what would have happened? I couldn't think about that and I tried to shake it from my mind. I had tears rolling down my face the entire time in the car.

So I had left all the furniture that we jointly purchased as I didn't want anything from him. I also left him our property that we had purchased together as I didn't want anything coming back on me. It was just Ava and I against the world again....

Chapter 52: Goodbye My Hero

The next few months were really hard. Grant and I had organised for Ava to stay one week with him when he was here and one week with me. We did this so she wasn't feeling the separation too much. Our main priority was to ensure she was OK and grew up feeling loved. I wanted Winnie but he wouldn't let me take her, he believed she was his even though he brought her for me. I felt safe with her around as she would never let anyone hurt us and with all I had been through I really needed to feel a little safe.

I was really happy about my friends moving in with me so Ava and I weren't alone, I always had the fear Jay would find us. He promised me the last time we spoke that no matter where I went he would find me. I was just hoping that being on the other side of Australia was far enough away...

Living in the house with Kerry and her partner was different. They were lovely people and always chipped in so this was good as there was no way I could have afforded to live in this house alone on my wage. The house was new and had a Mediterranean look, I loved it as it was very open plan but also gave me space to have Ava and I time away from everyone.

I had a great call from my cousin Tina she was moving over so she could be with me, she wanted a change. Tina and I had spent a lot of time together when I was in Sydney and I missed having my family around so having her move over suited Ava and I to the ground, we had a little bit of family in such a remote place. Ava always loved have our family around as she was spoilt rotten by them.

I took the day off work to go and pick Tina up from the airport. What I didn't realise is that she was a drinker and loved to party but that didn't change the fact that I loved her to bits. She didn't drink every day she just went all out when she was out clubbing. Typical for someone my age (Tina was a year older than me) Tina was so beautiful, she had dark skin, sun kissed dark hair and was petite. She looked a little like Jennifer Love-Hewitt. Everyone thought she was gorgeous, whenever we were out she turned heads. When Tina stepped out into the airport she was not walking straight and obviously had had a lot to drink on the way over but all the guys were swooning over her. I will guarantee that she did not buy herself one drink they would have been brought for her. Ava was ecstatic and Tina was just as happy when they saw each other.

The day Tina arrived I introduced her to all my friends, they loved her just as much as I did. Having Tina around was great we would go out on Friday and Saturday nights. These were my nights out. More on this later. I would wake each day get Ava's breakfast and get her dressed and take her to daycare then I would make the drive to the bank where I worked. I loved working at the bank as I had some independence and it felt good. I have never wanted someone paying for me and Ava, I always supported her and myself without the help of others. I would go without as many parents do so she could have all that she needed.

I always got to call Mum and Pa on Sundays. I never missed a call this was my life line and the only connection to my family back on the East Coast. I called Mum and spoke with her for some time about life and what was happening. She as usual was always comforting and told me not to worry and that everything happens for a reason. She didn't know it at the time but those words would be pondered and disbelieved for years to come. I was soon to start my spiral.

After one of the calls to Mum it was 7pm in New South Wales and much too late to call Pa. His routine was at 5pm to get Nan dinner then he would carry her up the steep stair case to the bathroom, bathe her then take her to bed all done by 7pm. I thought to myself '*I'll call him tomorrow*'

The worst day of my life so far...

As I woke this faithful day I felt a little ill. I had a strong feeling that I needed to call Pa. As I had to get Ava feed, dressed and to daycare and then get to work I thought to myself '*I'll call him tonight as soon as I get home*' I packed Ava in the car, dropped her at daycare then drove down to work.

At 11.12am (I will never forget this) the Bank Manager came to me and said "Emily, your husband is on the phone, you can take the call out the back". Out the back was behind a screen just behind where my teller window was. I walked to the phone and all I could think is '*What does he want now?*' Grant never called me at work but I was a bit jaded with him so I wasn't thinking much else.

"Hello" I said as I took the call waiting for him to argue about something stupid. What followed next dropped me to the floor quicker that any physical hit I had ever taken.

"Emily, your Grand Father is dead" Grant said, nothing more... no "You need to sit down", nothing. I dropped to the ground as my body felt so heavy that my legs could never hold it up. BROKEN!!! this was a call I never, ever expected. Pa was my everything.

"Not my Pa" I cried

"No! not Pa, Oh my god no!" I continued. I didn't think I was being loud but before I knew it I had the Bank Manager and two Tellers beside me whilst I held the phone to my ear with nothing but silence on the other end.

"Emily, was it your Dad?" The Bank Manager asked as he took the phone from my hands. I didn't want to let that phone go I just wanted the words to come out of Grants mouth to change and not be what he just said but there was no hope of that. I was shaking uncontrollable; I was physically sick.

"Emily, let's get you home" the Bank Manager said to me then after that I don't remember anything. I don't remember picking up Ava and I don't really remember much else at all that day. As I walked in the door the phone was ringing and Tina had answered it. She looked out at me and saw my face. I must have lost all colour but I know that day my eyes would have been swollen from crying.

"Emily, it's your Mum" Tina said with concern on her face. I took the phone and gave Tina a huge hug before speaking. I didn't want to talk to Mum as she was going to confirm what Grant had said however, I knew I had too. I told Tina I would take the call in my room. She held on the line in the dining phone until I walked in to my room and picked up the other hand set then I heard the click as she put the phone down.

"Hello" I said to Mum quite timidly not wanting conformation

"Emily, sweetheart Pa has passed away" Mum said choking back on her own tears.

"Not Pa, Mum please why wasn't it Nan" I broke down. I couldn't really speak. Mum was also a mess but trying to stay together for me as always she was the parent and put her feelings aside though she was crying and I could hear her tears. I know it sounds harsh but since Nan had her brain hemorrhage we had been expecting a call like this one but I did not expect my Pa. Mum and I sat silently on the phone for some until Mum told me that the funeral was in four days' time. There was no way I could afford to flight over for the funeral. This was killing me in more ways than one. After getting off the phone with Mum I went out and saw Tina. She knew this was bad.

"It's Nan isn't it?" she asked. I looked at her and broke down shaking my head no. I don't remember if Tina was as upset as me but she didn't live near Pa growing up so she only ever saw him on holidays. Pa was like my Dad not just a Pa and he was my hero. Tina was upset but she made the call to my Aunty her Mum. They spoke for some time and then when she got off the phone she told me she was flying back for the funeral.

That night Grant came and got Ava. I suppose this was his way of helping me out. He still didn't ask how I was or if I was OK. This made me hate him even more than him cheating on me. I went to bed that night and cried myself to sleep. I willed Pa to come and visit me but it didn't happen I was devastated, I couldn't understand how he of all people would not come and see me after he passed, If Nigel could and a stranger could surely my Pa could do it, he would have known the state I was in. The next morning, I didn't go to work. I stayed in my bed and wrote my Pa a letter. I can't remember every word but I do remember that I asked him to make sure he embraced the family and made then all hold hands and stay together. Pa was always our glue and now that he was gone I really was worried that it would fall apart.

The morning Tina was flying out I handed her the envelope and asked he to put it with Pa before they lay him to rest. I needed to say goodbye. This day I made a promise to myself. If I ever have the feeling I need to call someone I will... I honestly believe when you are that close to someone you just know when something is wrong.

I miss my Pa every day. This day was the beginning of my spiral. I had lost a part of me and the worst thing is that again like Nigel I felt guilty, guilty that I didn't call ....

UNBROKEN

My motto is 'NEVER SAY WHAT IF?' If your sixth sense kicks in follow it.

Chapter 53: Spiraling

From the moment I had the call that changed my world I spiraled almost out of control. I had given up cigarettes three years prior to this day and the next morning I went to visit my friend Denise at her house. She was smoking and I asked for one. I ended up buying a packet and I was smoking again.

Ava was in day care during the day and I was lost. My husband had cheated on me then he called and told me my Pa had passed, I wasn't going to the funeral so I couldn't see him or say goodbye. My letter that I gave to Tina was my only way to say goodbye.

The day of the funeral I was a mess. Everyone was going to be there but me! I felt terrible but there was no way I could afford to flight back home as I had rent, food and every other bill to pay by myself and raising a child by yourself is not easy when you have to pay for everything. I called Mum on the morning of the funeral and spoke with her a while. She knew I was devastated about not being there and I made her promise to say goodbye for me.

I didn't return to work after this as I really couldn't bring myself to get up and go. I got a single parents pension to help with the cost of living and raising Ava. Those that have had this pension will know that you have to stretch every penny. Looking back, I should have gone back to work and kept going but at the time there was no way, I could hardly function.

I started to go out with Kelly more often. We would go out every weekend Friday and Saturday nights. I started to drink a lot on these nights out (Ava was always babysat by an older friend of mine on these nights and I would pick her up in the morning). We would start drinking with friends at Kelly's house, a bottle of pink champagne kicked off the evening. We wouldn't get to the pub until

9:30pm when we went out. After a while I made so many new friends at the pub. As we lived in a Navy town there were always a lot of sailors out. The two Mauri bouncers at our local club loved me. Whenever I walked in to the club they would walk me to the bar and buy me a drink. I never had to take money with me, only enough for a cab as we were always tipsy before we got there and one of the guys would always buy me drinks, so by the time we were ready to go we all put in for a cab so the cost was always split. We would never leave before the pub closed at 3 am.

When Tina got back from New South Wales she joined in on the partying. She was always up for a party. Every time I went out there were guys trying to take me home. I was not up for this and there was no way I would bring them home when I had Ava in the house. I didn't want her to see this. I was a country girl that had never been able to go and party because I had responsibilities but Pa going broken me and too be honest I wasn't the same person I was before that little girl protected by her hero.

A little about Kelly. Kelly had beautiful strawberry blonde hair, blue eyes and was slim. She did fake tan before fake tan was popular and she always went all out when going to the club. Looking back, she thought she was perfect and if someone didn't pay her attention she would brush them off. She didn't like any of her other friends getting more attention than her. We got on but I didn't like that she had two kids at home and didn't spend any time with them. She was so into herself and always left them with a sitter and it wasn't the same sitter it was a different one every time. She and her husband split up just before Grant and I so I think I spent time with her because she understood what I was going through.

I remember going to her house one morning with Ava. The house was a mess, I heard her little girl crying so I made my way to where the noise was coming from. I entered this little girls room to see her sitting in her cot. She was a mess she had dirtied her nappy and taken it off she was covered in poo. The room stank as there were dirty nappy's everywhere, there were many bottles in her cot that had rotten milk in then. I picked that little girl up walked in to the bathroom and ran the bath. I bathed her and cuddled her so tight after I got her out. This poor little girl was not looked after at all. I couldn't understand how a mother could leave her child in this state. Since Kelly and her husband had split she was only interested in finding someone else so I guess her kids took a back seat. I did mention this to her and even said that if she wanted me to take the kids for a little while I would, she said no... Looking back, I should have called DOCS on her but I really truly didn't think this at the time.

During this stage of my life I was a real girly girl and always dressed to impress (maybe impress the opposite sex). I was nineteen and had a good figure. I wasn't up myself but I did know that I looked ok. I would wear short skirts and crop tops with a jacket showing off my lean body. My hair was dark, very long with spiral curls. When I went out I held my head high and was confident but inside I was very insecure. I guess this came from not having a real father around (apart from Pa). I made a good friend (Jodie) who I started going to the gym with. I had decided that I wanted to join the Police so I could protect myself and others like me and she wanted to join the Navy so we decided we would train together. We trained six days a week, twice a day. Ava would be at daycare all week so it was easy enough to do and she would come with us on Saturdays. I started training with the clearance divers over on the Navy base. Jodie cut her training back to once a day but not me I was focused. I won't brag but after a few months I was very toned and looking fantastic. This got the attention of more men when we were out.

UNBROKEN

We were walking home from the shop (Tina, Ava and Jodie) when I saw a white commodore, it was hotted up and you could hear that it had a V8. It stopped at a set of lights and the guy driving looked over at us, he didn't smile just looked. I said "I'm going to have him" laughing.

A few months later we all went out again and I had dressed to impress. I wasn't looking for anyone as I had finally got used to being on my own with Ava and was enjoying it. We were dancing and this guy walked past. I was a little tipsy so I turned around and pinched his bum. He spun around and looked at me. It was the guy from the car. He smiled then walked away. Not long after that he came back I didn't see him coming, he grabbed me around the waist and danced behind me. I spun around ready to slap him when I realised who it was. We danced for a bit then he went to the bar and got me a drink and brought it back. "Come with me" he said as he gently grabbed my hand and led me away from all my friends. Kelly gave us a death stare then she came over and pushed him away telling him I wasn't interested.

"Kelly! It's fine I'm a big girl" I said to her. I wasn't too worried as everyone knew us and I was always going to be safe here. He lead me out to the beer garden where all the pool tables were and it was a bit quieter.

"I'm Adam" he said to me whilst leaning down closer to my ear. Adam was over six-foot-tall, tanned, mousy blonde hair and blue eyes.

"I'm Emily" I said in to his ear as he was still leant down beside me. A lady walked past carrying a basket of roses and Teddy's (I had so many of these Teddy's as guys always brought them for me when I was out) Adam tapped her on the arm and brought a rose and a beautiful teddy.

Emily Reilly

"For a beautiful lady" Adam said as he handed me the gifts. My heart skipped a beat all I could think is what a gentle man. He leant in close again and asked if he could kiss me.

Chapter 54: Adam

Adam leant in and kissed me gently holding me close. Even though we were in the beer garden/pool area I did not hear a sound at this time, no noise I was lost in the moment. After I came back down to the ground I said "I have to get back to the girls, they'll be worried" Adam grabbed my hand and led me back to where my friends were still dancing. Adam and a few of his mates joined us, we danced all night. He was really impressing me. I leant in to Tina and yelled over the music into her ear

"What do you think?" she nodded her head. Jodie came over and asked me to go to the toilet. As all women know this is code for let's talk. I followed Jodie and following behind me was Tina and Kelly. We all got out to the toilets and all Jodie could say is

"He's hot! tell me what happened" as girls do I told them every detail.

"I'm not sure though, he seems too good to be true". Kelly piped up

"He's probably a creep, don't trust him" so negative for a moment where I was feeling awesome. I didn't feel any support from her but I also knew she would have been jealous because she was always the flirt and always had the guys following her because for some reason guys seem to like a bitch. I didn't enter into this I just continued to speak with Jodie and Tina. They supported me.

We decided to head home not long after this, all the girls were staying at my house so we walked inside and I walked up to Adam to tell him I was heading home with the girls. Adam offered to drive us as he hadn't been drinking much and was still sober. We all agreed and we got in the car, this was the car I had seen before when I told the girls I would be with him. Wow what a moment, I believe what you put out there does surely happen (in most cases).

When we got back to my house I asked if he wanted to come in for a cuppa and he agreed. That night we stayed up talking all night. I told him I had a beautiful little girl (Ava) and that I was separated. He told me he was in the Navy. I didn't go in to Grant as I wasn't really thinking about him at the time. This night I felt comfortable talking to this person, I didn't feel afraid or nervous as we were just comfortable talking. Before I knew it the sun was up and I was completely sober. Adam told me he had to go and that he didn't want this night to end. He asked for my number and asked if I would go out with him for a drive the next day. I agreed as I knew Tina wouldn't mind watching Ava for a few hours. Nothing happened between us at all that night. We got up and headed for the door. He turned around and without asking me this time he pulled me close and kissed me gently.

"I'll see you tomorrow Emily, I'll call a bit later and make sure you will be ready" I watched as he got in the car and backed out of my driveway. I watched him drive off down the street. I spun around and had a little laugh out loud and ran back in to the house. I was so excited that I ran down to Tina's room and jumped on her bed. She was asleep but not for long.

"Oh my god Tina I feel amazing, that was the best night, we didn't do anything, we just spoke, he is so nice, he's in the Navy, he's coming back later..."

"Slow down Emily" she said as she struggled to open her eyes. Jodie and Kelly also woke up. Kelly looked at me then just laid back down but Tina and Jodie sat up and tried to take in what I was saying. I didn't realise how fast I was talking but I was just trying to tell them everything all at the one time, I must admit I got a little dizzy because I didn't take a breath.

UNBROKEN

"I'm happy for you Emily, I really am" Tina said and she meant every word of it.

"Me too Emily" said Jodie. Tina agreed to watch Ava while I went out the next day, she said not to hurry back just have a good time. Kerry and her partner heard us and got up and I repeated the story to them. Everyone seemed happy for me. I told everyone I had to go and get Ava as my friend Sheryl was watching her from the night before.

I got in my car and drove over to Sheryl's house. Sheryl was an older lady who was in her late thirties she had two beautiful girls that loved Ava to pieces. They were more like her big sisters than her friends. When I got there I knocked on the door and Sheryl was a little amazed I was there so early after such a big night. Usually I got to her house at about 11am after going out but this night was not like any night I had had to this time in my life. I explained it all to Sheryl. She was excited for me but she also told me to just take it slow and be careful. Sheryl was one person I had told a bit about my past but not much as I didn't want people to know my past and judge me or feel sorry for me. I agreed that I should take it slow but wasn't sure how I was going to contain myself.

Ava came running out as soon as she realised I was there and gave me a big hug and kiss. This day couldn't have gotten any better. I had been with Sheryl for hours the time past so quickly, I said thank you and picked up Ava and her things and headed home.

By the time I got home the lack of sleep had gotten to me. I got Ava some snacks and put on a movie for us to watch. I laid up on the lounge and cuddled up with Ava and watched the movie then I could not resist closing my eyes for just a minute. Next thing I know I hear Tina in the kitchen cooking dinner. I jumped up and saw Ava at the table waiting patiently for her food.

"I am so sorry Tina" I said as I walked out still half asleep. She was fine she smiled and told me to take a seat dinner was ready. We sat and ate our dinner whilst talking about everything.

When I put Ava to bed I sang her the night song I always sung her (how much is that doggie in the window) this was a song that my Pa would play for me on his record player and he would sing it for me. I had tears in my eyes thinking about my Pa. The phone rang and Tina answered as I didn't leave Ava before she went to sleep. She was on the phone for about 15 minutes and I heard her say

"You had better have good intentions because if you don't then don't bother" I walked out and she looked at me.

"It's Adam" she said as she handed me the phone. I was so very nervous but I took the phone and spoke with confidence. We arranged for Adam to be here at 10am the next morning.

"I'll see you soon" he was his final words before I hung up the phone. Tina and I spoke for hours after my call, then we went and picked out the clothes for my date the next day. My room ended up a mess because every time I tried something on I took it off and threw it on my bed. I had settled on a skirt just above my knee and a three quarter tank top just showing a little of my tummy. I was getting nervous already. I didn't want him to get the wrong impression. By the time we finished it was really late and I needed to go to bed. I said good night to Tina, walked to Ava's room and walked over to her bed kissed her on the forehead and said my final good night as I did every night. I then got in to my bed snuggled with the teddy Adam had given me and fell asleep....

Chapter 55: The Other Woman

I woke to someone jumping up and down on my bed. Then I felt little lips kiss my forehead. "Good Morning Mummy" a little voice said. As soon as I felt this little kiss I quickly woke up and smiled at her. I then grabbed her and threw her on the bed and tickled her. Ava giggled so much she loved playing tickles but she wasn't very good at tickling me back then as her little fingers where too soft.

It then dawned on me that Adam was coming over and we were going out on a date. I immediately got up and organised breakfast for Ava and everyone else. Ava loved eggs on toast so that's what we were having. As we were eating and talking the phone rang. I wanted to run over and get it but at the same time I didn't want it to be Adam cancelling our date.

"Emily, are you going to get it? It's probably for you" Tina said as a matter of fact.

"Can you get it!" I said almost begging. Tina got up and answered it after she said hello she looked directly at me and held the phone out with a face that said I told you so. I was so nervous I really didn't want to take the phone, I did though. Tina was right, it was for me.

"Hi Emily it's Adam" he said and all I could think is who else would it be lol. It was as if he didn't think I would know who it was or maybe he thought I had men ringing me all the time. Adam said he would be over in an hour and just wanted to make sure I was ready to go. We said goodbye and as I hung up the phone I had a huge sigh of relief. I couldn't wipe the smile off my face, he wasn't cancelling he was just confirming our date, what a relief.

Emily Reilly

"Mummies going out for a little while Ava" were the first words I managed.

"Ok Mummy have fun" she replied. Ava didn't care as she was going to have the day with her Aunty Tina they had so much planned for the day already or at least Ava made the plans and of course Tina would comply.

"He's going to be here in an hour Tina, I have to go get ready. Are you sure it's ok for you to watch Ava?" I asked worried she may have changed her mind but Tina just smiled.

"Go! get ready! You don't want to be late" she said with a huge smile on her face. She really wanted me to be happy, I was so lucky to have her as a cousin. I only had an hour to make myself look irresistible and I am sure I won't come anywhere near it, I thought to myself. I straighten my hair the old way using only a hair drier (I wish we had irons back then). I did my make-up and then I got dressed in the clothes we had chosen the night before. I never used to get dressed before doing my makeup as I believed that you never look good in anything without your face on (weird I know but it was true for me) I rarely changed my clothes when I got ready this way. Finally, after 45 minutes (record time) I was ready. I walked out to the dining room

"You look pretty Mummy" Ava said. I thanked her and kissed her on the cheek

"You have lipstick cheeks" I said giggling at her as I knew what was to follow

"Yuck Mummy, you always do that" she said as she had many time before. I sat down and chatted with Tina and Ava for a little while then there was a knock at the door. My heart jumped and so did I.

UNBROKEN

Did I look ok?

Was I too dressed up?

Would he like me?

All these questions running through my head at the time. I froze, I couldn't move. Tina got up and went to the door. I heard voices and knew it was Adam. "Emily! It's for you" Tina yelled whilst guarding the doorway. She didn't want me to seem like I was waiting for him, she wanted it to seem like this was just another day in the life of Emily. I stood up straightened myself and kissed Ava.

"Be good for Aunty Tina Ava"

"I will Mummy" she responded with a smile. I really didn't need to say it because she was always good for Tina. I walked to the door and saw that Tina had not let Adam in and the door was only half opened so he really couldn't see me coming. When I reached the door it took all my strength to open it. I looked out he was in a surf shirt and jeans. Smart casual is how I would describe his dress. We said "hi" I hugged Tina, said thank you to her then told her I loved her.

As we got to the car I went to open the door and he run up and opened the door for me. I was a bit shocked as I have always opened the door for myself, it felt nice though. When I was younger I used to love movies where the man opened the door for the lady, as I got older I began to believe that there was no such thing as a gentleman any more, they died out after my Pa left this world. I got in to the car and put my seatbelt on. I hadn't paid much attention to his car the last time I was in it but it was a V8 and I later found out it was an ex pursuit car for the police. It was very comfortable though I could stop squirming for the first ten minutes or so. We drove north when Adam started talking to me like we had known each other forever.

"You look more beautiful today than you did the other night and that I cannot believe" he said to me. I blushed what a lovely thing to say, all I managed to say was

"You look nice too" then I thought to myself '*You look nice! Really! Couldn't you come up with something better*' but Adam just smiled at me and continued talking. Time did not seem to exist during the drive as before I knew it we were at Fremantle and he had organised for us to have a lovely seafood lunch. During lunch we talked about everything then he dropped a bombshell

"I have to tell you something" he said in a hushed voice. My mind raced.

What could it be?

Is he married?

Does he have kids?

I didn't say anything I just looked at him. "Emily I really like you" and at this moment I thought '*BUT*'

"I like you too Adam" I replied holding back what I was thinking.

"I have been dating someone for a few months" my thoughts then interrupted him and took over...

"But since the moment I met you I felt a spark that I have never felt before with anyone" he continued.

UNBROKEN

"Oh!" I said when I wanted to say WTF, that's wrong I can't believe I am the other woman, I can't do that to someone, no way never.

"She is in Victoria and has no plan of being posted here"" he said scanning my face to try and ascertain what was running through my mind.

"So she is in the Navy?" I asked.

"Yep she is but she has no plans to come here and it isn't going to work" Well I didn't know what to say but I managed something

"Adam I really like you and would like to see where this could go but I can't be the other woman, I can't be with you if you are with someone else" it took a lot to say that as I really did like him, he seemed like a gentleman and from what I had seen he was really nice and someone I could spend a lot of time with. We sat for a while and ate our meal then he looked at me, he reached over and grabbed my hand

"I am going to break it off with her, I want to see where this could go" he said moving his hand back and forwards between us. I told him I couldn't see him until he had as I couldn't be the one who broke up a relationship. I never wanted to do that to anyone as I had been there and it wasn't good. The only thing is that they had only been together three months and she wasn't looking at moving to Western Australia so I suppose it would be difficult to make it work. Long distant relationships rarely lasted.

As we got in to the car after our lunch Adam's phone rang he answered it and then I heard him on the phone, he was talking to her. They spoke for a while then he told her that he didn't think it would work with her there and him here. He was really caring when speaking to her and I could see it was hurting him. I could also hear her on the end of the phone and she was in tears. They talked for over an hour and I could hear her begging him as they had said last time they talked that they could fly and see each other once a month etc. or so I made out from what little I could hear. I was feeling really uncomfortable, I felt absolutely terrible this girls heart was being broken and it was my fault, If I hadn't pinched his bum that night they would probably still be together. The conversation didn't seem to go well. Adam finally hung up the phone and started his car. We drove back in silence and I didn't want to break this silence as he probably needed it. Just as we pulled in to my driveway Adam stopped the car and put his hand on my leg.

"Emily I'm sorry you had to hear that and I'm sorry I haven't talked all the way back but I didn't want to hurt her, she is a really nice person but you must know that what I feel when I'm with you is different, I have never felt this ever" he then leaned over and kissed my cheek.

"Can I call you later?" He asked.

"OK, and Adam thanks for a lovely lunch it was nice" I then exited the car and walked inside.

What was going on.....

Chapter 56: Avoiding Him

Adam called a few times after our date and I didn't really want to talk as I didn't know what to do. I didn't want to be the one who helped break someone's heart. I heard her on the other end of the phone whilst Adam was talking to her she seemed to be a mess, I had been there before and couldn't bring myself to do that to someone. Adam kept calling and speaking with Tina but each time I told her to tell him I wasn't in.

Each morning before I took Ava to daycare I would get up at 5am to go to the gym. Jodie and I would never miss a day. I was going three times a day at this stage. I was obsessed, it was there that I always felt at ease. At 5:30am I would train with the Navy Clearance Divers doing a circuit. We would train for 1.5 hours then I would go home and prepare breakfast and then get Ava ready for daycare I would drop Ava off and go back for two hours and do cardio whilst listening to music. Then I would go home clean and do the washing have lunch and head back and do weights.

One day when we were going back for round three Jodie was sitting on my feet whilst I did sit-ups with weights, I was up to about 80 when Jodie moved quickly and I fell backwards. "Jodie! I'm not finished" I said a bit shocked as she had never done this before.

"I'm going for a break" she said smiling then looking towards the door, I put the weight down and when I turned back I saw white pants and that oh to familiar smell of cooking. I slowly raised my eyes to see Adam standing in front of me with his hands out ready to give me a lift up. I just stared for a minute then I grabbed his hands and allowed him to help me up. I grabbed my towel and wiped my face as I had been perspiring quite a bit. I turned around to see him smiling at me.

"Emily, you have been avoiding me" he said quietly almost a whisper. There was no one else in the weight room thank god as I felt so embarrassed and completely not dressed to see Adam

"No, not really" I replied knowing I was lying. I had definitely been trying to avoid him.

"How did you know I was here?" My first thought was that Tina had told him as she was sick of lying for me.

"I remembered the first night we spoke all night, you told me your routine and considering you weren't answering my calls I decided to come find you here" he responded. Wow he actually did listen to me that night. *Where did this man come from? Was he even real?* my mind raced.

"I can't be the other woman Adam, I can't help break someone else's heart, I really do like you but I just can't do that to someone" I said as a matter of fact. I was being strong even though I wanted to run up and hug him and never let him go. I was trying really hard not to show my emotions. I don't know how well I was doing but I thought I was doing well. My entire being wanted to be with him but my head was saying "No".

"Emily! You're not that woman. I broke it off with her already. I have spoken to her since and told her it is just not going to work. We are ok now she had time to calm down and she understands" Adam really believed what he was saying but I was female and I knew that inside she would be breaking or at least I know I would be. We women are funny creatures, what you see on the outside is not always what is on the inside. I didn't bother saying it to Adam as he had made his mind up.

UNBROKEN

"I tell you what Emily. If you don't say yes to being my lady, then I am going to turn up here every day for the rest of my life until you do" he said to me so tenderly. I was melting inside (girls only dream of someone saying this to them) but still not convinced I was doing the right thing.

"Emily, please say something, anything, actually say you will be my lady" he wasn't begging he was just wanting me to say yes and to be honest that is exactly what I wanted to say.

"Can I tell you something?" he continued as I stood silently, I nodded.

"I was only seeing her a short while and to be honest if I loved her I would never have spoken to you or taken you out. I have never felt this way about another person and it scares me and usually I am arrogant but with you I couldn't do it. From the moment I saw your eyes I thought that is the girl I want to be with. If we don't give this a try I know we will regret it forever" he pleaded his case and he did it well. What girl wouldn't fall for this? I had never had someone speak that way to me. I truly melted he had me hook line and sinker. He didn't ask me this time he leant down and kissed me passionately. I melted in his arms.

"Yes" I said after our lips finally parted. He smiled this huge smile and said

"I am so glad you said yes, I would probably get charged for being AWOL if I had to come up every day and spend the entire time you trained trying to convince you to give us a chance" I smiled and we kissed again. Jodie walked back in after almost an hour. I am not sure where she went but she walked in as we were still kissing.

"Woah! Get a room you two" she said laughing as she walked towards us.

"Glad to see you two finally together. I can't believe it has taken you so long. You look awesome together" she said smiling. I could tell she meant it. It meant a lot to hear this from someone that I had told about Adam and his Ex and how I felt. She approved and I was to find out so did just about everyone else.

"I have to head back Emily but I would love to come and see you later if it's ok?"

"It's fine" I said we still had not let go of each other. He leant down and his lips touched mine again. I really didn't want to move now, he said goodbye and winked at me.

"I will see you soon" he said whilst walking towards the door he had my hand and our hand reached out until just our finger tips were touching. My heart raced and when I thought he was gone I jumped up and down quietly screaming

"Eeeekkkkk" (yes you can quietly squeal, all you girls know that). Jodie and hugged.

"I am so happy for you Emily, really you deserve this!" she said genuinely. I couldn't wipe the smile off my face.

"Now! Get down there and finish your sit-ups miss, we have so much more work to do" Jodie was laughing as she said it and I conformed but all I could think about was seeing Adam again and it was going to be that night......

Chapter 57: I'm Not Seeing Her Anymore

Adam came over that night but again nothing happened, he was a total gentleman. We went out for dinner, it was Ava's week with Grant. I missed her dearly when she was away but she really enjoyed going to stay with Grant.

I forgot to mention that when I had Ava I did not put a Father's name on the birth certificate so the only name on there was a Mother's name (mine) just before Grant and I got married he wanted to put his name on her birth certificate so we went in to the births death and marriages office in the city, where he told the lady a lie and said he was Ava's Father and now wanted to be recognised on the birth certificate. The lady just wrote his name on the birth certificate and later entered his details in the system. From that day forward he was on Ava's birth certificate as her Dad.

I didn't mind her going over as she wanted her Dad and this was the only one she knew. As much as I missed her it gave me time to sort myself out and get to know Adam.

Adam and I dated for seven months and we would go out every weekend to the club. I spent so much time with him that the only time I got to see my friends was when I went out and this was my decision I just wanted to spend every waking hour with him. Jodie and I went to the gym every morning but some mornings I would let her down as I just wanted to stay with Adam. After eight months of being with Adam Jodie had joined the Navy and had to leave Western Australia so the gym was of less importance and this put a stop to me joining the police force.

Adam moved in with Ava, Tina and I by this stage Kerrie and her partner had moved out as they didn't like Adam. They thought that Adam was taking too much of my time and were worried about me but I didn't appreciate it when they said it.

Adam had a best mate (Dave) that came over all the time. Over time he and Tina got really close and eventually started dating. Things couldn't get any better were my thoughts at the time.

One night we went to the club and as usual the girls would dance then Adam would slow dance with me. This night the J Babies were playing they sang cover songs from popular bands and most nights they would call me up to sing with them. This night when they did it the lead singer was flirting with me and when I got off the stage Adam was looking a little down. Dave came up to me and said "I have known Adam for years and I have never seen him in love or care about anyone like he cares about you. He's a little jealous of you and that guy"

"He has nothing to worry about Dave, why would I ever do anything to hurt him?" I replied. I had known the J Babies since I had starting to go out to the club, they were good guys.

"Don't say anything to him Emily" Dave begged and I didn't. When we wanted to chill we would go out to the beer garden and play pool. Adam was really good at pool but so was I thought I pretended not to be at the time (stupid but true). Whilst playing pool with the girls Adam came over to me and he looked upset, not sad angrier.

"Emily! Can we talk" he said in a cold tone. My heart sank, was he really that upset about the lead singer flirting with me? He grabbed my hand and took me around the side of the building. The entire time I was thinking 'it's over'.

"Emily!" he started, this didn't sound good

UNBROKEN

"Yes Adam" I said nervously tears welling up in my eyes and I felt like I was going to drop to the ground. After everything I had been through I had stupidly given myself to this guy. I hadn't realised that this whole time he had his hand behind his back. When he saw the tears well up and realised I was about to breakdown he moved his arm around to the front and in front of me was the biggest bunch of red roses I had ever seen. They were all individually wrapped.

"I love you" were the words that came out of his mouth. I cried automatically it was a cry of relief more than anything I was thinking the worst. He leant in and held me tight.

"Sorry Honey, I didn't mean to upset you I just wanted to give you these and let you know how I feel" I just held him tight and cried. Adam had brought all the roses that the flower lady had in total there were fifty roses. As you all know I had never ever had this in my life and I think I always expected the worst so when this happened you can imagine my relief.

After a while we went back to our group with me carrying all those roses. Since we had been together our two groups of friends had joined and now we had a massive group of friends that came visiting all the time. In this group of friends, we had friends that smoked pot and used ecstasy and other drugs. They never did it at our house only while they were out but one night when it was Grants week they all came over and we had a bonfire and some drinks. A couple of people had a joint and they passed it to me. I had bad memories from pot but I had a smoke and then ended up in the shower really sick. I didn't like the way it made me feel, it was like everything was totally delayed but after a while I just got really tired. This night I was that sick that I sat on the bottom of the shower for what felt like hours and all I could do was cry. Adam came to check on me and when he saw me crying he jumped in the shower, sat with me and held me. He was fully clothed. Looking back, it would have been funny if I wasn't so wasted.

A few days later Grant came to drop off Ava. When he came to the door Adam answered it. What I didn't know is that they were on the same submarine at one stage and I hadn't told Adam or Grant either person's name or what they actually did and to be honest I didn't really think about it. After Ava went inside and was out of earshot Grant lost it. He was swearing at me and calling me all sorts of names, Adam stood between us and he was not happy with the way Grant was acting. I had to step in as I really thought they were going to fight. I told Grant to leave "You cheated on me Grant, you have no right to say anything" I said to him as I walked him to the car.

"He's a fuck wit Emily, you'll see!" Grant yelled just as he was driving off. Adam was furious he had gone inside to get his keys. I asked Tina if she could watch Ava for a little while as I didn't want him driving in this state alone. I thought I could calm him down. We got in the car and before I knew it we were at Grants house.

"Adam!! No please, let's go" he was having none of it

"He cannot speak to you like that, I'm just going to talk to him and tell him that. It's ok Emily, trust me" well I did trust him so I sat in the car whilst he walked to the door and knocked. Grant came to the door. He was screaming all sorts of things at Adam then he started walking towards the car. I got out to try and calm him down and explain to Grant that Adam just wanted to talk to him but he wasn't going to listen. Adam followed him and said

"Grant this is between you and me not Emily" when Grant got close enough to me he pushed me in to the car and before I actually realised what had happened Adam grabbed him and pulled him away and punched him. There was a full blown fight right there in front of me. I tried to pull them apart but it wasn't going to happen. Adam kept hitting Grant

"Don't you ever lay a fucking hand on her" Adam yelled. Finally, I was able to pull them apart. Adam walked towards the car hardly a mark on him then he turned around and said calmly

"I just wanted to talk to you it didn't have to be like this" we got in the car and Grant was yelling as we drove off. Adam looked at me whilst driving

"No one can touch you Emily and I won't stand there and watch that happen" we got home and I explained to Tina and Dave what had happened. Tina was so angry she wanted to call Grant but I wouldn't let her. Grant called me later and out of spite he said

"I'm not seeing Ava again" I cried and tried to talk to him and explain it wasn't Ava's fault and that she needed to see him but he didn't care. I thought over time he would calm down and everything would be fine. This made me sick physically.

For weeks I was sick and finally Adam said to me "I'm taking you to a doctor, I think you are stressed and I'm not taking no for an answer". We got in the car and went to the doctors. Ava was at home with Tina, Tina was really worried about me I had lost so much weight.

Driving to the doctors Adam held my hand tightly. We arrived at the doctors and sat waiting our turn to go in when I got called in Adam said he would wait for me outside. I went in to see the doctor he asked a lot of questions "It could be stress but is there a possibility you could be pregnant?" I didn't think so as we had used protection. He wanted me to take a urine test anyway so off I went to the toilet. I walked back in and he did the test. The five minutes that it took for that test to show negative went for what felt like forever. Then I heard

"Congratulations! Your pregnant" I sat there and cried '*here we go again*' was all I could think at that very moment

"So you weren't planning this?" the doctor asked. '*Of course I wasn't!*' is all I could think. The doctor made me sit there until I had pulled myself together. How was I going to tell Adam? finally I had pulled myself together and stood up and grabbed the door handle slowly turning it and wishing with all my heart that it wouldn't   open..

Chapter 58: He Was Only Joking

As the door opened I felt it pull along the carpet and a slight creak which is something I didn't realise while going in to the doctor's office. It's funny how you notice the little things at a time like this. I walked with my head down to the counter to hand in my form. I was wishing that they would get me to stay there for as long as possible to do something so I didn't have to face Adam, anything at all not to lift my head and meet his eyes but no such luck. I stood there for what felt like an age until I finally got the courage to turn around. As I slowly turned I notice Adam stand up and my eyes met his. "What's wrong Emily? You've been crying! Are you ok?" he asked showing concern. I looked at the ground and my eyes welled up again. I felt his pointer finger touch my chin and lift my head so my eyes met his again.

"No matter what it is we can face it" he said again. I looked at him and mumbled quietly hoping the words would undo what I was about to say

"I'm Pregnant!" it was almost an embarrassed tone. I looked at his face to see the reaction but there wasn't one. His face stayed the same, it didn't change at all. He put his arm around my shoulder and said

"We can chat later" then he smiled. I couldn't read his reaction at all, we walked to the car. Adam opened the door for me and then closed it gently behind me. On the drive home when we stopped at a set of traffic lights Adam said

"It will be good to have a baby Adam" then he smiled. It lifted my spirits a little. I thought to myself '*Everything is going to be OK*' my thoughts went to the future which never happened for me. I thought of how Ava would be with a little baby brother or sister. Finally, things were going to be OK.

When we pulled in to the driveway Adam got out first and opened the door for me yet again. He put his arm around me and walked to the door. I was feeling a lot better. This is not what I expected when I told him. I don't know what I expected but this was not it. Adam opened the front door and walked through as soon as I got one foot inside I heard Ava "Mummy!!!" she was so excited to see me. I knelt down to give her a hug, I gave her a kiss and hug. She then ran off to play again. I walked to our room and got changed in to something comfortable. As I went to walk out the door I heard voices. I thought it was just Tina and Dave at home but when I got to our lounge room I notice that Powsey was there sitting on the floor with his girlfriend Donna, Tina and Dave, Adam had joined them.

"What did the doctor say Emily?" Tina asked Adam. I looked at Adam and he nodded and said

"We're pregnant"

"That's fantastic! I'm so excited for you both" she said truly excited and happy for us. Everyone was excited and we chatted for ages. Adam kept patting my tummy and talking to the little one like it was there with us. After a while I decided to make dinner for everyone. Adam offered to cook but I said I was alright and I set off to make dinner and get Ava bathed. I sat Ava at the table, fed her then bathed her and then she went to bed. Ava didn't like chilly and I really felt like chilly so she had steak and veggies one of her favourites.

When I had finished cooking I called everyone in and the conversation continued. The boys were teasing saying they couldn't imagine a little Adam running around etc. while the girls chatted like girls. After dinner I cleared the table and washed the dishes as everyone else went out the back and smoked some pot. After I had finished they came back inside and went in to the lounge room. The girls chatted with me at the table for a while. When we walked in to the lounge room I heard Adam say "It would be like killing a kangaroo" as I caught the end of a conversation I asked what they were talking about. Adam looked at me and said

"Well when you get rid of this kid it will be just like killing a kangaroo, nothing too it?" (My heart is racing as I write this). I didn't know how to respond but I thought it was just a sick joke, he defiantly couldn't mean that. He had been saying all afternoon that he couldn't wait for our baby to arrive and now this! I think I just stood there not able to respond. Tina looked at him and said

"Your sick Adam! that's not even funny" Adam laughed it off then they went on with a different conversation but I couldn't shake the heartache I felt.

Did he mean what he said? Time passed slowly and I don't remember the conversations that followed as my mind just kept playing Adam's words over and over again.

When everyone left we went to bed. When I got in I didn't say anything, I just rolled over to go to sleep. I was confused, scared to afraid to ask the question that was playing on my mind. Adam rolled me over on to my back and looked at my tummy. He lifted his hand, placed it gently on my tummy and started to rub.

"Hi there baby Adam, you'll soon be here" he then laid his head on my tummy and fell asleep.

Confused!! Just a little. Adam had never shown any signs of being a bad guy during the whole time we had been dating.

Well this proved it he was only joking...

Chapter 59: You'll Be Here Soon

Over the next few weeks Adam would rub my belly and say "You'll be here soon little one" these moments made me relax and feel comfortable. I was finally happy and could see a future with him. It would be Ava, Adam, Baby and me. He would walk in and hug me all the time and whisper in my ear

"We are going to have a baby and I can't wait" life seemed great. Nothing could bring me down. We would go to the beach and watch the sunset and if you have ever been to Western Australia you will know there is no better sunset then on the beaches there. We would sit on a hill at Warnbro and watch the sunset. I understand after seeing this sunset how the sun looks like it dances on water. The sun was so large that it seems like you could reach out and touch it (this was my place and time to think). The colour was something that is hard to explain but the water would be all shades of red, orange, yellow, silver and black, just magnificent. During these times Adam would rest his hand on my tummy and kiss my cheek. So comforting and any girl will know that this makes you feel special.

A few weeks later Adam came home from work with his mates and again went and smoked some pot out the back. Again we sat in the lounge room and chatted. I remember this one day so clearly as my entire world came crashing down after being so high. Tina, Dave, a few others, Adam and myself were all sitting there. Adam was rubbing my tummy and whispering in my ear the same nice comforting things he had been for the last few weeks when one of his mate noticed him rubbing my tummy (he knew I was pregnant)

"So Adam, you're going to be a Dad. Are you ready for it?" he asked. Without taking his hand off my tummy Adam replied

UNBROKEN

"Nope we're not having it. Emily's having an abortion" as the last words came out of his mouth I was up and running to our room. My mind was racing;

Why was he saying this after the last few weeks making plans?

Didn't he care how I felt?

My heart broke, I had to go and be physically sick in the toilet. As I lent down and started being sick I heard Tina yelling at Adam. I didn't hear the exact words but I knew she was not happy then I heard the door open followed by a hand on my back and Tina's calming voice "It'll be ok Emily. Don't worry about him he's wasted; he's being an asshole" I looked up from the toilet to where she was now standing

"Tina! I can't do this alone again" then I really broke down. My entire body was shaking and I couldn't lift myself but mostly I didn't want to move I wanted the floor to swallow me whole. As much as I loved Ava I couldn't do it again, I couldn't raise two children on my own. This is not the life I dreamt of as a little girl when I would play make believe games with Nigel about getting married and having kids. I know I came from a broken family but when I was little my dream was to marrying a really nice prince and living happily ever after., just like most little girls.

"You won't Emily, I will be here for you always!" she said whilst trying to calm me down. Luckily Ava was staying Sheryl and her girls that night. She had other kids to play with and she loved it there so every now and then she would sleep over.

Tina and I sat in the toilet for what felt like forever. She went and got me a drink a few times and always came straight back. All I did was cry and I really wondered why Adam didn't bother to come and check on me. I thought to myself 'why has this happened?

Emily Reilly

What have I done in this life time or the last that deserves me to be treated the way I have' this day I really truly wished I had not been born. I felt sorry for myself something I had never really done before. I don't know why but when Tina said anything bad about Adam I defended him. I really was a mess.

Finally, I heard the front door close, Tina went out to see what was going on. Everyone except Adam and Dave had left. I heard Tina and Dave talking then I heard the door to our room open and as I looked up from where I was seated towards the door Dave was standing there looking at me "Emily, don't pay attention to him he is wasted and he doesn't mean it" with my face red and my eyes swollen I replied

"He doesn't want this baby. This is the second time he has said something like this Dave and the most hurtful" Dave didn't say anything more, he walked over to me and brushed the hair from my face and wiped away my tears. This made me cry more as it should have been Adam! wiping my tears away. Dave then turned and walked away.

I sat in the toilet/bathroom for a long time then I heard the door again. This time when I looked up it was Adam "We need to talk Emily" he said to me. I had not long stopped crying and this made my eyes well up again. He reached out and grabbed my hands and walked me to the bed. He sat me down then he knelt in front of me.

"Why did you say that Adam? I am so confused it has been great for the last few weeks and now this?" I said through my tears. I didn't care how I looked but I know my nose would not stop running and tears did not stop flowing. Adam didn't say anything he just stood up and held me,

UNBROKEN

"It'll be ok Emily, don't worry" he said. I didn't eat this night, I just laid on my bed curled up and holding my tummy. Adam curled up behind me and wrapped his arm around me.

The next day Adam left for work as usual and Tina and I spent the day together. Sheryl brought Ava back but when she saw the state of me she said Ava could stay for a few days while I sorted this out, I was so very grateful. I missed Ava but I was a mess and I didn't want her to see me that way.

Later that day Adam called me "Emily! We need to go for a drive this afternoon" I thought this might have been his way of apologising so I got dressed nicely and waited with Tina until I heard his car pull up. Adam walked into the house, as he came in I thought he seemed to be in a rush

"Come on Emily or we'll be late" he said as he rushed in and got changed really quickly. *'Where were we going that we would be late?'* I thought to myself. *Maybe he is taking me for an early meal?* I really wasn't sure but I'm sure it was going to be lovely, I couldn't allow myself to think the worst. I walked out to the car and for the first time in just under two years he didn't open my door which I found very strange, so I opened the door and sat in the passenger seat. We drove for a while then we pulled into a driveway, as we pulled up I noticed right in front of me was the doctor's surgery, my heart sank and my mind raced

Why where we here?

Was Adam ok?

Was he sick?

I didn't know why we were here. Adam got out of the car and I followed him inside, when we got through the door he told me to sit down as he went to the counter. After a little while he came back and sat down. I didn't ask him what was wrong as I thought he must have been worried about something and I didn't want to upset him more. Adam didn't hold my hand which again I felt was strange.

After about an hour I heard the doctor call Adam. He stood up and then he grabbed my hand and led me into the office. He sat me on the chair closest to the doctor and sat next to me. For the first time that afternoon he put his arm around me "What can I do for you today" the doctor asked. I thought to myself finally I will find out what's wrong with Adam.

"Well Doc Emily is pregnant and we want to know how we can organise an abortion" he said as a matter of fact, like we had spoken about it prior. I didn't know how to react, I couldn't speak. The doctor said

"Well there is a clinic in town but can I ask why you want this?" as he looked directly at me for an answer. I was still frozen and just like the nightmares that I had had for a long time I couldn't speak, yell or scream.

"We are too young to have this baby, we don't want to have a baby" Adam responded with no emotion and without even looking at me.

What was happening here? I felt ambushed.

The doctor continued talking and to be honest I don't remember the rest of the conversation. I remember getting outside, getting into the car and the next thing I know I am at home and on my bed with Tina sitting there....

Chapter 60: The Clinic

This day couldn't have gotten any worse. All I could think was '*if Adam had beaten me I can handle that pain but to do this!*' this is more painful than a beating, the bruises go away from a beating but Adam's words and actions on this day will never leave me, they are forever embedded in my mind.

I heard Adam drive off, he hadn't even come in with me and to be honest I didn't remember getting out of the car or how I got inside at all. I was definitely messed up. I got up from where I was sitting, walked past Tina and pulled the curtain back to see Adam drive away. I remember thinking to myself '*Why! What have I don't in this life or another to deserve this?*' again, a question I had asked myself one too many times.

Tina came over and sat me down on the bed. When I finally realised she was still in my room I looked her in the eyes. She looked so confused and worried. I just sat there looking right through her. "Emily! What happened?" I heard Tina say. Tears ran down my face and I started to blubber like a child, I couldn't get the words out. How could I put into words what had just happened when I couldn't understand it myself. Tina walked out, got me a tea then came back and just held me till I was in a state that I could relay what had happened. When I had left the house I was really high she was thinking that we were going somewhere we could talk and spent time together but for us to come back and I'm like this it must have really confused her, not as much as it did me though.

"Adam took me to the doctors" saying these words hurt my throat trying to get them out.

"Why? What's wrong? Is everything ok? You haven't said anything to me. Are you ok?" all of these questions rolled off her tongue in quick succession.

"Tina!! Stop!!" I yelled. I was taking my pain out on her, I didn't mean to yell at her, it just happened. She looked at me wide eyed, she knew there was something else going on, something serious.

"I am so sorry" I said to her as I started to cry all over again.

"Adam took me to the doctor" I paused as I couldn't bring out the words. Tina didn't say anything she just sat there quietly and waited with anticipation. Through my blubbering and gasping for air I spat out

"Adam has organised for me to have an abortion" that was it as I said those words my entire body collapsed.

"Who the fuck does he think he is?" obviously Tina was angry but she looked at me and realised that her reaction was not what I needed right now. We sat there for hours then I called Sheryl who was watching Ava so I could say good night to her and make sure she was ok. As I heard her voice it took everything to hold back my tears. She was having a ball and I was so happy she didn't have to see me this way.

Later that night as I lay awake in my bed I heard Adam's car pull up. He came inside and sat on the bed next to me, I pretended to be asleep. He leant down and kissed me on my cheek then he wrapped his arms around me. Even after everything that happen this day I needed him to hold me and explain why? I turned over and faced him. He could see I had been crying since I got home as the red swollen eyes were a dead giveaway "Adam, I need to know why?" I said looking him in the eyes. His eyes welled up as he said

UNBROKEN

"I'm not ready to be a Dad, we need to have more time together before we think of having a baby" I didn't know what to think. We talked all night and didn't sleep. All night he was talking about our future and what we will be doing in ten years but right now he wasn't able to have a baby in his life he wasn't ready and he wanted us to have a house and be settled before we had a baby. I didn't speak much that night. What I can say is that he had me worried he would leave even though he didn't say it at all.

If you have ever felt this way you will know, mental abuse can be so much worse that physical abuse. I honestly believe now looking back that's what it was mental abuse. I finally found a guy that treated me like a princess after all the bad things I have endured or so I thought until I found out I was pregnant. It seemed to me that pregnancy changed a man's perspective and your entire relationship.

The next few days he went back to the same loving person I had met and for a while I thought he might change his mind. It was a Thursday a day I will never forget (This is hard) I drove down to a local surgery where Adam had booked me in. Tina came with me this day. She was there to support me no matter what she would be there for me. As we parking the car I just sat there staring at nothing, I felt Tina put her hand on my arm. "You OK Emily?" she asked knowing that I wasn't, that nobody could be when they feel cornered like this. I faked a smile and pulled the keys out of the ignition, opened the door and walked to the clinic.

When we got to the clinic I couldn't open the door I was shaking too much. Tina came over and opened the door for me so I could walk in. I felt dirty, sick and generally shit. As I got to the desk a nurse asked for my details and walked me into a change room. I got changed in to the blue robe she had given me and walked back out where they checked my temperature and blood pressure before putting a drip in my hand. The whole time Tina stood next to me rubbing my arm, she knew this was killing me. As they wheeled away my bed to the operating theatre I started to cry silently. They move me to a hard bed then before I knew it I was out.

When I woke up the first person I saw was Tina, I woke crying. I didn't talk or make a sound. I laying was there a while when the doctor came and told me I could go and get changed and that everything had gone ok, it seemed extremely insensitive, he seemed to look at me like I was the worst person in the world. As soon as I heard his words I thought '*OK!! nothing is ever going to be OK again*' he asked how I got there as I was not supposed to drive after surgery, Tina looked at me a little worried as she couldn't drive and she didn't want me to "Let's call Adam"

"No it's all good Tina you can drive my car" I said knowing that Tina didn't have a license and had no idea how to drive. I got myself up and changed then went out to the car, go into the driver's side and drove us home very slowly as I was still groggy from the general anesthetic and worried that we would have an accident on the way.

When we arrived home I walked into the house and collapsed on my bed. I was numb. No emotion, no thoughts I was blank. I had done something that I didn't want to do, never in a million years would I have thought I would be in that situation.

Later that night Adam came home with Dave, I was on my bed and all I could hear was Tina losing it with him....

Chapter 61: The Hickey

A little about Powsey and Donna (his partner).

Before I met Adam I was out with friends and met Powsey. We danced together and he asked me on a date. We went out one night and while we were out he told me he was engaged to a girl called Donna but he didn't love her. He complained about her the entire night. She was not living in Western Australia she was in another state. He asked me how he could break it off with her because they were not going to work out. He said she was too needy and wouldn't let him out of her sight. I said from experience that it would probably be best to be honest with her but do not do it over the phone if that is what he intended to do. I was so uncomfortable giving relationship advise to someone I had just met. This was a weird conversation considering we were on a date and I didn't realise until this moment that he had a fiancée. It was a very long night and this conversation completely turned me off. I liked him as a person but not in a romantic way so we stayed friends. I didn't know at the time he knew Adam until after I met Adam.

Imagine my surprise when I came home one day and Adam and Powsey were sitting listening to music in my lounge room, I was a little shocked. I had kissed Powsey and now he was sitting with Adam. I didn't lie to Adam and later that night I told him what had happened, he was a little funny I would say he was jealous. He didn't treat me badly but from then on he was a little funny with Powsey.

Donna moved to Western Australia and they stayed engaged. The first time I met Donna, Powsey had invited us over for dinner. When we arrive Powsey took us inside, he and Adam decided to leave me in the house alone with her while they went to the shop. I didn't know this person from a bar of soap but I did know that her partner didn't want to be with her. She chatted to me and told me that she didn't really like the meals Powsey cooked but not to tell him because she didn't want to make him feel bad. We became friends (not overly close but friends) it was good because when the boys went out we would have each other to talk too. We took Ava to the beach and park together. Because the boys were close we spent a lot of time together. Adam and I would spend a lot of time at their house and vice versa.

Back to the night I got back from the clinic. Adam had a shower and came to bed. He didn't say anything he had his back to me the entire night. This is the time I needed a hug the most but it wasn't coming. I didn't sleep at all. My body and mind had become numb. I hated myself for what I had done but for some reason I still wanted to be with Adam. I couldn't see what was wrong with him only what was wrong with me.

For weeks I ate very little and lost a lot of weight. I didn't go to the gym or out much at all. I stayed home and spent time with Ava and Tina. I had lost myself.

Christmas time came around again and this time Adam was going back to Queensland to see his family. I knew I would miss him but I wasn't too worried about anything else. Adam had been treating me well again which made me feel better about us. He got over what had happened and never spoke about it, I couldn't but I tried really hard not to show it.

Adam was gone for a few weeks and called me almost every night. On the last night he told me he was going out with old friends and that he couldn't wait to get back to me. I was feeling good because when I got up in the morning I could go and get him from the airport.

UNBROKEN

I woke the next morning and for the first time in a long time I got dressed up, most of my clothes didn't fit me anymore due to the amount of weight I had lost. I did my make-up and hair. Tina was going to watch Ava so I could go to the airport "I am so glad to see you smile again" Tina said. I smiled and gave her a hug. I then gave Ava a massive hug and told her I would be back soon with Adam. She was excited, she loved Adam.

I arrived at the airport and had to wait half an hour for the plane to land. I was nervous and I couldn't understand why. I was also excited for the first time in a long time. When the doors opened I stood and waited for Adam to walk out. It wasn't long before I saw him. He ran out the door straight over, picked me up kissed me and spun me around "I've missed you so much" he said. I told him I had missed him too. We walked out of the airport and he drove us home. When we got home we spent time with Ava and then had dinner and went to bed. Adam took off his shirt and what I saw shocked me. He had a hickey on his chest and then when I looked closer he had one on his neck too.

"What's that?" I asked sheepishly not really wanting him to give me an answer unless he was going to lie to me.

"Nothing" he replied. He looked guilty.

"Adam what is that?" I asked again, this time a little more firmly.

"Did you get with someone while you were away?" I wasn't happy at this stage. I wanted him to say something anything that made sense just not what I knew it was. He looked at me and said

"Your crazy! It's not what you think, fuck this I'm going to Powsey's" and with that he put his shirt back on and walked out to his car and drove off.

Emily Reilly

I ran the shower, sat on the floor and broke down. I was shaking and in a terrible state. I could not control myself, I had completely lost it. I wasn't thinking only sitting there drenched hoping that I would be sucked down the drain. I'm not sure how long I sat there but I know that as soon as I got up of the bottom of that shower, I walked out grabbed all of his clothes and threw them in a box. I knew that when he got back he had to go even though my heart was breaking, I was broken I couldn't do this anymore.

I heard a car pull into the drive in the early hours of the morning. I got up as it wasn't Adam's car and looked out the window, I saw that it was Donna's car. Adam got out and he was really wasted, I watched him stumble to the door. I got back into bed and pretended to be asleep as I couldn't deal with this now. He came in and got into bed fully clothed. My back was too him and he cuddled up to me. He thought I was asleep and he started talking to me telling me how much he loved me and that he was sorry then I heard snoring. I didn't sleep again this night but when he got up in the morning all his clothes were in a box.

"Emily! What's going on?" he asked.

"I can't do this anymore Adam, they are hickeys on your body, you cheated on me after everything we have been through. I can't do this" I said through choking tears.

"Emily you're being stupid, nothing happened it was a stupid dare the boys had when I was over there, I haven't done anything" I don't know why but I let him stay again. Actually I know why, I was broken and in my mind I couldn't lose another person (sad but true).

Adam started going over to Powsey and Donnas more often without me. I heard Adam on the phone one day "No, can she stay with you! I will come and visit soon". When he got off the phone I

340

UNBROKEN

asked who he was talking too and who is she? He wouldn't say but then Tina walked in and she asked him also. Finally, he told me that his ex had move to Western Australia and she needed somewhere to stay and that he asked Paul if she could stay there.

What was going on?

Why was he helping her and going to visit her?

At least he didn't lie. He told me she didn't know anyone here, he was still her friend and he wanted to make sure she was ok. I let him go as I had to trust him. He went visiting her over and over. One day he came home and told me she wanted to get back with him but he told her no, that they could be friends but he was with me. I believed him as I didn't ask him about his visits he came to me with it. I didn't like that he was visiting her but he was honest enough to tell me about this so that in itself made me feel secure....

Chapter 62: It's Over

For the next few weeks Adam kept asking me to go out and visit Powsey and Donna and each time I said I wanted to stay home. I didn't feel like socialising after everything that I had put myself through.

One night I overhead Dave calling the Navy base asking at the mess if Adam's ex was there. Dave had been friends with her also. Adam was standing next to him whilst he made the call. Dave asked the person on the end of the phone "Is there a short, beautiful blonde there?" Well I knew this night that Adam was going to visit her as I was sure he had asked Dave to call and see if she was there.

Not long after hearing this Adam came into our room, had a shower and got ready to go out I asked him if he would mind staying home with me as I wasn't feeling the best. To be honest with you my sixth sense was going in to over drive. He told me he had to go and meet up with his ex, Powsey and Donna. He had promised he would take her out to meet people. He told me not to worry that they were just friends but I wasn't buying it. Adam left the house for his night out without me and didn't look back. This night I got to spend time with Ava. Tina had gone with them so I felt a little better knowing she was there as there is no way he would do anything with my cousin there. After Ava had gone to bed I went in and laid down, my mind was in over drive. I had all sorts of thoughts going round and round in my head. I was worried he would cheat on me and break me more than I was at this point. I really couldn't take much more heart ache.

Early in the morning I heard Adam's car Tina, Dave and Adam got out of the car, they were laughing and had obviously had a good night. I on the other hand was not so happy, I was just terribly broken. I felt more alone then I had in my life. I got up and went

UNBROKEN

out to meet them. They had all gone in to the lounge room by this stage. Adam called me over and sat me on his lap. We chatted together for a while but I was really miserable. I tried not to be but it was eating me up inside that he had chosen to go out with this ex and his friends and have a good night rather than stay in with me. Tina called me to the kitchen and she said "Emily, you don't have anything to worry about. She is lovely, but she is not interested in Adam at all. Really she is lovely" I smiled and felt a little better but why was my heart beating so fast and why did my mind race to the worst conclusion. I had to take her word for it.

The next day I wanted to do something nice for Adam so Tina and I went to the shop and I put a surfboard on lay-by for Adam.

He loved to surf but his board was at his parents' house on the other side of Australia. When we got home I was so excited that I couldn't wait to tell Adam, this was the first time I had been happy about something in weeks. When he got home I ran up to him and with excitement in my voice I said "I put a board on lay-by for you today, it is an awesome board" Adam looked at me strangely

"No, Emily you shouldn't have done that" I was a little confused with his reaction, I truly thought he would be ecstatic.

"I wanted to do something nice for you" I said to him. Without any further reaction he rushed out past me and called out to Dave

"Dave! we have to go" he yelled on the way through. Dave looked a little confused also but they walked to the car in silence. I had no idea where they were going or why Adam had reacted this way.

Later that afternoon Adam walked back into the house with Dave. Dave called out to Tina and asked if her and Ava wanted to go for a drive. I said it was ok as I wanted to spend a little time with Adam anyway, maybe I could find out why he reacted the way

---

he did to his surprise. After they left the house Adam grabbed my hand and walked me to our room, he sat me on the bed. "Emily, here" he handed me money.

"What's that for?" I asked a little confused *'Why was he giving me money?'*

"It's the lay-by money, you shouldn't have done that" this was weird

"I wanted to Adam, I know how much you love surfing" *'What's going on here?'*

"Emily, I don't know how to say this but we are not going to work out" I saw his mouth move but I couldn't hear his words. *'What was happening? What had I done so wrong?'* If I wasn't broken before I was now.

"Adam what are you talking about? Why? I don't understand" I cried. He stood up and pulled out a suitcase and started packing his bags. I was begging to know what and why. He wouldn't answer me, I cried so much and he didn't care not one little bit.

"It her isn't it!" I screamed at him

"It's got nothing to do with her we are never going to be together, I can't be a Father Emily, I'm not ready" At this time all I could think was *'I know that is why you made me have an abortion'* but I didn't spit that out.

"What are you talking about Adam?"

"I can't be a Father"

"I don't expect you to be a Father Adam and I never have" I spat at him by this time I was angry.

UNBROKEN

"I love you Emily but we can't be together" were the last words he said to me before he walked out the door.

I sat on my bed in shock. I don't remember doing it but I grabbed a bottle of pain killers and took the lot. I don't remember much more after this, the next thing I know I am drinking charcoal with Tina sitting beside me in a hospital ward. When I saw her the first thing I said was "Where is Ava?" she looked at me with swollen eyes and told me she was at Sheryl's house, I was relieved Ava wasn't around when I did this. *What had I done?*

I got released from hospital and was feeling sorry for myself for some time. My friends all came around to visit and tried to make me feel better about myself. It was good to have such great friends and support. I couldn't talk to Dave even though he still lived with us, I tried but every time I looked at him I was reminded of Adam.

A few weeks later I got a call from my Mum. She was upset, she wasn't crying but I could hear in her tone that something wasn't right. She chatted about all sorts of things then final she got to it. "Emily, sweetheart" she said timidly, I had heard this tone before.

"What's wrong Mum, is it Nan?" Mum went silent then I could hear her gulp

"I have been diagnosed with breast cancer" I know this sounds bad but all I could think is '*what did I do to have such a shitty life*'.

"Why Mum?" I blubbered, I said so many things that I can't remember I can remember Mum saying

"Emily! Stop! This is happening to me sweetheart" I must have been making it all about me and for that I am sorry. I wasn't thinking that this was happening to her.....

Chapter 63: Breast Cancer

I spoke to Mum every night checking on her. She sounded completely drained. Mum was working full time at the Hospital as an Administration Manager. She would start work two hours early and take a two-hour lunch. During her lunch she would have her radiation treatment then return to work to complete here day. She couldn't afford not to work.

One night during our call she broke down. This was heartbreaking as I was so far away. I prodded her enough for her to tell me what had happened "The other ladies I work with are giving me a hard time for having a two-hour lunch break as they don't know why I take two hours for lunch. I can't tell them Emily as I don't want them to treat me differently" she cried. I hadn't heard Mum cry in a very long time. Mum was always the brave one. She held it together no matter what so we didn't feel her hurt or pain so I knew this was bad when she let it out.

"Mum, you have to say something" I said calmly and softly

"My boss knows but not the others" she replied

"Well they don't matter Mum, they are work colleagues not friends and they don't have to go through what you do and if they did they would take time off" was all I could say to try and make her feel better. I wanted to be there more than anything but I didn't have enough saved to go back. Another time when I needed to be somewhere I couldn't.

"Barry is not taking it well Emily, he is acting out" she was opening up and telling me everything. Right now she and Barry needed me there more than anything.

UNBROKEN

"Mum if I can make it back soon I will" I promised. This would mean that I would have to save what little money I had as quickly as possible. Mum told me she had to go in the next week and have a part mastectomy and the lymph nodes removed from under her arms in a hope that they can get it all. This cemented it for me, somehow I was going to get back in the next few weeks. I told Tina what was happening and she was very supportive and extremely worried as Mum was also her Aunty. She said she would help me get back.

The night of Mum's operation she called me from the hospital she was crying and I thought that she was hurting or had bad news after the operation. I tried to calm her but I couldn't. Finally, she told me that the police had turned up at the hospital and advised her that Barry had taken her car for a joy ride "He stole my car Emily! and got caught"

"Fucking hell Mum I am going to kick his arse big time, he doesn't think of anyone else but himself" I ranted. I didn't mean what I said but I felt guilty that I wasn't there for Mum and Barry.

"No Emily! He is acting out, he is worried about me just like you are and this is his way of handling things" she interjected. She was right as always she knew us too well. We chatted for a little while longer then I said good night to her and told her I would call again in the morning. I didn't bother trying to call Barry as he wouldn't be home and back then we didn't have mobile phones. I called her again at the hospital in the morning, she was going home that day. I felt terrible for her and still ever so guilty for not being there with her through this time. Over the next few weeks I got all the money I had and booked a flight for Ava and I to return home to support Mum and Barry.

The morning we were to flight out I call Mum and I told her I would be there that night, that we had our fares booked. Mum tried to stop me as she didn't want me interrupting my life and spending money I didn't have. Can you believe that? she always thinks of us always even when she is going through all of this. I packed our bags and my girlfriend took us to the airport. Tina told me not to worry about anything here and to give Mum all her love.

It was a very long flight back to Mum and Ava got really sore ears during the flight so I kept tricking her in to yawning so her ears would pop. Finally, we landed and as soon as we got out to the terminal Mum was there waiting. I didn't see her until I saw Ava running so fast I couldn't believe her legs would hold her up right, I swear I thought she was going to trip over herself and slide along the ground. "Nannyyyyy!!!!!!!!" she yelled so loudly that it echoed through the whole terminal and made people stop in their tracks she was not stopping for anyone. Mum's eyes lit up and the biggest smile took over her face. I couldn't help that single tear roll down my face. It had been years since we had seen her and she hadn't changed accept for the fact she had lost weight.

On the trip home all Ava wanted to do was sing the song My Girl with Mum, that song is very special for the both of them. Mum used to dance to this song with Ava since she was a baby. Ava really was Nannies girl.

When we got home Barry was there. Wow he had changed. He was so much taller than I remembered. Mum made us all a cup of tea as I put my bags away and went to see my Great Uncle J. He hadn't changed one bit; he was exactly like I remembered. I had a chat with Barry and asked what was going on with him. He didn't say much he closed off.

There was a knock at the door. Barry jumped up and ran out to the door. When he came back he brought his girlfriend Rhonda. Rhonda was so very special. She had a softness and kindness that made her who she was. She kept Barry in line though and for this it made us love her. They were so in love. I had never seen someone tame Barry but this girl was in control in a good way. Ava loved her so very much. Rhonda was great with her, she came from a large family and to her family always comes first. She would not allow Barry to disrespect Mum in any way.

I loved this girl. With her and Barry together I knew I would never have to worry about him again as you could tell when they looked at each other that this was true love and both of them felt the same.

On the first day there I felt relaxed and at ease for the first time in a very long time.

Boy it was good to be home, if only for a little while ...

Chapter 64: Returning Home

Every day I was home Rhonda would come over. She was a god send for Barry. She kept him in line her dark eyes would sparkle every time she looked and Barry. When I saw them together I was so very glad they were and I knew that this would be forever. I had seen Barry with other girlfriends but this one was special with a capital S. Rhonda came from a very traditional family and to her family came first and she thought of us as family. Her family liked Barry but he was not Lebanese so they would not allow them to marry.

During my last week there I called Tina to make sure she was ok "Emily, everything is fine. There was a call for you the other day from a guy but when I told him you were back with your Mum for a break and asked who he was he hung up".

My heart sank. Tina didn't know his voice but she knew it was not a long distance call. Back then if you called long distance there was a sequence of beeps as you answered the call before you spoke. My first though was that it was Jay. If it was not long distance than that meant, he was in Western Australia and he had my number so I would assume that he knew where I was living. We continued to speak for a while and I told her my thoughts. I told her to make sure she always had someone there. Tina had not had to deal with Jay but she knew all about him. Before hanging up I told her I loved her and to stay safe. When I got off the phone Mum looked at me. She knew something was wrong and asked me to go with her to the shops she asked Barry and Rhonda to watch Ava. Barry knew Mum's tone as well as I did and he knew Mum needed to talk to me without even speaking a word.

We got in the car and Mum asked me immediately "What's wrong sweetheart?" I looked at her and a single tear rolled down my cheek as I told her about my conversation with Tina. Mum told me not to worry it could have been anyone. She knew as well as I did that my gut feelings were usually right. I really couldn't believe that this was going to happen all over again. We went to one of the major shopping centers and Mum just tried to keep my mind off of it. She always knew how to make me feel better. I never needed her to buy me things or spoil me with material possessions I just needed her to be there, just stand beside me and she always was. After spending hours away we got in the car and returned home.

That night we all sat down to eat Barry and Rhonda were talking about getting engaged soon. We were so excited. They were glowing, oh so very happy, I had never seen Barry like this. He had not a care in the world. They were perfect. It was so wonderful to see them together. Rhonda and I were talking about dresses etc. she couldn't wait. Barry was going to get her a ring. He wanted I pick it himself. Rhonda went home that night and was going to tell her parents. She didn't care what they said she was going to be happy and marry who she wanted. Barry dropped her off.

They were young but who's to say young marriages couldn't work, after all my Nan and Pa were young and were married till Pa passed away. I looked at Rhonda and Barry and saw my Nan and Pa. Their relationship was so very special, together forever that's what I saw when I looked at them.

The next day Barry called Rhonda's house and her Mum answered the phone. Barry asked for Rhonda and after a while he came out to us and said "They said Rhonda has gone away for a while?" he looked blank I could see the complete and utter confusion in his face, he was gutted.

"She'll be fine she's probably gone to the shops or something" I said to him.

"Just give her a call a little later" I didn't want him to worry about nothing so I changed the subject so that he didn't dwell on it, I knew there had to be a reason he was concerned as he was pretty intuitive.

Later that day he tried again and he got the same answer, again he can out and told me what was said. I told him not to worry again and I made him some lunch. These calls continued until the day before I left and I told him we should go and check on her. I drove as he wasn't in a state to drive. The entire time I was at Mum's they spent every waking moment together so it was strange, I could no longer sit around and tell him it was going to be OK. I had to take him to her house so he could speak to her family and ask the questions he needed to ask face to face.

When we arrive we pulled up out the front of Rhonda's parents' house. I saw the door open as Barry went to get out an older lady came out. It was Rhonda's Mum I found out later. Barry stood speaking calmly with her, I sat in the car and waited as it was not my place to interfere. He spoke with her for about ten minutes then returned to the car looking more confused than I had ever seen him. He slumped down on the seat and I didn't want to ask but I knew I had too "What's happened Barry?"

"She's the oldest child so they have sent her to Lebanon to sell the family land" he responded.

"I can't believe she didn't call me and say goodbye or come around and tell me" he continued. The rest of the trip home we sat in silence and when we got home he walked straight to his room and slammed his door. Mum looked at me and asked what had happened. I walked her to the table and explained what was said. Mum did not believe this story and she was right not to.

UNBROKEN

The next few days Barry didn't leave his room. He was hurting and couldn't figure this out. I didn't blame him. Ava was the only one who could really speak to him as he didn't want to talk. Him speaking with Ava was a release for him he didn't have to tell her his feeling he just had to have a kid chat.

The day we flew back Barry didn't come to the airport. He said his goodbyes and went back to his room. This must have been the first real broken heart he had ever had. I told him it would be fine as soon as she sold the land she would be back and they could kick off where they started. I knew how much they truly loved each other and that doesn't just stop in a minute, a day, a year, a decade or even a lifetime. I think it sank in a little but he still couldn't put the pieces together and to be honest I couldn't blame him.

With all of that happening I didn't have time to worry about what I would be going back too but the minute we pulled up at the airport I felt my drama landing on my shoulders again.

Ava cried so much her little body was shaking when we had to say goodbye. I tried to keep it together but I knew that it would be a very long time before I saw my Mum again. The breakdown was inevitable. It was a very hard goodbye.

As we sat on the plane I calmed Ava with a book and crayons and looked out the window. I contemplated what we were going back too. My broken heart returned, was Jay going to be waiting?

Chapter 65: Careful What You Wish For

The plane landed at the airport in Western Australia. When we got off the plane there was no one waiting for us. We walked outside and waited for a taxi in order to get home after such a long flight I was ready to feed and bathe Ava then hop in a shower myself. We were lined up waiting for a taxi when I heard someone yell out to me. It was Tina and Mandy a good friend of mine "Do you really think we would let you arrive without a welcome party" Tina said. At that moment I walked over and held her and tears rolled down my face. I felt so alone after leaving Mum and Barry and my emotions were all over the place. Whilst holding Tina everything I had bottled up and was worried about when I returned came flowing back. It felt like a freight train had hit me. Whilst we were with Mum it was like I had left everything on the otherwise of Australia and could just be me for a while, now I was back and all my problems returned. I knew I should have been stronger but I really couldn't control it. We got in the car and Ava would not stop talking, not unusual for her she was a very confident little girl and extremely intelligent she still is to this day. I was in the passenger seat and Tina sat in the back seat with Ava. I looked back at them and they were both as happy as each other to be right where they were at this moment. It looked like Tina missed us as much as we missed her.

When we got home I took Ava's bag to her room and put mine in the lounge room. I got her fed and bathed and we called Mum to let her know we got home safely. After we had finished on the phone I tucked Ava in to bed and kissed her good night. I walked out to the lounge room and Tina was sitting there waiting for me. Mandy had left so we could settle in "Emily, we need to have a chat" Tina said.

UNBROKEN

"Go and have a shower and I will get us a cup of tea" I looked at her and thought this was strange behavior for her but obviously she needed to tell me something. I was oh so quick to leave the room dragging my bag in to my room behind me. As I entered the room I walked over to my cupboard and as I opened the sliding doors it hit me like a ton of bricks that Adam was no longer here. His side of the cupboard was empty. I quickly put my clothes away so I could close the cupboard and hopefully not think about it. I got in to the shower and cried uncontrollably I did this so no one could see me, I'm sure a lot of people do this. My mind was racing thinking what Tina needed to discuss and then I realised that Dave was not home. I finally pulled myself together got out and dress in my PJs. I walked out to the lounge room and said down next to Tina.

"Emily, Dave has moved out to a unit we have decided that for the time being this would be best. We are still together but this is best for now" Tina started. I didn't know how to respond but I felt it was because Adam and I had broken up and maybe it made him uncomfortable.

"There's more" she continued.

"I don't know how to say this!" she said sheepishly. I looked her in the eyes I couldn't let he drag this out any longer

"Just say it Tina! I can't handle people hiding things from me" I snapped. I didn't mean too but I did.

"Well" she paused and took a big gulp. I gave her the look.

"Um, well Adam is with Donna" she finally spat it out. At this point my heart broke not just broke but shattered in to a million pieces. I was angry, pissed off and all together broken. I didn't say anything but I thought about a lot of things but mainly

How long has this been going on?

All those times she sat with Adam and I, she flirted with him were they doing something then?

I listened to her when she needed it and kept her secrets!

Bitch!

I didn't say these words out loud or asked Tina as she couldn't answer these questions even if she wanted too "They moved in together" she continued. My silence said it all. I got up and walked to the kitchen without saying a word. All I wanted to do was sink into the floor below me. Tina followed me out to make sure I was ok. I think she might also have been checking I hadn't done something stupid. I walked over to the phone picked it up and rang a girlfriend of mine.

"Hey do you want to get the girls together, I want to go out tomorrow night" she was more than happy too so we arranged a time and I called Sheryl who has the two little girls that Ava loved spending time with and asked if she would watch Ava and she agreed. I turned and looked at Tina

"Well are you going to come?" smiling at her though she looked confused. In my mind I wanted to go out and prove I was too good for him and this was my way of getting on with life. Tina smiled back and said she was in. She wanted me to be happy and if this is what it took well she would support it.

The next morning, I found a modelling academy and signed Tina and myself up. Funnily enough it was on Thursday afternoon which just happened to be that day. I dropped Ava off that afternoon to Sheryl and Tina and I headed out to our first modelling class together. We dressed to impress, I had a black pair of skin tight short shorts and a tank top showing off my tummy, long black boots and did my make-up and hair not only for modelling but also for the night ahead.

I had so much fun at modelling and we had our first assignment to do for the next week. We then headed over to the pub that was adjacent to the club we went too and had a drink and played pool. We were getting a lot of attention. I know this sounds vein but that is how it was when we went out. I hadn't paid that much attention when I was with Adam but now it was really obvious.

I walked in to the toilet area to make sure my makeup was ok and went in to the stall as I was walking out I heard a voice. I had never heard it before but one of the two people talking called the girl by her name which just happened to be Adams ex who had moved to WA. I walked out of the stall and said "Are you Rebecca?" she looked at me nervously then took a step backwards

"Are you Emily?" we both said yes at the same time. We got to talking and walked out together. Tina saw us and thought that there was going to be trouble and rushed over. She said hi to Rebecca and said

"Is everything ok here?" we both laughed and said we were fine.

"Rebecca told me Adam had told her that I was going to beat her up if I met her?" I couldn't believe it as that is not who I was and she noticed that what he had said was a load of shit. We must have talked for hours then she joined us in going next door. As I walked in I scanned the room and it was packed with people, it had been a long time since I had been there. I walked around with my head held high and walked with confidence. All my girlfriends were out the back as I went to walk out I walked past Adam and didn't even noticed until I heard

Emily Reilly

"Here's the slut!" I recognised that voice straight away as I turned in the direction of the voice I was shocked at what I saw. Sitting at a table was Adam and next to him was Grant! I was furious. I walked over to them both and pointing at Adam I said

"How's it feel to be second best to Powsey?" then I turned and pointed at Grant

"You know me better than that and as you both know I am far from a Slut!" I then turn and walked confidently outside, I strutted as I didn't want them to think, especially Adam that this had affected me. I was here to show him what he was missing.

When I got outside I told to girls what happened and they wanted to go and say something but I wouldn't let them. We went to the dance floor and had to walk past them both again. This time I didn't speak or look at them I just held my head high and strutted on. We danced and I had so many guys coming up to talk to me whilst I was dancing offering me drinks and wanting to dance with me. Somewhere really hot so I agreed but I made sure the other girls were close by. As I danced with these guys I took a quick look in Adam and Grant's direction and Adam was staring, he was not happy and this made me feel fantastic that was exactly what I wanted to happen.

That night I wished that he would hurt as much as I did. I wished a lot of bad things for him. I couldn't believe what he said as I wasn't the one who did something wrong. I didn't break his heart!

My Mum always told me be very careful what you wish for and over the next few weeks Adam was going to be affected greatly by   my   wishes...

Chapter 66: Karma

For the rest of the night we danced and drank. We met some really hot guys and decided to go on to a late night club. I had been there many times with the girls and the owner had a little crush on me. Every time I walked in he would get his girls to get me drinks. I never paid and either did anyone with me. I always flirted a little but back then I was just being me. This night one of the guys with us wanted to try a flaming Lamborghini, I got it for him and if you have ever seen this drink in action you know that you NEVER! Drink this when you have had drinks previously. No sooner had he downed the drink he free fell backwards. There were giggles but also some concern. He wasn't out for long but after that he stuck to water for the rest of the night.

Adam had followed us to the club and one of the girls pointed it out to me. I did have a lot of drinks that night, I saw a guy that I knew from my time with Grant. He had attended our engagement party. Jamie was a looker over six-foot-tall, dark hair, tanned and dark eyes. He was such a nice guy and I had always had a secret crush on him. I walked up to him as I knew that he was no longer with his girlfriend and we danced together. I was making Adam jealous and it felt good. Jamie was monopolising my time so the girls dragged me away. Jamie got my number before I left. The club was about to close so we decided to go back to our place and continue our night. We all piled in to a taxi.

When we got back the girls told me how upset Adam look and as girls do we laughed about it. I wanted to hurt him like he hurt me. I seemed strong but to be honest inside I was feeling sick that I was doing this as it was not me. When I finally got into bed I cried and wished only bad things for Adam. I wish he would hurt like I did. I wished him nothing but pain and as far as Donna was concerned she was very lucky that I didn't see her that night.

The next weekend we went out again. The pub was packed. I hadn't seen so many people in the club for a very long time. We all strutted around as we did exuding confidence. I may have come across as a bit of a snob to men as I really didn't want anyone to hurt me again. Tina and I walked upstairs to play on the pool tables there as the one in the beer garden were taken. We put our money on the table and waited for all the other girls to join us. When the music died down I heard Adams voice. Funnily enough I could make out that voice anywhere. I spun around and saw Donna standing there with him. She walked over to me "Stay away from Adam bitch!" she shouted. I walked in close to her put my face about an inch from her face and said very calmly

"Let me tell you something for nothing sweetheart! Turn yourself around and waddle off or I am going to take your head off your shoulders. If you EVER come near me again or speak a word to me again I will not be having this conversation and that is a promise" I took a step back still staring at her. She spun around really quickly and ran over to Adam. Tina and Kelly were right there and just heard what I said as I turned around they smiled

"Handled well Emily! Very well" Tina said she was so proud and maybe just a little surprised that I didn't attach Donna there and then. We started to play pool and the entire time Adam and Donna were watching us. I looked up every now and then. After about an hour Donna had disappeared and Adam walked over to me.

"Can we talk Emily?" he said standing close to me. My heart raced, my emotions were everywhere. I wanted to cry and ask him why but I knew I wouldn't get an answer.

UNBROKEN

"Go away Adam, you scumbag" Kelly projected her voice from behind me.

"It's ok Kelly" I said. She was about to step in and I don't know what she was capable of doing.

"What do you want Adam?" I managed to say.

"You need to leave Donna alone" he said. That was the last straw

"ME! Leave her alone!! Fuck me!! She came over to me and told me to stay away from you! I will tell you what I told her. If she comes near me again or I hear she has spoken about me I will deal with her myself. DON'T tell me to leave her alone she is the one who started this but I promise I will be the one to finish it" wow I can't believe that came out of my mouth to Adam.

"She will not come near you again, I'll make sure of it" he said he spoke so softly and it felt like he still cared. He looked at me for a while then he turned to walk away.

"Adam" I said stopping him in his track.

"I want you to know you broken my heart, but I have learnt a lot in my short life, those who hurt others will get what is coming to them, karma has a way of biting people. Remember what you put out comes back three fold and because you have hurt me so badly I am sure Karma is on your back. Whatever happens from here on in is your Karma" it hurt to say these words but I meant every word and as I said my Mum told me be careful what you wish for.

A few weeks later I got home and there was a message on my phone, it was Adam.

"Emily, can we please have a chat" I didn't return the call but later that day I heard his car pull up. I looked out the window and saw him getting out, his arm was in a sling. I didn't open the door until a few minutes after he knocked.

"What do you want Adam?" were the first words out of my mouth.

"Can you please take this curse off me" he said with tears in his eyes.

"What are you talking about?" I asked a little confused.

"Emily, in the last few weeks I have broken my arm, smashed two motorbikes and smashed my car, you said Karma would get me and it has" he was almost crying out loud. I looked him in the eyes

"It's not me who has done this! It is all you" I closed the door and walked away. I did have a little smile on my face but deep down I didn't want him physically hurt.

I guess it's true though be careful what you wish for.....

Chapter 67: Moving House

A few weeks after my last discussion with Adam Tina, Ava and I moved house. It was not far from where we were. The house was a lovely three-bedroom house with a formal and casual lounge room. Ava was really happy she had a new room and loved the back yard after we assembled her swing set. It felt good to be out of the old house, leaving all of those memories behind. We could start a new here.

I started going out one night each weekend. I was becoming stagnant and feeling down so the girls always got me hyped up for a big night, they didn't want me sitting around all the time thinking about Adam, it was time to make a change and just live. Ava didn't mind me going out as she loved staying with Sheryl and her girls, it was a little time out for her also.

Every time we went out Adam was not there and that suited just me fine as I didn't have to have my heart break when I saw him with Donna and I didn't have to act strong I could just be me. I would always have guys buying me drinks, flowers or teddies. I finally was starting to become strong and confident again. My girlfriends were always ready for a laugh and to dance which is something I loved to do. I really started to let my hair down.

After a while I met lot of new people who were really nice and we had a lot of fun together. We had become really good friends with the band (The J Babies) so when we were out we always got up on stage and sang with them. One night we all went back to our house and someone had some pot, I decided to try it again and this time I was not sick at all it made me relax. I seemed to help me escape the stress and worry, my mind was working so slow that I could only focus on what was right in front of me and luckily for me it was my friends so we laughed and had a great time. I know

now it is not great to do but back then I only wanted to escape the world and this helped me do just that. This became a regular event when Ava wasn't around.

One weekend that I will not forget I left Ava with Tina whilst a friend (Charlene) and I went for a drive to get some pot as she knew people who had it. When we came back home I saw Adam's car parked out the front. I had changed my hair colour to a dark chestnut brown by this stage. When we pulled in to the driveway I said to Charlene "I'm going straight to my room, I don't want to be around him" she tried to convince me it would be ok and he would probably leave when I got there but I didn't want to take the chance so I opened the car door and got out walked in to the house right past Adam without saying a word. I walked straight to my room as I said I would. My heart was breaking seeing him again, I had worked so hard to get over him then he turns up at my house and all those emotions came back filling me to the brink. Why would someone who broke your heart come to your house? was it just to hurt you all over again? A clean break would have been so much easier.

"Who was that hot chick with Charlene?" I heard Adam say he was obviously talking to Tina as I then heard her say

"That was Emily you dickhead"

"Really! she looks so hot, she's changed her hair and has lost so much weight" Adam responded. I then heard a knock on the door, my heart raced thinking that the door would open and it would be Adam standing there. I could not have handled seeing him in my new room. I just wanted to hide, I didn't need him anywhere near me.

"Mummy, can I come in?" a little voice asked. I dried my eyes and opened the door to see my beautiful little girl standing there waiting to come in and see me I knelt down gave her a huge hug and told her I loved her.

A little while later I heard the Adam drive away so I picked Ava up off my bed and we went out to the lounge room where everyone was sitting. I didn't mind sitting on my bed talked with Ava though as it was really nice having kid chats. She had no idea that Adam and I weren't together or so I thought. As I put Ava down she ran to the window "Where's my friend gone Mummy?" she asked. I looked over at this little girl who was looking out the window obviously looking for Adam.

"Adam's gone Darling" was all I could manage. This little girl looked almost as heartbroken as me, it was so very sad but there was nothing I could do to take that away or bring Adam back.

In the lounge room everybody just sat there looking at me to see if I was ok but didn't say a word. My face must have told them if they said anything I would break. Later that night when every one had gone home and Ava had gone to bed Tina looked at me "You got him good Emily, he couldn't believe it was you that walk right past him, you should hold your head up and be proud" she said. I really didn't care about getting him, I just wanted it to all be over as I knew never again would we be together. The thought of him visiting us more often was killing me. I didn't want him anywhere near me, I needed my heart to heal and that was going to be impossible if he was around. Even after everything he had done I still cared, stupid I know I should have kicked him to the curb a long time ago but when you have been with the Devil (Jay) anyone who treats you like a princess when you first get together is a god send. I had only known evil before this. Tina and I chatted for hours about just about everything. It was nice to just talk we could just be Tina and I, we were always so busy entertaining everyone else who came around that we forgot that it is important to have us time. For the first time we smoked a joint together with Ava in the next room. We sat and laughed for ages.

After being in our house for about six months we really had settled in and everything was running smoothly. I hadn't seen Adam and it is true when they say out of sight out of mind. I really needed this time to heal. We continued going out once a week and having friends over and I was almost back to me, the real me, the one I had lost so many times.

One night the phone rang, I jumped up to answer it thinking it would be one of the girls checking to see what we were up too. "Is that you Emily?" fear engulfed me. I froze I felt my body shake from the inside. That voice was the only voice that could make me fear to speak.

"I know it's you Emily" the tone changed again

"I know where you are and I will be there soon" I looked around to make sure the door closest to me was locked. The fear made me hang up the phone and ran around the house closing all the windows and making sure all the doors were latched. I was obsessed with making sure everything was secure. I then rang in to Tina's room and told her that I had just received a call I never wanted to get ever again.

JAY WAS BACK!!

UNBROKEN

CPSIA information can be obtained at www.ICGtesting.com
Printed in the USA
BVOW06s0603100916

461740BV00010B/72/P

9 781326 701154